MARVELOUS MYTHS

To Robert T. Dalton Jr., who lived a heroic life.

Marvel Superheroes
and Everyday Faith

RUSSELL W. DALTON

CHALICE
PRESS

ST. LOUIS, MISSOURI

Bible quotations, unless otherwise noted, are from the *New Revised Standard Version Bible*, copyright 1989, Division of Christian Education of the National Council of the Churches of Christ in the United States of America. Used by permission. All rights reserved.

Cover image: Scribe Inc.
Cover and interior design: Scribe Inc.

Visit Chalice Press on the World Wide Web at
www.chalicepress.com

10 9 8 7 6 5 4 3 2 1   11 12 13 14 15 16 17

EPUB: 978-08272-23608 • EPDF: 978-08272-23615 • Paperback: 978-08272-23387

Cataloging–in–Publication Data

Dalton, Russell W.
Marvelous myths : Marvel superheroes and everyday faith / by Russell W. Dalton.
   p. cm.
Includes bibliographical references.
ISBN 978-0-8272-2338-7
   1. Comic books, strips, etc.—Religious aspects. 2. Superhero comic books, strips, etc.—History and criticism. 3. Christianity and literature—United States. 4. Marvel Comics Group. I. Title.

PN6712.D35 2011
741.5'382—dc22   2011004902

Printed in the United States of America

Contents

Figures

Preface

Living Heroic Lives

The Purpose of This Book

The superheroes of Marvel Comics have become some of the most recognizable characters in popular culture. They are featured not only in comic books but also in major motion pictures, animated television shows, and video games. As these stories entertain us, they also present us with their own particular perspectives on what it means to live a heroic life. This book is an attempt to reflect on those perspectives in a thoughtful manner, putting them into dialogue with insights from the Bible and Christian scholars.

Superheroes may seem like an unlikely source for reflection on the life of faith. People of faith do not believe that we solve the world's problems by dressing up in spandex costumes and beating people up. We should question the entire premise of stories in which our problems are solved by having someone in a costume come in and clobber villains in order to preserve law and order. Like the ancient myths, however, the stories of Marvel superheroes also offer readers and viewers some positive models of how extraordinary people face challenges and struggle to overcome adversity in order to live out heroic lives.

The Marvel superheroes discussed in this book, as conceived by Stan Lee, Jack Kirby, and others, were not perfect people who lived charmed lives. They had to deal with family affairs, anger issues, money troubles, and a whole host of other problems. Like most of us, they had to overcome everyday problems in order to live out heroic lives. Because of this, their stories provide us with opportunities to reflect on our efforts to do the same.

This book opens with an interview with Stan Lee, who was the co-creator of most of the heroes discussed in this book. Insights from my interviews with three other Marvel creators, Chris Claremont, Herb Trimpe, and Kurt Busiek, appear throughout the book. The introduction examines some of the inherent problems that stories of superheroes present for people of faith and then provides a brief history of Marvel Comics. Each chapter focuses on a particular Marvel superhero or team of superheroes. With nearly half a century's worth of stories for many of these characters, it is not possible to explore every story or every hero. This book focuses on the heroes created by Lee, Kirby, and others in the 1960s and examines the characters' origins, some of their better-known story lines, and the popular motion pictures that feature them.

Each chapter explores the particular issues and obstacles each hero or team faces in their efforts to live heroic lives. It then reflects on how we might face those same issues and obstacles as we strive to live our own heroic lives in the real world. While none of us will ever put on a costume and go around punching out criminals, we can still do our best to live heroic lives by loving others, doing what is right even in hard times, controlling our anger, doing our civic duty, using our gifts and talents to help others, and more. Although I hope that this book will speak to readers from a variety of backgrounds, I am writing as a Protestant Christian and I put the issues raised by the stories of these superheroes into conversation with insights from Christian scholars and the Bible. Each chapter then ends with some questions for reflection, which can be used by individuals or in group studies.

Dedication: What Makes a Life Heroic?

I dedicate this book to my big brother Bob Dalton. Bob was one of the earliest members of Marvel's first fan club, the Merry Marvel Marching Society. In 1969, when I was seven years old, he walked with me nearly a mile to the one store in our small hometown to help me buy my first comic book, a copy of *The Incredible Hulk* #119 (September 1969). In those early years, Bob shared with me his enthusiasm for comic books, but he also encouraged me to think critically about them and all popular culture from the perspective of my faith. Encouragement became a recurring motif in Bob's life. Bob was gifted with a very intelligent mind, and he used it to do research, teach Sunday School, and be a thoughtful Christian. As the oldest of five siblings, he inspired the rest of us to take our studies in school seriously. Bob was also a gifted musician. When he was still a teenager he could write songs and play the guitar like few others in northern Michigan. It seemed to us as if he had a superpower. Bob used that power to encourage others, first by playing early Christian rock songs in our small Baptist church. Then, while a student at Central Michigan University, he used a very long extension cord to play lead electric guitar as he also played the role of Judas in a traveling production of the musical *Godspell*. Later, he wrote his own songs of faith and performed them at churches and Christian coffee houses throughout the Midwest. Bob was also a gifted writer. He wrote novels and newspaper columns that challenged readers to be thoughtful about their faith. Later in his career, Bob became a multimedia professional, and he and his family took vacation time to travel to Jamaica to help produce a video for the New Vision City of Refuge children's home. Bob was not a world-famous musician, novelist, or video producer, but he used the gifts and talents that he had to encourage others and to minister for his faith. Along the way, in day-to-day interactions with others, Bob found ways to encourage others and share with them his enthusiasm for God's creation.

Bob encouraged me to write this book and was excited to share his thoughts, read through my early drafts of the chapters, and offer advice. But life intervened in ways we had not planned. Just as I started to write this book, doctors discovered a tumor in Bob's brain. At age fifty-four, Bob was diagnosed with glioblastoma multiforme, an advanced form of brain cancer. Soon after the diagnosis, I visited Bob in the hospital. He said, "You know, some people might say how sad it is that this is happening to someone so young, but the way I look at it, I've already had such a full life." He talked about how he had the chance to write and make his own music, how he was able to write newspaper columns and novels, how he got the chance to do multimedia work, and how he was able to use his various gifts for the work of the church. Most of all, he talked about his family. He loved his wife Renée, and he was amazed that he was blessed with three children, Lindsey, Rob, and Kaitlyn, who, as he put it, had more creativity in their little pinkies than he had in his whole body. During our visits in those last months of his life, Bob shared with me his thoughts on Marvel superheroes. Even near the very end of his life, when it was hard for him to talk on the phone, he would gather up the strength to talk to me and share some new ideas. Bob would not have agreed with all the opinions or perspectives that I share in this book, but our conversations led to some of the book's better sections.

After Bob died, I had the privilege of serving as the minister who officiated at his funeral. I was moved to hear how Bob had touched so many people in so many ways. Sometimes he touched them through his creative gifts, but often he touched them simply through the ways he found to encourage people every day. During the service, his youngest nephew Jack came up and shared with the congregation a picture of Marvel superheroes that he had drawn and colored for Bob while he was in the hospital, and he told us how Bob had talked to him about superheroes. Bob's friend Phil was the song leader and soloist for the service, and after hearing all the testimonies, Phil noted that what he had been hearing were stories not of a life cut short but of a life fulfilled.

My brother Bob would have been the first person to say that he was not perfect, but by using his gifts to serve God and encourage others, he lived a fulfilled life. He was my hero. My brothers Dave and Tim and my sister Ann are all heroes to me in different ways, but this book is dedicated to my big brother Bob who loved Marvel superheroes, loved God, and lived out a heroic life that touched many lives. 'Nuff said.

Acknowledgments

I wish to thank Cyrus White, publisher and president of Chalice Press, for his support of this project and encouragement along the way. I wish to thank my student assistants at Brite Divinity School, Greg Henneman and Jon Reeves, who helped track down articles and quotations and did some helpful initial proofreading of the text. I have great respect for the theoretical depth and practical implications of the work of my colleagues at Brite Divinity School in Fort Worth, Texas, and my former colleagues at United Theological Seminary in Dayton, Ohio. Savvy readers will recognize that many of my chapters draw on their work. Many of the classic superhero stories discussed in this book are available in Marvel Masterworks reprint editions. I am thankful for the Marvel Masterworks Resource Page at http://www.marvelmasterworks.com, created and maintained by John Rhett Thomas, and for the contributors to the site's message boards. It is one of the more helpful, thoughtful, and civil message boards I have found.

A special word of thanks goes to Marvel Comics legends Stan "the Man" Lee, Herb Trimpe, Chris Claremont, and Kurt Busiek for allowing me to interview them and share their thoughts with you.

I am indebted to my own fantastic four—Nathan, Anna Grace, Maria, and Joseph—for giving their father time to write this book. Finally, I wish to thank my amazing, incredible, uncanny, invincible, and mighty wife Lisa. She was my first editor and most trusted advisor and treated this book as part of a family project that we all played a part in completing.

Prelude

A Conversation with Stan Lee

As editor-in-chief and primary writer, co-plotter, and co-creator of most of the heroes discussed in this book, Stan Lee was the driving force behind the resurgence of Marvel Comics in the 1960s. He was born Stanley Martin Lieber on December 28, 1922, in New York City. As a teenager he became assistant editor at Timely Comics (the precursor to Marvel Comics) and created the pen name "Stan Lee" in order to preserve his birth name for what he thought would be his later, more serious writing. At age twenty, after serving in World War II, he returned to New York City and became the company's editor. Publisher Martin Goldman gave him the position temporarily, intending to replace him soon with someone older and more experienced. Instead, Lee remained in that position for several decades and guided the company through some rocky periods for the comic industry. Lee is best known for his work in the 1960s, when he worked with artists such as Jack Kirby and Steve Ditko to create a new kind of superhero that took the world of comic books by storm. He has received many honors, including a National Medal of the Arts presented to him in 2008 "for his groundbreaking work as one of America's most prolific storytellers, recreating the American comic book. His complex plots and humane superheroes celebrate courage, honesty, and the importance of helping the less fortunate, reflecting America's inherent goodness."[1] A new generation of fans knows him for his Hitchcockian cameos in the Marvel films that feature his co-creations.

From 1967 to 1980, Lee wrote "Stan's Soapbox," brief two- or three-paragraph musings about superheroes and life in general, which were featured as part of the bulletin page that appeared each month in every comic book that Marvel published. In these "Soapboxes," Lee often said that Marvel did not take sides on the issues of the day but, especially from 1967 to 1972, his "Soapbox" columns contained increasingly urgent pleas for tolerance and understanding.[2]

Lee does not consider himself to be a religious man in the sense that he formally practices any one religion. He was born into a Jewish family and has been married to his wife, Joan, an Episcopalian, for over sixty years.[3] While he does not adhere to any particular world religion, in the interview that follows one can see that he has some serious thoughts regarding several issues that concern people of faith, including issues of good versus evil and the nature of humankind.

In the interview below, I refer to Lee's poem "God Woke," which was written circa 1970 but was only recently published.[4] In the poem, Lee describes the way people make a show of submitting themselves to God but are actually trying to turn God into a slave who is at their beck and call, answering their every prayer and giving them whatever they want. Lee imagines God looking down on the wars being fought over issues of religion, race, or a piece of coveted land and being distraught at how people use God as part of their justification for war. He sarcastically writes, "The mayhem, the carnage, the slaughter won't cease / But no need to worry, God's in his corner, he's killing for peace."[5] The poem is a plea for humankind to take responsibility for its own actions, a theme that also was important to Lee's longtime partner Jack Kirby.[6]

This interview was conducted by phone on March 3, 2009. Mr. Lee was in his office at POW! Entertainment in Beverly Hills, California, and I was in my office at Brite Divinity School in Fort Worth, Texas. We talked about his characters, living a heroic life, and the difficulties with seeing the world as simply a battle of good guys against bad guys.

STAN LEE: Russell W. Dalton, this is Stan Lee.

RUSSELL DALTON: Hi, Stan. You can call me Russ.

LEE: OK [*laughs*], you prefer that to W.? [*laughs*]

DALTON: Yes! [*laughs*]

STAN: OK!

DALTON: Well, it's a privilege to talk to you, sir. I'm a divinity school professor, and I'm writing a book that reflects on how Marvel heroes, and we ourselves, need to overcome obstacles in our lives to live out our mission in life, to live a heroic life. And I know our time is brief, so I will get right to the questions, if that's OK.

LEE: OK.

DALTON: Well, I've heard comments and I'm sure you've heard comments from those who read the Marvel Comic books that you wrote while they were growing up, and they talk about how your stories and characters influenced them in ways that they find hard to put into words. But the general theme of their comments is that the stories you wrote made them want to be better people and perhaps, some say, gave them a helpful perspective on life. I have my own theories as to why your characters and your stories had such a profound impact on people, but what is your theory? Why do you think that those Marvel heroes' impact went beyond entertainment to influencing the way people lived out their lives?

LEE: Well, you know, I am probably no better a judge of that than anyone else because I wasn't really trying, at least it wasn't my main objective, to help people live their lives when I wrote these stories. I was just hoping the stories would be entertaining enough and people would enjoy them enough that they would keep buying the magazines and I would earn a living. But if people really did find something beneficial in the stories, I would imagine it might be because I tried to make the heroes easy to relate to, in the sense that they weren't all perfect human beings. They had their own problems, their own personal problems, their own devils that they had to overcome. And maybe the average reader was able to empathize with those characters because the average person has plenty of problems also that he or she is trying to overcome.

DALTON: And Peter Parker is an excellent example of a hero with whom we could empathize. He dealt with a lot of problems. And I have a theory that part of what made Peter Parker keep going, despite the odds, is that he was not motivated by a sense of revenge, not even a sense of guilt, and certainly not out of a desire for fame and glory, because he definitely did not get that.

LEE: No.

DALTON: Instead, he had this sense that "with great power comes great responsibility." So even though he wanted to quit, it was that sense of responsibility that kept him going. Do you have any thoughts on that, Peter's motivation as responsibility?

LEE: You hit it pretty close. It was mainly the responsibility, although I think a tiny bit of guilt also, because he did feel a sense of guilt in that he hadn't been there for his uncle when his uncle was killed. But the responsibility, to me, was a very important part of it. Because I've often thought, what would make a superhero, if there were such things as superheroes, risk his life day after day, fighting bad guys, putting his life on the line all the time? It would have to be a very compelling reason. So, in Peter Parker's case, it was the feeling that he had the responsibility to do this. When he gained this power, because he didn't use it correctly in the beginning, he blamed himself for his uncle's death. He became very much aware that, when having any sort of an ability, you are almost compelled, you have to use it, you have to be responsible, because you have that talent, that ability, that superpower if you will. And with that power comes the attendant responsibility.

DALTON: One thing you are well known for is humanizing heroes, but another thing that struck me as I reread many of your stories was that you created empathy for so-called villains as well. You showed the possibility of redemption. You had many former villains become heroes, especially in *The Avengers*. And it seems as though the 1971 Attica State Prison riots tragedy seemed to have a big effect on you. You wrote an issue of *The Amazing Spider-Man* #99, in which you had Spider-Man help stop a similar prison riot tragedy and you wrote a "Soapbox" column on it about the dangers of committing injustice in the name of "right." Would you talk a bit about your concern to avoid splitting the world into just good guys and bad guys, and your empathy for criminals?

LEE: Well, I'm not really all that sympathetic with people who are dangerous criminals, of course. But I do feel that so often people tend to divide other people into groups: good guys or bad guys. Very few people are all bad. Most people, there is a chance for them to become good.

There is a chance for them to redeem themselves, I think, unless they are totally hopeless, and I don't know how many of those there are. And even most good people occasionally may yield to temptation or may do something that they regret later. People are very complex, and it just doesn't seem right to take the very simplistic attitude, "This guy is good, this guy is bad, and that is the end of it." That's too unrealistic, I think. If I can do a story that shows that somebody who had made some mistakes in his life, or done some wrong things in his life, that there is still hope for this person, that he can be redeemed, that he can be turned around, so to speak, and become a good guy, it's kind of nice. Those kinds of stories I find satisfying.

DALTON: Well, quite frankly, I think that makes for good theology as well. I loved your "Soapboxes," and I loved where you pointed out the limits of the superhero genre. You talked about how, for example, bigotry and racism "can't be halted with a punch in the snoot, or a zap from a ray gun" but that the best way to destroy them is to expose them and reveal them. And as we've been discussing, you wrote about how "nobody is all good, or all bad." Did you have this in mind with your approach to Marvel Comics—the danger of comic book superheroes oversimplifying society's problems and trying to help people think about them in a more complex way? Today we would call what you did a "deconstruction" of the superhero.

LEE: Wow!

DALTON: Well, I wonder if you had that in mind.

LEE: Well, I would love to take credit for that, but I honestly don't think so. It might have been subconscious. As I mentioned before, the only thing that was uppermost in my mind, and I think it is uppermost in most writers' minds, is "I hope people will like these stories and that the books will sell." Because you always worry, what if you do a story and no one cares for it and nobody buys the book. So my first thought always was "I hope I can make these stories entertaining enough that people will want to read them and want to read more of them." That's always the primary goal. Now beyond that, in writing the stories, you always get different thoughts and different ideas. That's when I might think to myself, I can put in a few sentences here that would make somebody stop and think. But again, to be perfectly honest, that was never my overriding intention when I started. It was just to hopefully write something that people would enjoy reading.

DALTON: Well, you succeeded on that point. In 2007, you returned to work with John Romita Jr. and wrote *The Last Fantastic Four Story: World's End*. In the story you returned to a common theme in your work. After thousands of years humankind is as warlike as ever. Crime, poverty, and bigotry still exist. So a cosmic tribunal decides that we deserve to be destroyed. But it is the compassion of humankind, as seen through the example of the Fantastic Four who fought to save those who would destroy them, that proves we are worthy of existing. Why was that particular story an important one for you to tell?

LEE: Well, when I was asked, if I were to write the last story of the FF what would I write? I felt it wouldn't be seemly to just have a story of them fighting some supervillain as they had done so many times in the past. If this is going to theoretically wrap up the series, it ought to be a story with a point to it, with a moral, or something that would make people think with a philosophic angle. That is why I did it that way. I worked a little bit harder in trying to think of an angle that was different from what I might have written before.

DALTON: Many have asked you in the past about the Silver Surfer being a Christ figure, but personally I don't see him that way.[7] I see the Surfer as having much more in common with the God of the Hebrew prophets who looks down and sees how crazy the world is and says, in effect, "Why are you doing this to each other and to my world?" And that's really the same god as the God in your poem "God Woke," isn't it?

LEE: Oh, you read that poem? Wow!

DALTON: Yes, well, the poem presents an outside perspective, with God looking down on us and seeing both our faults and our great potential. And I wonder what you thought of that in general and in terms of the Silver Surfer?

LEE: Well, I think you hit the nail right on the head with the Silver Surfer. I never thought of him as a Christlike figure, although other people have written that. I agree with you, he's just somebody from another world that can't understand why we don't appreciate this world and take care of it and take care of each other as we should. I'm sorry, what was the other part of the question?

DALTON: In general, I was wondering about that perspective in "God Woke," with God looking and seeing how people act. I was wondering about your vision of God in that poem.

LEE: Well, you know, I was a little nervous about ever making that poem public, because I thought it might offend some religious people, but I was very happy that it didn't seem to have. Most people who read it seemed to like it. It's just that I have often felt that people spend too much time just asking God for things all the time in their prayers. It's hard for me to just imagine some divinity up above us who is doing nothing but listening to us twenty-four hours a day. I feel that after a while he'd get pretty bored or pretty annoyed that we were harassing him this way. And I feel, have any religion you want, that's fine. But kind of do things on your own, don't depend on some invisible power somewhere to accomplish things for you. I feel it is sort of a cop-out.

So anyway, that's the way I feel about it.

DALTON: Well, I know that one thing you've made clear in many interviews is that you did not want Marvel Comics to be religious in the sense that it would advocate for any one religion.

LEE: Oh, absolutely. And, certainly not even for my philosophy, which wouldn't be fair to inflict on people.

DALTON: You did, however, feel strongly about some ethical and religious themes such as "Do unto others like you would have done to you."

LEE: Well, to me, I don't feel that is religious. To me, that is probably the greatest sentence ever written since the world began. If you think about it, if everybody would just live according to that precept, this would be heaven on earth. If you treated people the way you'd want to be treated you'd never lie, you'd never rob, you'd never cheat, you'd never do anything to hurt anybody else, because you wouldn't want anybody to do that to you. As far as I am concerned, that should be the sum of all religions right there in that one sentence.

DALTON: And it is a principle in many of the great world religions, to have that attitude.

LEE: Yeah.

DALTON: On a more personal note, one could say that you've lived a heroic life of your own.

LEE: I don't know about that.

DALTON: Well, I know that, as with anyone in any business, you've had disagreements with people, but I've found that it's hard to find people who say anything other than what a generous and great person you are to be around and to work with.

LEE: Well, they are great judges of character, obviously! [laughs]

DALTON: Well, I know you want to be humble about it, but if, in any way, you have lived a heroic life, I wonder what you think are some of the keys for doing so?

LEE: Well, I certainly don't know that I have lived a heroic life; all I did was write stories for most of my life. I got married and had a daughter, love my wife, love my daughter, love the work that I do. And for the most part, I have loved the people I have worked with. I've always been very lucky because I have worked with some of the most creative people you could find anywhere—artists, writers. Now that I am in Los Angeles, I work with screenwriters, actors, directors. So I have been a very lucky guy, because I have always been incredibly interested in my work. I have been lucky enough to love what I do. In fact, I think one of the tragedies of the world is that so many people do work that is meaningless to them. They just do it because it is a means to earn a living, but they get no joy or satisfaction from it. There are so many people who just have jobs, a fellow who is a clerk in a store or a deliveryman. There are so many jobs that bring very little satisfaction. But you do them because you have to make a living. I feel very sorry for people who [do not have careers in which they] can't wait to get up in the morning and go to work because they love what they do so much. I realize, proportionately, there are very few such people in the world and there are very few of such jobs, you might say, that you could love going to. So in that sense I consider myself incredibly lucky. Not heroic, just lucky.

DALTON: That's a good perspective. It is a perspective that reflects on a real strength you gave to the characters you created. To some extent, they were real people. You alluded to this earlier, when you mentioned that your heroes faced normal problems. They were in families that bickered, or they were teased at school. But still, despite all of these things, they found a way to do what is right and to continue to do what is right. I wonder if you had any thoughts on that.

LEE: Well, I think you summed it up perfectly. Just wanting to do what is right is one of the greatest qualities a person can have. If only more people had that. If only it were easier to tell what is right. You take politics. You take the liberals and the conservatives for example. So many of them think that the other one is the closest thing to Satan. Here people who live in one country cannot agree on how things should be done. If you think about it, it shouldn't be that hard to figure things out. Yet, you have these two political parties who never agree with each other. Each acts as though the other is terrible, almost evil. You wonder how can there ever be real peace in the world when even members of the same country with different political philosophies can't ever see eye to eye. It seems that there is something inherent in human nature that we think of ourselves and the people who think like us as the good guys, and the people who disagree with us as the bad guys, which can get me to another subject altogether. I have often thought I'd like to write a book about this, which I never will have time to do. When I was a kid and I lived in New York City, we had neighborhoods, more than neighborhoods. The kids who lived on one street, on one block, were a little different from the kids who lived across the street on the other block. Not different, but we thought of ourselves as the good guys, and the kids who lived across the street, hell, they were the kids across the street. They weren't so great. If ever we played ball with them, we wanted to win and we better win to show that we were better than they were. There is always that feeling of me and my group, we are the good ones, and anybody different . . . I think if there was no such thing as politics, people who are blondes would hate brunettes, and tall people would hate short ones, and vice versa. It's almost as if it is some inborn thing in human nature that makes us want to feel that anybody just like us is good and anybody different isn't good. I think that is since Adam and Eve. It is just part of what being human is, I think.

DALTON: You dealt with that a little bit with the X-Men, where you had people hating them and mistrusting them because they were mutants.

LEE: That is right, because they were different. Everyone loves sports and thinks that sports are so wonderful and good for people. I often wonder if they're that good. Again, when people are rabid sports fans, you always cheer for your team. But the other team, they're the bad ones. You've read there have been riots when the wrong decision has been made after a game, or people will start rioting in the street if their team loses and they feel it is unfair. It's ridiculous the way people feel that they have got to be the winners; they've got to ally themselves with the winners or with the good guys. These people, when a team wins a series, whatever their hometown is, everybody drives around waving their hand and saying, "We're number one." Well, what do you mean you are number one? Your team beat another team. It has nothing to do with you; it has nothing to do with your city; it has nothing to do with anything. You just happened to hit a few more homeruns. So, again, I have nothing against sports, but it seems to be ingrained in the human condition that you've got to be for something and the people who aren't for it are the enemy.

DALTON: And unfortunately, when you add religion into that mix . . . Well, there is a philosophy called Manichaeism. And it can come with this sense that God is good and, since we are on God's side, we can just trample our enemies, since they are the enemies of God. And it's very tempting to go there.

LEE: Well you see it even at a prizefight. If two fighters are religious, each one of them will cross himself and look up and pray to God. And God can't be rooting for both of them!

DALTON: Right. But, of course, we want to believe that God is always on our side.

LEE: I think I even mentioned that in my poem somewhere.

DALTON: Yes, I think you did . . . And that leads to a profound theological question. Who would win in a fight, the Incredible Hulk or the Mighty Thor, I mean really?

LEE: Wow! You know, I think probably the fight would go on forever. Because, being a thunder god, you couldn't really defeat Thor, but the Hulk gets stronger the more he fights. So maybe you could compare it to God versus Satan, it just goes on forever.

Lee and I then concluded the interview after talking about some more personal matters. After the interview, I was left with a couple of lasting impressions. The first was how friendly and generous Lee was, well deserving of the reputation he has for being a gracious man. It also struck me as ironic that this man, best known for writing in a genre filled with stories of muscle-bound heroes punching out villains, had such thoughtful concerns both about how we can overcome obstacles in our lives and about the danger of labeling others as our enemies. Lee introduced themes that do not easily fit into the superhero genre into his stories, lending them more complexity than most superhero tales of the time. This may be one of the reasons for Marvel's success. Those themes certainly make his stories and his characters rich sources for reflection in the chapters that follow.

Introduction

Mythology and the Peril and Promise of Marvel Superheroes

Myths served an important function in ancient cultures. The stories were often exciting and entertaining, telling of extraordinary heroes with special powers who overcame great obstacles to save their people. As myths entertained people, however, they also passed on particular ways for people to understand their lives and the world around them. The stories reflected or challenged the values of the culture, modeling particular virtues and suggesting ways that people could live meaningful and virtuous lives of their own. As the stories were retold over the years, certain aspects of the stories changed and new stories were added to reflect or challenge the changing values of the times in which they were told.

The stories of the heroes of Marvel Comics can be viewed as a sort of present-day mythology. In the 1960s, Stan Lee and artists Jack Kirby and Steve Ditko created most of the heroes of the Marvel Universe described in this book. Those stories set the foundation for Marvel's characters and its world. New stories have been added to this mythology every month since that time. Like the myths of old, these are exciting and entertaining stories of extraordinary heroes doing extraordinary things. At the same time, the average reader can relate to the hero's struggle to do the right thing and to persevere in the midst of adversity. In some cases, these stories have helped people reflect on how they might live heroic, meaningful lives of their own. As such, they are valuable because they explore values and beliefs not just in the abstract, but as they are put into practice in life.

Like the ancient myths, these stories of superheroes carry with them values and virtues that people of faith might affirm, and others that people of faith might question. By reflecting on the values inherent in the superhero genre and the stories of Marvel Comics in particular, we can use these narratives as an opportunity to reflect on our values and how we are choosing to live out our lives.

The Problem with Superheroes

Superheroes are great fun. Their stories appeal to our sense of wonder, our enjoyment of fantasy, and our sense of right and wrong. As mentioned in the preface, much of this book will focus on the positive reflections that can be inspired by these characters and their stories. Every time we see a hero punch out a villain, however, it raises a concern for people of faith. We generally do not think that violence is the best way to overcome conflicts. Aside from an incident involving a whip and some money changers (Jn. 2:13–17), Jesus generally did not go around addressing society's ills by punching out villains. He told his followers that, rather than fighting a Roman soldier who struck them, they should turn the other cheek and walk the extra mile (Mt. 5:39–41). Instead of flying off to win the day, Jesus humbly washed his disciples' feet and told them to follow his example (Jn. 13:1–210). Instead of using repulsor rays to overthrow the oppressive Roman regime, he told his disciples that greater love has no one than this, than that he lay down his life for his friends (Jn. 15:13), and then he went out and did it. When he met a potential enemy, Zacchaeus, he affirmed his worth by going to his house to share a meal before asking him to change his ways (Lk. 19:1–10). When one of Jesus' followers drew a sword and cut the ear off a member of the crowd who came to arrest Jesus, Jesus said, "Put your sword back into its place; for all who take the sword will perish by the sword" (Mt. 26:52). Jesus fought his battles not with superhuman strength, adamantium[1] claws, optic blasts, enchanted hammers, or great agility, but with love, understanding, forgiveness, and sacrifice.

J. M. DeMatteis, who wrote *The Silver Surfer* comic in the 1990s, has talked about his frustration in working under the constraints of the superhero genre. He says that he would have the Silver Surfer give a long impassioned discourse on the futility of violence but then, since it was a superhero comic book after all, he would feel compelled to have him go fight someone a few pages later.[2]

While Marvel comics have many stories of love, forgiveness, and heroic sacrifice, many more of the stories resolve their conflicts through beating up villains. Stories in which the world is divided into good people and bad people, and in which the bad people are defeated through strength and power, should make people of faith a bit uncomfortable. Are we supposed to be glad that our "good violence" is stronger than the bad guy's "bad violence"? Do we believe that might makes right?

Of course, humankind's fascination with stories of violent resolution is not unique to stories of superheroes and it is certainly not new. Humankind has used violent stories for thousands of years to try to explore internal conflicts in external and concrete ways. One of our earliest myths, the ancient Babylonian creation myth known as the "Enuma Elish," is quite violent. It tells the story of a bloody battle among the gods. According to the myth, humankind was actually born from the blood of Kingu, one of the slain gods.

Stories of violent resolution persist today. They are common in R-rated action films, in which the villain is revealed to be truly evil and the protagonist must simply get mad enough, determined enough, and perhaps self-righteous enough to destroy the enemy. This same motif is also present, however, even in many G-rated family films. Disney's *Beauty and the Beast* (1991), *The Lion King* (1994), and *The Hunchback of Notre Dame* (1996), for example, all tell stories that lead viewers to empathize with the heroes and despise the villains as truly evil. When the villains force their hand, the hero and his often comical sidekicks realize they must fight back. The films present the viewers with dramatic, colorful visuals and rousing music. An emotionally satisfying battle ensues, as the hero physically defeats the enemy. The conflict is ultimately resolved and the community is redeemed when the villain dies. Theologian and Bible scholar Walter Wink writes, "This Myth of Redemptive Violence is the real myth of the modern world. It, and not Judaism or Christianity or Islam, is the dominant religion in our society today."[3]

The danger in these stories is not simply that they will lead to copycat violence, but that they will, in subtle and subconscious ways, lead to a viewpoint that divides the world and suggests that the only way to resolve conflict is to destroy our enemies.

Seeing good and evil as two equal and competing forces struggling for control of the universe can be appealing. It may even sound like a spiritual approach to the world. The name theologians have given this approach to good and evil is *Manichaeism*. It is based on a popular belief system taught by the Persian prophet Manes in the third century C.E. Dating back to that time, St. Augustine of Hippo and most Christian traditions through the years have considered this view of the world to be heretical. They argue that good and evil are not two equal forces in a struggle for control of the universe but that God is ultimately in control of the universe. Put another way, the force of evil is not equivalent to the one good God.

Critics of Manichaeism argue that this approach has problematic philosophical and ethical implications. They argue that those who believe there is a universal struggle between good and evil are tempted to see themselves as fighting on the side of good, or the side of God, and therefore see their enemies as evil ones who are part of the universal force of evil. Consequently, they may begin to see themselves as totally good and begin to demonize their enemies. As a result, say its critics, those who take a Manichaean approach are tempted to justify all sorts of methods to defeat those whom they see as evil. Works of fiction are sometimes criticized as being Manichaean when they present one side, the heroes, as totally good and the other side, the villains, as totally evil. The conflict in these stories, as previously described, is resolved when the heroes simply get angry enough or determined enough to stand up to evil and destroy their enemies.[4]

Most Christian theologians contend that the Christian faith calls for a very different approach to confronting evil than Manichaeism. Christians know that all have sinned and that no human is totally good. Likewise, they know that everyone is redeemable and no one is totally evil. If people do not view their enemies as totally evil, or on the side of some cosmic force of evil, then they are less tempted to demonize them or destroy them in the name of God. Instead, Christians are compelled to practice virtues such as mercy, sacrifice, and forgiveness. Christian thinkers refer to New Testament commands such as "love your enemies" (Mt. 5:44), "do not repay anyone evil for evil" (Rom. 12:17a), and "overcome evil with good" (Rom. 12:21b).[5] They may also be more inclined to leave the ultimate results of a conflict to the hand of God.

The stories of superheroes raise other concerns. John Shelton Lawrence and Robert Jewett trace the role of stories of heroes in the United States in their book

The Myth of the American Superhero.[6] The book is more about stories of heroes in literature, films, and television than about comic book superheroes,[7] but their analysis of western films, novels, and thousands of other stories of American popular culture is insightful. They offer for consideration a description of what they refer to as "the American monomyth." The basic plot is as follows: "A community in a harmonious paradise is threatened by evil; normal institutions fail to contend with this threat; a selfless superhero emerges to renounce temptations and carry out the redemptive task; aided by fate, his decisive victory restores the community to its paradisiacal condition; the superhero then recedes into obscurity."[8] Lawrence and Jewett say that heroes even renounce relationships. They are not able to have close friends or a spouse or even be a part of the community. Instead, at the end of the story, they ride off into the sunset.[9]

Lawrence and Jewett explain that the problem with this myth is that it reinforces the status quo. The normal institutions of society are unable to solve a problem, and over the course of the story the society is not reformed and society still does not work. To solve the problem, an individual comes in from the outside, saves the day, and then leaves.[10] The American monomyth celebrates the stranger who saves the day, but it is an inadequate and hollow myth. It does not call us to take action and work together to reform society's institutions and create long-term solutions to our problems.

It is helpful, then, to acknowledge that the genre of the superhero story has some inherent problems for people of faith. Our faith teaches that we should not continually try to solve our problems through violence. We believe that we should not repay evil for evil. We also believe that we should not wait around for some outside hero to come and save us but should work together as a community to address society's ills and to change our society accordingly.

Now, given their potential pitfalls, should we reflect on stories of superheroes at all? Do they contain any helpful insights for people of faith? I believe that the stories of the Marvel heroes, especially those created by Stan Lee, Jack Kirby, and other early Marvel writers and artists, contain many positive lessons as well. Unlike most superheroes that came before them, Marvel's superheroes were given distinct, complex personalities. Their stories often dealt with how they were growing in character and how they lived their lives in relationship to others. The heroes of Marvel Comics faced complicated moral dilemmas. They were not perfect people, and their struggles to overcome life's complications in order to live out heroic lives can help us reflect on how we might do the same. Still, it is important that we acknowledge the problematic aspects of the superhero genre right up front, realizing that some readers and viewers might be fans of the stories because of the very aspects that thoughtful viewers and readers may find problematic.

A Brief History of Marvel Comics

To see how these heroes of the Marvel age of comics fit into the overall history of comic book heroes, it is helpful to understand the history of the comic book company that became Marvel, from the 1940s, when it was known as Timely Comics; to the 1950s, when it was known as Atlas Comics; to the emergence of the Marvel Universe in the 1960s; and finally to Marvel Comics and Marvel Entertainment today.

In 1938, National Publishing, the forerunner to today's DC Comics, featured a new type of character in *Action Comics* #1 (June 1938). On the cover, a man dressed in colorful tights held an automobile over his head. Comic book readers had never seen anything quite like it. The man's name, of course, was Superman, and he was an immediate hit. In those early days, Superman was not the super-Boy Scout he is often thought of as today. He had no qualms about threatening crooks with electrocution or a drop from an upper-story window. National Publishing soon followed with other popular heroes such as Batman and Wonder Woman.

Other publishers saw National Publishing's success and quickly began to publish superhero comics of their own. Martin Goodman, publisher of Timely Comics, rarely saw a successful idea that he did not try to copy. Seeing the popularity of Superman, he quickly decided to broaden his pulp-magazine offerings to include comic books. So Timely Comics entered the superhero comic book fray with *Marvel Comics* #1 (October 1939).

Timely Comics' first superheroes did not fit the mold of other heroes. It was not clear at first whether they were heroes or menaces. The first issue introduced the Human Torch, a different character from the teenage member of the Fantastic Four who would be introduced over twenty years later. This Human Torch was not human at all. He was an android that burst into flames and ran amok after being brought to life, burning down the city around him. The comic also featured the Sub-Mariner, a powerful being who lived under the sea and was a menace to surface dwellers. The Human Torch soon settled down and took a job on the police force. The Sub-Mariner, however, continued to have a more ambiguous relationship with the human race.

The appearance of Captain America, created by the young Jack Kirby and Joe Simon, was a turning point for the new comic book line. The cover of *Captain America Comics* #1 (March 1941) featured the new hero, Captain America, dressed in a red, white, and blue costume and punching Adolf Hitler in the jaw. Remarkably, the cover was drawn a year before the United States declared war on Nazi Germany, and at a time when a majority of Americans did not want their young men involved in a war in Europe. The cover struck a chord with readers, however, and that first issue sold over a million copies, giving Timely Comics a hit on par with Superman and Batman. Like many of the comic creators of the time, Kirby and Simon were both Jewish. Their anti-Nazi stories made them the target of anti-Semitic hate mail and death threats from Nazi groups, but they were determined to continue telling the best stories possible. The two partners soon left Timely Comics to pursue other opportunities, but their exciting action scenes and dynamic visuals had already had an impact on the industry and influenced nearly every superhero story that followed. As comic book writer and historian Mark Evanier put it, "Simon and Kirby did ten issues of Captain America and super hero comics were never the same."[11]

When the Japanese military bombed Pearl Harbor, Timely Comics really hit their stride. There was no question of their heroes' loyalties. The Timely heroes, including Captain America, the Human Torch, and even the Sub-Mariner, fought on the side of the Allies. Their comic books became pro-American propaganda. The Nazis and the Japanese army became the enemy to beat. At times the stories seemed to reflect Manichaeism at its worst. Nazis were all portrayed as sadistic and Japanese villains were often portrayed with disturbingly yellow skin and dripping fangs for teeth.[12]

Not long after World War II was over, comic book superheroes seemed to fade in popularity and take a backseat to other genres such as comedy, funny animals, romance, and western comic books. In the 1950s, with the advent of the new medium of television to entertain children, comic books hit even harder times. Comics also came under attack for being a corrupting influence on children. In 1954, a psychiatrist named Fredric Wertham wrote the book *Seduction of the Innocent*[13] and testified before the Senate Subcommittee on Juvenile Delinquency. He warned parents and the U.S. Congress that comic books were corrupting the youth of the day. Horror comic books, especially those published by EC Comics, were his primary target (Wertham especially hated pictures of needles poking toward eyeballs), but superhero comic books were not immune from his attacks either. Many of the lurid images Wertham saw supposedly hidden in the folds of superheroes' clothing seemed to say more about what was on his mind than what was on the minds of the comic book writers and artists, but his book and his congressional testimony frightened parents and helped lead the comic book industry to create the Comics Code Authority, a self-censoring agency that certified comic books as appropriate for children. Timely Comics, now known as Atlas Comics, tried to regain some of their lost young readers by reintroducing Captain America, the Human Torch, and the Sub-Mariner. The time for superheroes seemed to have passed, though, and the revival was short-lived.

As the 1950s came to a close, Atlas Comics was a small company consisting mainly of writer and editor Stan Lee, artist Jack Kirby (who had returned to the company), and artist Steve Ditko. Goodman, who was still the company's publisher, had the small staff create comics that fit into genres that were successful for other comic book companies, including western, romance, and horror comic books. By the early years of the 1960s, Atlas Comics had become best known for stories of giant monsters and science fiction tales with twist endings that bore titles such as "I Was a Prisoner of the Martians!" in *Tales to Astonish* #4 (July 1959); "Sserpo, the Creature Who Crushed the World!" in *Amazing Adventures* #6 (November 1961); and "The Terror of Tim Boo Ba!" in *Amazing Adult Fantasy* #9 (February 1962).

Goodman kept hinting that he was going to close down operations, but Lee, Kirby, and Ditko's stories kept selling just enough issues to keep the company profitable.

According to Stan Lee, it was during this time that DC Comics publisher Jack Liebowitz happened to tell Goodman that he was having good sales of a new superhero comic book *The Justice League of America*. The comic book featured popular heroes such as Batman, Superman, and Wonder Woman, along with other heroes that DC Comics had revived and retooled, teaming up to battle new threats. Always eager to copy successful ideas, Goodman told Lee that they too should put out a comic book about a team of superheroes, even though the company was not publishing stories of any superheroes at the time.[14] The assignment did not sound that interesting to Lee.

In the comic books of the late 1950s and early 1960s, the image of the hero was quite formulaic. A hero had a square jaw, a muscular build, and a quick smile. Most heroes looked the same and talked the same, and their biggest personal problem was trying to keep their girlfriends from guessing their secret identities. If they exchanged costumes, no one could tell them apart. As a matter of fact, beginning with *World's Finest Comics* #71 (July/August 1954), Batman and Superman would occasionally switch costumes to fool their enemies or even Lois Lane. Even without a mask, people did not seem to notice that it was Bruce Wayne's face in the Superman outfit. Creating more cookie-cutter heroes in order to keep the company afloat was not an exciting prospect for Lee.

At age thirty-eight, already with over two decades of work in the comic book industry, Lee was ready to quit and start a new career. According to Lee, his wife Joan urged him to give it one last chance, but to do it his way. As Lee recalls it, "She said to me, 'If you're planning to leave anyway, why don't you just turn out a couple of books the way you think they should be done, and get it out of your system before you actually quit.'"[15]

Meanwhile, Jack Kirby was determined to do all he could to keep the company going. Although he was universally hailed by other artists and writers working in the industry as the man who had helped create or recreate almost every genre of comic book,[16] what he really wanted was work and a steady paycheck. Always the family man, Kirby felt a great responsibility to take whatever task he was given, do his best to produce quality work, and, because he was paid by the page, to complete as many pages as possible. Kirby would often sit on his hardback chair at his beat-up desk for twelve to fourteen hours a day, completing page after page.[17]

The cover of *Fantastic Four* #1 (November 1961), the comic book that resulted from Goodman's request for a superhero team, may not have looked that different from other Atlas comics of the time. It featured four people in plain clothes battling a giant monster. The story contained within its pages, however, revolutionized the genre of the superhero comic book. What came to be known as the Marvel Age of Comics had begun.

If Goodman thought he was going to get a Justice League of America knockoff, he was sorely mistaken. What Lee and Kirby did was a kind of deconstruction of the genre. Superheroes were supposed to have costumes and secret identities. The Fantastic Four had neither. Although Lee and Kirby conceded to give them blue jump suits in issue #3 (March 1962), the Fantastic Four still did not wear masks, and everyone knew their identities.

Most superheroes were strapping men with identical athletic builds, but the members of the Fantastic Four had distinct body types that readers could easily tell apart even if they just saw them in silhouette. In the comics that followed, Lee, Kirby, and Ditko would repeatedly defy the convention of the physically robust hero. Bruce Banner (the Hulk) was a frail man, Don Blake (Thor) walked with a cane, Peter Parker (Spider-Man) was a scrawny bookworm, Matt Murdock (Daredevil) was blind, Professor Xavier of the X-Men used a wheelchair, and Tony Stark (Iron Man) had a weak heart.[18]

Most superheroes at the time had the generic personality of an affable professional athlete or friendly neighborhood policeman. The Fantastic Four, however, represented different types of people than those who normally appeared as superheroes. As Lee has put it, Mr. Fantastic is "the world's greatest scientist, who is also a little bit of a bore. He talks too much, he's too ponderous and he drives the others crazy."[19] Most women in comic books, with the notable exception of Wonder Woman, were not heroes themselves, but girlfriends of the heroes. Lee wanted Sue Storm, the Invisible Girl, not to be just the girlfriend but rather an equal member of the team and Reed Richard's fiancée.[20] Sue's younger brother, Johnny Storm, the new Human Torch, was a teenager. But while most teenagers in comic books were sidekicks who tagged along with the heroes and idolized them, Johnny was a full-fledged member of the team and often argued with the adults. Perhaps most shocking to readers of the day was Ben Grimm, the Thing. The Thing certainly did not fit the mold of a handsome or erudite hero. He talked as though he had just stepped out of the rough New York neighborhood in which he grew up, and his orange, rocklike skin made him grotesque in his own estimation. He was a monster and his power, as he saw it, was a curse. Ben blamed Reed for the accident that gave him his powers and Reed continually attempted to find a cure for Ben's condition.

The immediate popularity of the Fantastic Four was due, at least in part, to the depth of characterization that Lee and Kirby gave to their heroes. This element was quickly recognized by fans as a strength of Marvel Comics. According to Lee, "First I thought of what kind of character I wanted, then I figured out what kind of super power he'd have."[21] Kirby took the same approach, saying, "I was really interested in the characters as people . . . I have a genuine feeling for real people and what I do is recreate them in a fantastic formula."[22] Lee's dialogue provided a distinctive voice for each member of the team. Even if the characters were just seen in the distance, readers could tell who was saying which piece of dialogue because they knew which distinctive voice went with each character. Through Kirby's artwork, readers could tell a great deal about the characters just by looking at them, even if there were no voice balloons or thought balloons. Kirby's artwork gave the characters body language and facial expressions that conveyed emotions and personality. This combination of characterization in dialogue and in artwork gave greater depth to the Fantastic Four and other Marvel heroes and made them seem more realistic and more interesting to readers than anything they had seen before in the superhero genre. Readers came to empathize with the characters and care about them. Furthermore, the emphasis on character shifted the focus of the stories away from battles and toward the relationships between characters. While Marvel comic books contained a great deal of action, they also explored how the characters struggled to live out their virtues in their relationships with friends, with strangers, and even with enemies.

A year after the introduction of the Fantastic Four, Lee collaborated with artist Steve Ditko to create Marvel's most famous superhero, Spider-Man.[23] Although teenager Peter Parker wore a mask and kept his identity a secret, he defied the typical image of a superhero in other ways. While most heroes never had any personal problems beyond keeping their identities secret, Peter had to face money problems, girl trouble, health issues, family problems, and classmate problems. Spider-Man was the Charlie Brown of superheroes, with almost nothing in his life going right. Lee had some trouble convincing his publisher, Goodman, to allow him to publish the story. He recalls some of the arguments against his idea:

> You can't name a hero "Spider-Man" because people hate spiders!
> You can't ever feature a teenager as a super hero. Teenagers can only be sidekicks. (Spidey *was* a teenager when the series started.)
> You can't give a hero so many problems. Readers won't think he's heroic enough.
> You can't have a hero who isn't big and glamorous and handsome. (Peter was just your average nerdy student in those early days.)
> You can't have a hero whose Aunt May is always wet-nursing him. It's not macho enough.[24]

Lee was finally able to sneak a short eleven-page origin story for Spider-Man into the last issue of *Amazing Fantasy*. Because the series, which had been up to that point filled with monster and suspense stories, was being cancelled anyway, Goodman did not mind letting Lee publish his Spider-Man story in that last issue. As it turned out, that issue sold surprisingly well and Spider-Man soon received his own comic book. The stories that followed continued to depict Peter Parker as an unpopular teenage science nerd with a whole host of problems.

Because Marvel's heroes had somewhat realistic personalities and faced real-life problems, they served as relatable models of heroism for a generation of readers. Furthermore, while neither Lee nor Kirby practiced organized religion as a member of a church or synagogue, they both had solid cores of values that infused their stories. Both grew up in families with values drawn from the Jewish faith.[25] Perhaps because of their service in World War II, Lee and Kirby also brought to their stories a more thoughtful approach to violence and defeating evil than many comic book creators.

In the documentary "Jack Kirby, Story Teller" included on the second disc of the *Fantastic Four: Extended Edition* DVD, award-winning artist Barry Windsor-Smith notes, "That's Jack Kirby's action. Not violence, action. There's a big difference. Nowadays it's violence. When Jack did it, it was action!"[26] It may seem a fine distinction, but Kirby and other Marvel artists in those early years emphasized the action leading up to a punch and rarely depicted a bruised or bloodied face or wounded villain.

Lee, meanwhile, repeatedly depicted his villains as redeemable people and began to explore some of the social issues of the time. After the Attica State Prison riot in the early 1970s, Lee wrote about it in one of his "Stan's Soapbox" columns that appeared in every Marvel comic book. He seemed to share many of the same concerns that the critics of Manichaeism have about the way some people approach the struggle with evil. He wrote, "Is it possible that too much harm, too much injustice has been caused in the name of 'right'—in the pursuit of combating 'wrong'? In every human conflict, isn't each disputant completely convinced that his particular cause is wholly 'right' while the opposing view is totally 'wrong'?"[27]

While stories of superheroes battling villains certainly raise many concerns, these aspects of Marvel Comics' early characters and stories make them rich fodder for reflection. More recent developments in the stories of Marvel superheroes, however, may prompt people of faith to approach them more cautiously.

In 1986, DC Comics released two critically acclaimed series, Frank Miller's *The Dark Knight Returns* and writer Alan Moore and artist Dave Gibbon's *Watchmen*. These were thoughtful deconstructions of the superhero genre that included adult themes and graphic violence. What followed from DC Comics and Marvel was a barrage of grim and gritty comic books that seemed to use violence and adult content simply to appeal to readers' more lurid interests. These new writers and artists seemed to miss the point of Miller's, Moore's, and Gibbon's commentaries on vigilantism, and their stories often seemed to celebrate their heroes' use of violence rather than question it. Marvel Comics began to specialize in vigilantes like Wolverine, Punisher, Deathlock, and the new Ghost Rider. As comic book writer and historian Mark Evanier has suggested, it seemed as though Marvel's superheroes of that era were no longer super or heroic.[28]

Even the original characters, those co-created by Stan Lee, have taken a different turn. While Marvel does publish a Marvel Adventures line for children today, those who think of superheroes as child-friendly fare should be aware that many of the comic books of the mainstream Marvel Universe today are rated Teen+ and often feature graphic violence, highly sexualized bodies in skin-tight spandex, and other so-called mature content.[29] Most of the films based on Marvel heroes are rated PG-13 or R, and most of the video games based on them are rated Teen for violence, language, and other content.

Perhaps most disturbing is the change in the inherent values of the heroes in many of these comic books. In *X-Men* #9 (January 1965), the X-Men capture a villain named Lucifer, the person who caused the injury that resulted in Professor

Xavier becoming confined to a wheelchair. At the end of the story, however, Xavier refuses to harm him. He explains, "We X-Men are pledged never to cause injury to another human being . . . no matter what the provocation!"[30] (Figure 1). Contrast that sentiment to those expressed in the X-Men's 2008 story Messiah Complex. In *X-Men* #207 (January 2007), the X-Men's Emma Frost says she takes pleasure in an enemy's pain. In *New X-Men* #46 (January 2008), Cyclops sends Wolverine off on a mission and tells him, "Kill anyone who gets in your way"[31] (Figure 2). Throughout the rest of the violent and bloody battle, Wolverine and other X-Men sometimes kill others as acts of war or in self-defense, but at other times they seem to kill simply out of a desire for revenge.

The transition of superheroes to the medium of film raises its own set of issues. The job of the filmmakers is to bring the heroes out of the four-color fantasy world of the comic book page and into our world. Thus, the X-Men wear black leather outfits in their films instead of brightly colored spandex. The action of punching out a villain becomes very violent and very real in a film. One does not see just the action leading up to the punch or the result of a punch, but sees and hears the whole action in real time. In an audiovisual medium, this sort of battle can have a visceral appeal to a more violent part of our natures.

The typical action-adventure film uses camera angles, well-framed shots, acting performances, and soundtracks to rouse one's sympathy for the hero and ignite one's anger toward the villain. When the heroes of a film finally get angry enough and determined enough, they set their jaws and ultimately defeat the enemy using the force of their wills. *Iron Man* (2008), for example, makes an attempt to tell what is, at least in part, a story about the dangers of advanced weaponry. Yet concern for the dangers of weapons seems to take a backseat when Iron Man uses that same technology to blow away some terrorists. Before Iron Man leaves, he grabs the terrorist leader, throws him down in the midst of those he had held hostage, and says, "He's all yours." In *The Incredible Hulk* (2008), viewers are led to be repulsed by the savagery of the Abomination, but soon afterward they are treated to a visceral thrill when the Hulk unleashes his fury on the Abomination, savagely beating him and pounding him into the pavement. At the theater where I watched the film, the audience had been led into an experience in which they cheered and laughed rather than cringed at the violence. These scenes of revenge and violence certainly do little to nurture our better natures, but they are often the very aspects of these stories that are embraced by fans of the films and related video games.[32]

If Marvel's earliest heroes seem more violent in their films, their newer grim and gritty characters are often even more violent. The film *Punisher: War Zone* (2008), for example, features well over one hundred people being killed, many in graphically brutal ways. The scenes of ruthless revenge, gore, and dismemberment were justifiably panned by most critics but the film, disturbingly, found a significant audience.

Figure 1. *X-Men* #9 (January 1965), page 20, panels 6 and 7; Marvel Comics. Stan Lee script and Jack Kirby art. Professor Xavier solemnly explains that X-Men never cause injury to human beings. Copyright ©1965 Marvel Comics, all rights reserved.

Marvel Comic Book Creators on the Influence and Inspiration of Their Stories

From the perspective of faith, then, the stories of Marvel heroes seem to be a mixed bag. Some aspects of the stories offer positive values and others seem to appeal to our worst natures. Rather than embracing these stories as though they were sacred texts or rejecting them as having no redeeming value at all, we can engage in a thoughtful dialogue with them and critically reflect on the helpful and harmful messages they are sending us.

As with many stories of our popular culture, it is helpful to understand that these stories are commercial entertainment products. They are created primarily to entertain consumers and make a profit rather than to preach or teach certain values.

In preparing this book, I had the opportunity to interview four Marvel comic book creators: Stan Lee, Chris Claremont, Herb Trimpe, and Kurt Busiek, in separate interviews. My interview with Stan Lee is included in full in the Prelude to this book, and sections of my interviews with the other creators are included throughout this book, including in the chapters on the characters that they wrote or illustrated.

I opened each of my interviews by telling these creators that I have heard many people talk about how the comic books that they created have had a great influence on them and have led them to live better lives. I asked each creator if they had heard the same thing, and if so what their reaction was. As can be seen from their responses, each of these creators made it a point to say that they were primarily trying to tell good stories and entertain their readers. Stan Lee said this explicitly, and the other creators shared similar sentiments. I asked each of them to share their thoughts on the subject.

Figure 2. *New X-Men* #46 (January 2008), page 23, panels 1 and 2; Marvel Comics. Craig Kyle and Chris Yost script and Humberto Ramos art. How times have changed. A stern Cyclops instructs Wolverine to kill everyone who gets in his way. The story is filled with much blood and much killing. Copyright ©2008 Marvel Comics, all rights reserved.

Chris Claremont

Chris Claremont is best known for his award-winning seventeen-year run (1975–1991) as the writer of *Uncanny X-Men* and for his ongoing work in comics and novels today. I spoke with Claremont about how the comic books he writes have influenced readers.

> RUSSELL DALTON: The book that I am writing explores how we struggle to overcome obstacles and remain true to our mission in life and direction in life. One of the strengths of Marvel superheroes is that they didn't live perfect lives and struggled, but still found a way to do good in the world. That is what my questions reflect upon. One of the first things I wanted to ask about was the way in which your stories and characters have influenced others. Many people I have talked with have said that your stories have made them want to be a better person.
>
> CHRIS CLAREMONT: That is incredibly flattering.
>
> DALTON: Have you heard that feedback from fans and is that [theme of living out a virtuous life] something you try to put into your stories?
>
> CLAREMONT: It is a multipart answer. Yes, I have heard that on a number

of occasions over the years. It is always immensely flattering and, to a small extent, intimidating, because it raises the bar in terms of my own sense of responsibility to the audience. I take that much more care in putting a story together and presenting the characters, not because they are so important or significant, but because if a portion of the audience is willing and prepared to take them seriously, then they have to be treated with a similar respect. That said, the essence of the game is to tell a story, possibly even a great story. One does not sit at a desk, at a typewriter, and say, "I am going to write a great, classic, important piece of work." You want to give the reader enjoyment. There may be other elements in it, but the essential thing is to provide, in the best sense of the word, entertainment.[33]

Herb Trimpe

My next interview was conducted by phone with longtime Hulk artist Herb Trimpe. For many fans, Trimpe is the quintessential Hulk artist. Trimpe drew the Hulk's adventures from 1968 to 1975. Trimpe is now an ordained deacon in the Episcopal Church and received the 2002 Comic-Con Humanitarian of the Year Award for his work as a chaplain for the recovery workers at Ground Zero in New York City. We spoke by phone on November 20, 2008. I started off the interview by asking Trimpe the same question about how his work touched the lives of readers.

HERB TRIMPE: Yeah, I can't figure it out. I've had people tell me at shows about particular issues they read. Not only the Hulk. You know, former readers are coming back now, and they have families. They're in their 40s and 50s. Some are younger, but they've still got their collections. They still reminisce about individual stories. I had one person tell me that one of the Hulk issues actually saved their life. So it's very difficult to know how to respond to something like that, especially when working in the business where you have your own family and you have your own interests and you have deadlines and the check is paying for the mortgage and the food. So when someone tells you [that your stories have changed their life] it's quite astounding. I had someone else tell me that the series itself got them through college. Another guy—who was actually reading the *GI Joe Special Missions* comic books I worked on—he said that the first issue, which he had clutched in his hand, got him though a very difficult time in his life. And I tell you, I took that book home, Russ, and I looked at it, and I couldn't see for the life of me why that would be an inspiration to anybody. Because we didn't pay that much attention to what we were doing because we were all meeting deadlines. That was probably the most important thing, because the printers were unionized and if you missed a print date the company was charged extra fees that were pretty phenomenal.[34]

Trimpe went on to make clear that, as far as he was concerned, there was no conscious intent to inspire readers or to impose certain moral values on them. He simply wanted to entertain them. At the same time, he recognized that his values, and those of the writers with whom he worked, influenced the way they told their stories, which, in turn, may have had an impact on readers. Trimpe said that while he was working in comics regularly, he worked hard at his job but did not have much respect for the work he was doing. Today, however, after meeting fans who were influenced by his work, he says he has gained greater respect and appreciation for the work that he did. He called it a blessing that fans have given him.[35]

Kurt Busiek

My third interview was with award-winning writer Kurt Busiek, who is perhaps best known to Marvel Comics fans for his work on the groundbreaking miniseries *Marvels*, his long runs on *Avengers* and *Iron Man*, and his creator-owned series *Astro City* and *Arrowsmith*. Mr. Busiek sent his responses to me by e-mail. I initially asked him about the values inherent in his stories.

> RUSSELL DALTON: Many of your characters can be seen as good models for how we overcome the challenges before us in order to do what is right. Is this on your mind when you write? Do you ever approach your writing consciously thinking about how people need to overcome obstacles and stay true to their convictions, and try to have your characters model that in a realistic way, or is it more a function of trying to write a believable and entertaining story?

> KURT BUSIEK: Probably the latter. I write not to instruct, but to make people feel something—so I'm less concerned with using Captain America to show people that loyalty to principle is worth something so much as me knowing that loyalty to principle is at the heart of who Captain America is, so if I'm going to write him honestly, we're going to see that in him. If that inspires someone to follow a similar path, that's great, but what I'm really doing is writing Captain America the way I think he should be. I wouldn't write, say, Wolverine or the Punisher the same way. They each have their own sense of principle and morality, and if I'm writing them, I want to get that across, and make them feel like honest, affecting portrayals of those characters.[36]

One common thread in all these responses is that the storytellers did not intentionally insert the values inherent in the creator's stories in order to try to teach the readers moral lessons. Instead, the stories grew out of a desire to tell entertaining stories about realistic characters facing conflicts and responding in heroic ways. In many ways, this makes these stories more valuable than if they were written consciously to impart certain values. Many works of Christian fiction, for example, are merely heavy-handed sermons strung into narrative form, and as such they are neither good narratives nor good sermons.

Each of the chapters that follow examines one Marvel superhero or team of superheroes. The chapters explore these characters and their stories and examine the issues and obstacles they face as they attempt to live out heroic lives. While acknowledging the problematic nature of some of the stories, each chapter uses them to reflect on how we might face some of the same issues and overcome some of the same obstacles as we strive to live meaningful lives in the real world. These issues are then placed into conversation with insights from Christian scholars, the Bible, and my own thoughts and experiences. It is worth noting that the Bible itself is a large collection of inspired texts that presents many different perspectives and insights and that can be read from a variety of contexts and perspectives. The connections I draw between the stories of Marvel superheroes and certain passages of scripture are not meant as simple "proof texts" to validate a particular point of view, but as connections that might inspire the reader's own reflection on the issue at hand. Each chapter ends with questions for reflection that can be used by individuals or for group study.

Questions for Reflection

- Have you ever wished you could just punch a problem (or a problematic person) in the nose and solve the problem that way?
- Have you ever seen someone else as an enemy to be defeated, only to view them as a colleague or friend later?
- If you are a comic book reader, what era of comic books did you read growing up? What were some of the values inherent in the comic books of that time?
- Do you think artists and writers have to be trying to impart religious values in order for a narrative to have religious values?
- One of the strengths of Marvel heroes is their well-developed personalities and the problems that they face. What heroes do you identify with and why?
- Have you ever had a positive reflection or learned a good lesson from a movie, television show, novel, or comic book that you thought was offensive in other ways?
- What do you think is your mission or are your missions in life?
- What obstacles do you face in carrying out those missions?

The Fantastic Four

Relating to Friends, Strangers, and Enemies

The Fantastic Four are Marvel's first family. They were the first heroes of the new Marvel Universe that began in the 1960s and their comic book served as Marvel's flagship title for many years. As discussed in the introduction to this book, writer Stan Lee and artist Jack Kirby defied many of the conventions of the superhero comic book when they created the Fantastic Four and launched the Marvel Age of Comics. Other superhero teams had various superpowers, but the Fantastic Four is one of the few teams whose members knew each other before they gained their powers. Perhaps because of this, the Fantastic Four put more emphasis on coordinating the use of their various powers than superhero teams that had preceded them. The most significant innovation of the book, however, was the emphasis that Lee and Kirby placed on the characterization of their heroes. Because of this, the Fantastic Four's stories were less about their physical battles with villains than about the way they related to each other, to strangers, and even to their enemies.

Since each member of the Fantastic Four has distinct powers, their stories provide us with an opportunity to reflect on the powers that we have and how we use them. What gifts and abilities have we been given? How do we work together to use the gifts and abilities that God has granted us? Since the characters in the stories have distinct personalities, the stories often concern personality conflicts and can help us reflect upon our relationships with others. How well do we work together with the people we know the best, including our families, our church families, and our communities? How well do we relate with people of different cultural backgrounds than our own? Are we suspicious of people whose ways are different from our ways, or can we recognize them as potential allies and friends? How do we work to understand our enemies and resolve our conflicts with them? Can we really be expected to follow Jesus' call to love our enemies? The adventure awaits us.

Origin

In *Fantastic Four* #1 (November 1961), Dr. Reed Richards asks his old college roommate, war pilot Ben Grimm, to fly a rocket ship to the stars. Ben worries that cosmic rays might pass through the ship and kill them, but as Reed's girlfriend Sue Storm says, "Ben, we've got to take that chance . . . unless we want the commies to beat us to it!"[1] So, along with Sue's teenage brother Johnny, the four of them sneak onto a spaceport to fly Reed's rocket into space. Ben's fears seem to be realized when the cosmic rays have a strange effect on the four of them and cause them to crash back to earth. They survive, but they are all changed. Sue discovers that she can turn invisible, Johnny bursts into flames and can fly, Reed can stretch his body at will, and an enraged Ben turns into a grotesque monster covered with orange rocklike skin. While each of the four adventurers has a different reaction to his or her transformation, the scene that follows reveals that they all ultimately respond to their circumstances in a heroic manner (Figure 3).

Reed somewhat pompously begins to say to the group, "Listen to me, all of you! That means you too, Ben! Together we have more powers than any humans have ever possessed!" Ben stops him there. "You don't have to make a speech, big shot! We understand! We've gotta use that power to help mankind, right?"[2] The four of them pledge to work as a team to help the world, and together they become the Fantastic Four.

Superpowers

Superpowers are a key feature of most superhero stories. The Fantastic Four have an intriguing diversity of powers. Ben Grimm, the Thing, has great strength and his rocklike exterior protects him from attacks. Johnny Storm, the Human Torch, can burst into flames, shoot fire at enemies (but somehow never burn them), and fly. Sue Richards, the Invisible Woman, can turn invisible, construct powerful invisible force shields, and even project those force shields as weapons at her enemies. Reed Richards, Mr. Fantastic, can stretch his elastic body to great lengths and into almost any shape, though his most valuable asset is his brilliant mind. Fans have often pointed out that these four powers parallel the four classical elements, earth, fire, air, and water. The Thing's rocklike skin represents rock or earth, the Human Torch's flames represent fire, the Invisible Woman's invisibility represents air, and the fluidity of Mr. Fantastic's stretching power represents water. Others have pointed out that the Fantastic Four's powers fit their distinct personalities. Ben Grimm's rocklike skin serves as a symbol of his rough exterior. Johnny Storm can be a hothead, and his flame power corresponds to his fiery personality. While Reed Richards may seem to have a rigid personality in some ways, his brilliant mind is as fluid and expandable as his body. When Sue Storm started out as the Invisible Girl, her power of invisibility fit her personality well. Like Marvel Girl, the Scarlet Witch, and other Marvel female heroes of 1960s, Sue's powers were more passive and defensive than those of her male teammates. You also did not see many Marvel women throw a punch in those early years. Even when Sue gained the power of an invisible force shield, it was a defensive power. She constantly waited for Reed and would pout when he was so engrossed working on some new invention that he did not notice her new hairdo. Along with America's understanding of women,

Figure 3. *Fantastic Four* #1 (November 1961), page 13; Marvel Comics. Stan Lee script and Jack Kirby art. While the art and dialogue seem relatively crude compared to their later comics, Lee and Kirby quickly established four distinct personalities, excitable teenager Johnny Storm, pompous professor Reed Richards, a surly and resentful Ben Grimm, and (in the previous pages) a frightened Sue Storm. Despite their differences, the four quickly agreed to join forces to help humankind. Copyright ©1961 Marvel Comics, all rights reserved.

however, Sue's powers and personality eventually evolved. She married Reed in *Fantastic Four Annual* #3 (1965), becoming Sue Richards, and later adopted the name the Invisible Woman. She now often uses her force shield power to project assaults on the enemy. Dr. Doom himself has said to the rest of the Fantastic Four, "I always said Susan was more powerful than the three of you put together."[3] As her powers grew, she became more forceful in her personality as well, often serving as the leader and a driving force of the group.

While we do not have superpowers, according to the Bible we have been given a variety of gifts and talents that we can use to serve others for God's sake. When we put these to their proper use, they can help us do heroic things as well.

Spiritual Gifts

Spiritual gifts, as their name suggests, are spiritual in nature and given to us freely by the Holy Spirit of God. They are not special abilities that are earned or awarded to individuals for their own benefit. The word "gift" used in the New Testament is the same as "grace" and it is by grace that these gifts have been given. According to 1 Corinthians 12:7, these gifts are given in order to build up the whole Church and facilitate its work in the world. According to the apostle Paul, the members of the Church have been given different gifts including prophecy, ministry, teaching, exhortation, generosity, cheerfulness, leadership, and the speaking in and interpretation of tongues (Rom. 12:3–8; 1 Cor. 12:1–11). Since the lists of spiritual gifts in Romans 12 and 1 Corinthians 12 are not identical, neither list should be taken as an exhaustive list or a comprehensive explanation of the nature of these gifts today.

How do we know what gifts we have been given? One way to identify our spiritual gifts is to think about how we have been used to build up the Church and others in the past. We can also ask other people what gifts they recognize in us. If we can recognize the gifts we have been given, we may gain a better idea of how we might best help the Church, others, and the world. Reflecting on our spiritual gifts can also help us thank God for the gifts we have been given by God.

A key to the Fantastic Four's success was that they learned to use their powers as a team and coordinate their efforts. By working together, the four heroes became greater than the sum of their parts. If all four members of the Fantastic Four had the Thing's strength, for example, or all four had the same flame power of the Human Torch, they would not be as effective as they are when they are able to draw upon four different powers.

The Super Skrull is a villain who has been bioengineered to have the powers of all four members of the Fantastic Four. Though he is able to coordinate his efforts very efficiently, in this case four heads are better than one. The Fantastic Four repeatedly defeat the Super Skrull by working together.[4]

The apostle Paul explained that the Church also needs people with different kinds of gifts to function properly, and that no gift is more important than the others. To make this point he develops an analogy to the human body. He makes the case that the eye is not more important than the ear, for example, because if the whole body were an eye, we would not be able to hear. He argues that every part of the body, and every member of the church with every different gift, is indispensible to its effectiveness in ministry (1 Cor. 12:12–26).

The Fantastic Four use the superpowers that they received from the cosmic rays, but they also make use of their own natural talents and abilities in order to successfully complete their missions. Reed's stretching power is helpful, but the way he uses his mind to create inventions and find solutions is much more important to the team's success than his stretching ability. Ben's superstrength is a great asset, but his ability as a pilot also helps the team achieve their goals. In a similar fashion, while the New Testament does not list being a brilliant student, talented musician, or good organizer and planner as spiritual gifts, many people of faith have nurtured these God-given abilities and used them for God's purposes rather than for personal gain. While spiritual gifts are an aid to the church, they are not the magic solution that will solve every problem. Many times, we carry out our missions in life by effectively using the other talents and abilities that we have been given.

Fruit of the Spirit

Along with the gifts of the Spirit, Paul writes that the members of the church have also been given the fruit of the Spirit. According to the book of Galatians, "the fruit of the Spirit is love, joy, peace, patience, kindness, generosity, faithfulness, gentleness, and self control" (Gal. 5:22). While the gifts of the Spirit are particular to each believer, the fruits of the Spirit are available to all. Love, joy, peace, patience, generosity, kindness, and self-control may not seem like the sort of powers or weapons that a superhero might use to their advantage, but the Fantastic Four have discovered on several occasions that it is these very characteristics that have helped them win some of their most important battles.

In 2007, Stan Lee returned to work on the Fantastic Four with artist John Romita Jr., on a special issue titled *The Last Fantastic Four Story: World's End*. In the story, the powerful Cosmic Tribunal assembles and determines that, after thousands of years, humankind still is involved in crime, poverty, bigotry, and war all over the world. Therefore, they judge that humankind must be eliminated. They send the seemingly all-powerful Adjudicator to do the job. The giant Adjudicator arrives, appearing in several places at once all over the world, and gives humankind one week to make their peace before they are destroyed. The world's heroes, villains, and armed forces all try to stop him, but with no success at all. The Fantastic Four launch an attack, but to no avail. As it turns out, the only beings in the universe that could ever destroy the members of the Cosmic Tribunal are the mindless Decimators. To help Earth, Galactus and the Silver Surfer tell the Decimators of the Cosmic Tribunal's existence, and the Decimators immediately attack them. At first the Fantastic Four are very glad that the Decimators have entered the fray, because the Adjudicator leaves Earth (at least temporarily) to try to stop them. They are shocked, however, when they are told that the mindless Decimators will not stop their attacks until they have killed all the members of the Cosmic Tribunal. Upon hearing the news, the Fantastic Four race across the universe to save the Cosmic Tribunal. After the Fantastic Four have fought off the Decimators, the Cosmic Tribunal is moved to reconsider its judgment. The collective voice of the Cosmic Tribunal tells them, "You have saved us and our world. We shall be ever grateful. In fact, you have saved us twice! Once from a deadly alien foe. And a second time from making an enormous mistake . . . from destroying a race that possesses such great compassion."[5] It is not the Fantastic Four's great power but their virtues of love, peace, kindness, gentleness, and self-control that ultimately save the world.

When Jesus performed miracles it must have seemed to those around him as though he had superpowers. According to the gospels, Jesus Christ did not use these miraculous powers against his enemy or for his own benefit. Instead, he used them to confront the power of evil in the world by helping others. He did not attack those who oppressed others with a power blast or by miraculously inflicting them with a disease. Instead, he healed those who had leprosy and those who were blind, publicly criticized leaders of an oppressive system, and called his followers to acts of compassion and justice. In the end, he won his battle with evil not through acts of strength but through the power of love, generosity, faithfulness, and self-control.

Truth be told, the sort of superpowers that superheroes have would not help us much in performing the sorts of tasks we are called to do as people of faith. The fruits of the Spirit are much more helpful. The ability to shoot flames is not going to help us comfort someone who has lost a friend or loved one as much as love, gentleness, and kindness. The ability to stretch our bodies would probably not help us work for justice while we try to get a political prisoner released as much as faithfulness and dedication. The ability to turn invisible would probably not help feed the hungry as much as a compassionate heart and willingness to give our time and money to the cause. Superstrength is not going to help us forgive someone who has wronged us as much as peace and self-control. The fruits of the Spirit are powerful resources for our work in the real world.

Commitment and Faithfulness

Often the success of our efforts depends more on our determination and commitment to the cause than our powers or abilities. While the Fantastic Four and other Marvel heroes had amazing powers, their powers did not solve all of their problems or allow them to win all their battles.

In the 1950s and early 1960s, most of the comic books published by Marvel's competitor, DC Comics, featured heroes who had powers that were a kind of wish fulfillment for the readers. Readers imagined that they were as strong as Superman or could fly like him, or that they were as fast as the Flash. During those years, DC Comics' heroes often won their battles by ultimately proving themselves to be stronger or faster than their enemies. Their fans cheered them on as they proved themselves to be the most powerful heroes of all.

In contrast, Marvel's heroes, as often as not, saw their powers as a curse. Readers identified with Marvel heroes not just because they liked to imagine that they had the same powers but because they empathized with the struggles the heroes faced in their personal lives and in their battles. Furthermore, Marvel's heroes often found that they were not as strong as their enemies. The drama in their stories lay in seeing whether the heroes could find ways to use their powers wisely and have enough determination and perseverance to win the battle even when they were outmatched. In the Fantastic Four's adventures, it was often the case that Sue, Johnny, and especially Ben would let themselves get beaten up by an enemy in order to stall him or her until Reed could finish creating some invention that would bring them victory.

In "The Battle for the Baxter Building," *Fantastic Four* #40 (July 1965), the group temporarily lost their powers and Doctor Doom took over their Baxter Building headquarters. Though they did not have their powers, with the help of the superhero Daredevil, they tried to take back their headquarters anyway. They used their wits and natural fighting skills to stay in the fight long enough for Reed to find a machine that gave them back their powers.

It is even more often the case in our lives that true victory does not come from having the greatest gifts or most amazing abilities but by having the right attitude and committing ourselves to using the gifts and abilities that we have been given wisely, faithfully, and for the right causes. As people of faith we know that might does not make right. In our spiritual battles, it is our faithfulness to God's call that matters more.

God has provided us with all that we need to live heroic lives. We have gifts of the Spirit, our natural talents, and the fruits of the Spirit to aid us in our quests. But just like superheroes, we must choose whether we will use these gifts and abilities to do good deeds or whether we will allow them to go unused. In *Fantastic Four* #1 (November 1961), once Reed, Sue, Ben, and Johnny overcame their shock at gaining their powers, they immediately committed themselves to using those powers to help humankind. The challenge before us is to find ways to use our own abilities to do good things in the real world.

Loving Others

In *Fantastic Four* #72 (March 1968), Sue Richards, the Invisible Woman, refers to the Silver Surfer as "all-powerful." The peaceful cosmic being the Watcher challenges her, saying, "All-powerful? There is only one who deserves that name! And His only weapon . . . is love!"[6]

Love is the primary Christian virtue. The very first fruit of the Spirit listed in Galatians is love. After discussing the various gifts of the Spirit in 1 Corinthians 12:13–26, Paul goes on to say that these gifts, as important as they may be, mean nothing without love (1 Cor. 13:1–3). Moving a mountain seems like quite a heroic act that would be difficult even for the Thing or the Incredible Hulk to achieve, but Paul writes, "If I have all faith, so as to remove mountains, but do not have love, I am nothing" (1 Cor. 13:2).

Love is to be a primary sign of being a follower of Jesus Christ. According to the Gospel of John, Jesus gave a new command for his followers. He said, "I give you a new commandment, that you love one another. Just as I have loved you, you also should love one another" (Jn. 13:34). He added, "By this everyone will know that you are my disciples, if you have love for one another" (Jn. 13:35).

Love is a wonderful sentiment. Most people think that love is a good thing. We like the idea of loving others, and most people would agree that the world needs more love. The problem with following the Scriptures' call to love occurs when we have to apply it to real people. The kind of love that our faith calls us to have is not just a warm fuzzy feeling. It goes beyond the kind of affection we naturally feel for someone whom we find attractive or someone with whom we always see eye-to-eye. The challenge comes in loving others even when they are different from us and when we disagree with them. Real people with real personalities can be difficult to love. They see things in a different way than we do. They disagree with us. These are the kind of people we meet in the real world. How, then, can we love them?

Stan Lee and Jack Kirby made it a point to emphasize the characterization of their heroes, villains, and supporting characters. They gave each of their characters a distinct personality, and while these personalities may not have been as fully formed as those in a great novel, they were nuanced enough to create interpersonal conflicts. Their stories, therefore, focused not only on action but also on relationships as well. Because their stories deal with personality conflicts and relationships, the Fantastic Four provide us with an opportunity to reflect on how we can learn to love other people even when it does not come easily for us. We can examine the ways in which the Fantastic Four strive to get along with each other, to get along with strangers, and even to get to know and understand their enemies. These efforts parallel our own calling to love our neighbors, strangers, and even our enemies.

Loving Friends and Family

While many of the heroes in American popular culture renounce romantic relationships or family relationships,[7] the Fantastic Four have been, from the start, a family. Johnny and Sue were brother and sister, Reed and Ben were college roommates, and Reed and Sue were engaged to be married. They make for a nontraditional family, but a family nonetheless. The powers they gained after their ill-fated space flight served to link them even more closely together. In *Fantastic Four Annual* #3 (1965), in a turn of events unprecedented in the history of superhero comic books, two members of the team, Reed Richards and Sue Storm, got married. Most of the heroes of the Marvel Universe were present at the wedding ceremony, and naturally most of the villains of the Marvel Universe took the opportunity to crash the wedding and attack them. It made for a very exciting ceremony! In the end, however, the villains were defeated and the minister pronounced Reed and Sue husband and wife.[8]

Even though the members of the Fantastic Four were not all related by blood or by marriage, they have been a family for each other. Jon B. Cooke, editor of *Comic Book Artist* magazine, writes that the wedding "solidified the group in domestic terms."[9] He adds, "Codified by the nuptials, there was now no doubt about it: Reed was the dad; Sue the mommy; Ben, the oldest son; and Johnny, the baby boy of the cosmic-powered unit, all told giving the phrase 'nuclear family' a delightfully inspired parlance."[10] The family would grow with the birth of Franklin Richards in *Fantastic Four Annual* #6 (1968) and the addition of his sister Valeria years later.

That the Fantastic Four were a family did not mean that they always got along with each other. Being part of a family is great, but it is not always easy. As a matter of fact, one aspect of the Fantastic Four that shocked many readers when it first appeared was that the members of the team were constantly bickering among themselves. Up until that time, comic book readers were used to superhero teams being perfectly civil to one another. From the start, however, Ben resented Reed and blamed him for the accident that turned him into a monster. Also, as a plain-talking man, Ben was often irritated by Reed's professorial loquaciousness. As early as *Fantastic Four* #3 (March 1962), the Human Torch quit the team in a fit of teen rebellion, saying that he was tired of taking orders from the adults. After he returned, he and Ben argued constantly, pulling pranks on each other and fighting each other, often trashing their living quarters in the process. Reed got so caught up in his scientific research and experiments that he often neglected his relationship with Sue. Sue thought that Reed could be too cold and detached, while Reed thought that Sue was overly emotional. Although they loved each other, the two got on each other's nerves. Over the years, each member of the Fantastic Four has temporarily quit the team or taken a leave of absence from the others on more than one occasion.

Still, through all of their conflicts, the four of them know that they belong together. They are family. Despite their bickering, they share a common goal, and they find a way to work together. Their loyalty and their family bond is a true strength of the team, and one of the aspects of the team that make them appealing to their fans.

Ben Grimm has always been a bit of a tragic figure. With his power comes a monstrous appearance that frightens men, women, and children alike. He often is despondent and wants nothing more than to become human again and to have a normal life. In the film *Fantastic Four* (2005), directed by Tim Story, Ben gets his chance. Dr. Doom uses a machine to change Ben's body back to its human form. He does not do this out of a sense of generosity but in order to eliminate the threat of the Thing's strength so that he can then easily destroy the rest of the Fantastic Four. When Dr. Doom threatens the rest of the team, however, Ben selflessly turns himself back into the Thing to give himself the strength to defend them.[11] By the end of the film, Ben has embraced his place on the team and as part of the family. When Reed promises Ben that he will fix the machine that will cure him, Ben says with conviction, "Forget about it, egghead. I'm good as is."

In *Fantastic Four*, vol. 3, #60 (October 2002), writer Mark Waid and artist Mike Wieringo tell a story that recalls O. Henry's poignant short story "The Gift of the Magi," in which a husband and wife each make sacrifices for the other. A public relations agent arrives at the Baxter Building to find out what the Fantastic Four are all about, but he is left wondering why it is that they do what they do. He discovers that Ben, Sue, and Johnny really do not have a great interest in being adventurers, but they do so because it allows Reed to do his amazing scientific explorations and research to help humankind. They have sacrificed some of their own personal goals in order to support Reed's work. Meanwhile, Reed has made his own sacrifice. It has always seemed quite uncharacteristic for someone with Reed Richard's personality to dress up in a jumpsuit and call himself "Mr. Fantastic." At the end of the story, however, Reed reveals to his son Franklin that he did it in order to give the others some measure of celebrity. Even though the life of a celebrity adventurer is the last thing Reed would want, he feels that it is his small way of making up for the odd life he thrust upon the rest of the team through their ill-fated flight.

The Bible repeatedly calls us to demonstrate this sort of sacrificial love for those around us. According to Luke 10:25–27, Jesus affirmed the Hebrew Bible teaching that we should love our neighbor as ourselves. As a matter of fact, according to Jesus, there are no other commandments greater than the command to love God with all our heart, soul, and mind, and the command to love our neighbor as we love ourselves (Mk. 12:28–34).

Loving our neighbors, even when that just means loving those who are closest to us, can be difficult. It often calls us to give up our own interests for the sake of others. Those who heard Jesus' words would have thought of a neighbor as a friend or a companion, or perhaps more broadly as someone who was a part of their own community. One might think that it is easy to get along with those to whom we are closest, such as those in our families, those in our churches, and the people who live in our neighborhoods. To have the sort of selfless love for others that Jesus calls us to have, however, and to care as much for their well-being as for our own can be quite a challenge.

We are called to make sacrifices for our families and our neighbors as well. If we truly love them as we love ourselves, we must look to their interests as well as our own. We understand that even though we have different personalities and are, therefore, bound to have interpersonal conflicts, we are still to be loyal to each other and remain a family. The members of early Christian churches were said to have bonds like family members and referred to each other as brother and sister. First Timothy 5:1–2 instructs church members to treat each other as family members. Sometimes there are great tensions in church families, but these conflicts should be worked through as though we are a family and not adversaries in a political power game. The church is to work together because its members share a mission and a calling.

Sometimes, our loyalty to our family can come into tension with our work with our church and community. How do we balance our commitment to family with our commitment to our mission outside our home? A couple of scenes in the film *Fantastic Four: Rise of the Silver Surfer* (2007) explore a similar issue.[12] The Fantastic Four's continuous earth-saving efforts have created tensions in the group. In the middle of the film, Reed and Sue decide that once the present crisis is over they will quit the team. As Sue puts it, "We will never have normal lives as long as we do what we do. How can we raise a family like this?" Reed is willing to give up their Earth-saving activities and take a quiet faculty position so that they can raise their family in peace. When Ben and Johnny hear about it, they feel abandoned and betrayed. By the end of the story, however, after facing the threat of Galactus, both Sue and Reed are ready to embrace their work with the team. All four put aside their quarrels and reaffirm their commitment to each other and the work they do together. As Reed puts it, "Who says you have to be normal to have a family?"[13]

Do we put the needs of our family aside to do our church, charity, and social outreach work? Or do we devote ourselves completely to the needs of our family and put aside any good work or mission outside of our home? I knew of a deacon who was involved in every aspect of the life of his church who said that he had sacrificed his family for the sake of his church. To some extent, he had neglected his children and his home life in order to be at the church practically every time its doors were open. It is hard to imagine that God would ask that of us, as responsibility to our family is a primary duty for people of faith. Parents have a responsibility to raise their children, children have an obligation to their parents, and spouses have a duty to each other. We should not use our work with a church or with community organizations as a way to escape or neglect our family obligations. At the same time, we should not hunker down in our homes with our families, wearing blinders to the needs in the rest of the world. As parents, when we serve our church and community, we are teaching children to live lives of service rather than to just take care of their own. Ideally, we can find ways to put time and energy into both family and our work for the church and in the world and even find ways to serve together as families in our churches and our communities.

Loving Strangers

During the years 1965 through 1967, Stan Lee and Jack Kirby produced a series of *Fantastic Four* comic books that many comic book critics still consider to be the best of the superhero comic book genre. These issues include the wedding of Reed and Sue in *Fantastic Four Annual* #3 (March 1965) and the classic tale "This Man, This Monster" in *Fantastic Four* #51 (June 1966). Those years are best remembered, however, for introducing the Fantastic Four to a series of people from different cultures who would become key characters in the Marvel Universe, including the Inhumans, Galactus and the Silver Surfer, and the Black Panther.

The Inhumans

In *Fantastic Four* #44–48 (November 1965 to March 1966), the Fantastic Four meet a mysterious, long-hidden race of superpowered beings known as the Inhumans. The Inhumans have their own culture, values, and political system. They live in a kingdom hidden from the rest of the world, which they call the Great Refuge. They are ruled by a royal family that includes the green-scaled amphibious Triton, who can swiftly swim the depths of the sea; the goat-hoofed Gorgon, who can create an earthquake with a stomp of hooves; martial artist Karnak, who can recognize and exploit the weakness in anything and anyone; Medusa, whose long, red hair becomes alive and can grab anything at will; and their giant dog, Lockjaw, who can transport them anywhere with a simple thought. Their king, Black Bolt, is the most powerful and enigmatic of all. He can fly and his strength is greater than that of the Thing. His greatest power, however, is found in his voice. A mere whisper from Black Bolt creates powerful sonic blasts. For this reason, he cannot speak without destroying nearly everything nearby, so he usually remains silent. This adds an eerie tone to the Inhumans' interactions with others and serves as a metaphor for the communication challenges that so often exist between people of different cultures.

The Fantastic Four meet the Inhumans as the result of a chance meeting between the youngest member of the royal family, Crystal, and Johnny Storm. Crystal's family has taught her to fear and avoid all those outside of her Inhuman community. She happens to see Johnny using his flame power, however, and assumes he is an Inhuman like herself, and feels attracted to him. The two teenagers quickly become infatuated with each other. When Johnny and the rest of the Fantastic Four follow Crystal to the Great Refuge, the Inhumans see them as intruders and prepare to fight them off. When Black Bolt orders them to leave immediately, Reed makes an impassioned plea for the Inhumans to join the rest of the human race rather than stay hidden away. Their tenuous peace is interrupted when Black Bolt's unbalanced brother Maximus suddenly creates an impregnable barrier between the Great Refuge and the Fantastic Four, seemingly separating Johnny and Crystal forever. In later issues the barrier is eventually crossed, and over the years the Fantastic Four and the Inhumans have made small but significant steps in understanding each other's cultures and values. On several occasions, Medusa and Crystal have even come to live with the Fantastic Four and joined the team on their adventures. At times they are the best of allies, but at other times there continue to be tensions over the very real differences in their cultures and moral values.[14]

Silver Surfer and Galactus

As the issues that introduced the Inhumans came to an end, the famous Galactus trilogy, *Fantastic Four* #48–50 (March–May 1966), began. The story is one of the most well-regarded superhero sagas ever told and serves as the source of the film *Fantastic Four: The Rise of the Silver Surfer* (2007). In the story, a supremely powerful being known as Galactus comes to Earth to feed. He is literally a devourer of worlds and uses a giant machine to suck the life force out of planets.[15] Comic book writer and historian Mark Evanier notes that Galactus was so powerful, so grandly envisioned, that many people think of this story line as "The Fantastic Four fights God." But as Evanier points out, Galactus is nothing like God. He writes, "I mean, think about it: Galactus is a powerful menace but he does not create Life. Quite the opposite. He sucks planets dry, killing all that inhabit them and leaving each world a hollow, inert shell. The depictions of God across the world's religions are many and varied but none even come close to that interpretation. It certainly doesn't fit either Lee's or Kirby's image of the Almighty."[16]

In the story, Galactus is guided to Earth by his herald, the Silver Surfer, a silver alien who rides through space and sky on a silver surfboard. The Silver Surfer has scouted the galaxy and found Earth to be a planet with sufficient life energy to feed his master. The Fantastic Four's initial efforts to stop the giant Galactus are futile. At one point, after the Thing vainly tries to punch Galactus' shin, Galactus drops a small gas bomb toward him. The Thing says, "Yiccch! My eyes . . . my nose . . . what izzit? What the blazes is happenin'??" Reed explains, "Can't you tell? He's treating us like some sort of bothersome gnats! It's a type of cosmic insect repellent!"[17] For Galactus, the fate of the people of Earth is beneath his concern. They are like the ants that people tread upon as they walk in their yards.

The Fantastic Four have no chance of holding off Galactus without some significant help. Unfortunately for Earth, the only being nearby who is remotely as powerful as Galactus is his herald, the Silver Surfer. In the comic book story, the Silver Surfer happens to meet Alicia Masters, the Thing's blind girlfriend. Her simple hospitality to the Surfer, her thoughts on nobility, and her plea for mercy touch the Surfer. He says, "There is a word some races use . . . a word I have never understood until now! At last I know beauty!"[18] In the film version, it is Sue Storm who shows compassion to the Surfer and is even willing to sacrifice her life to protect him. In both versions of the story, the women's words of grace and acts of compassion and hospitality inspire the Silver Surfer to stand up to Galactus. In the comic book, the Silver Surfer flies over New York City and pleads with Galactus to cease his plans for destruction. He says, "These are not ants, Master! They think . . . they feel . . . they have even created the primitive civilization which we see all about us!"[19] The Silver Surfer has met a person of Earth and has learned to appreciate her for who she is. He joins the Fantastic Four and helps hold off Galactus until Johnny can return from a trip to outer space with the one weapon that can stop Galactus, the Ultimate Nullifier. Johnny gives the weapon to Reed, but rather than use it to destroy Galactus, Reed uses it as a bargaining chip to negotiate a truce with Galactus. Reed gives Galactus the weapon and in exchange Galactus agrees to leave Earth in peace. This is the start of a strange and strained relationship between Galactus, the Fantastic Four, and the Silver Surfer.

As punishment for his betrayal, Galactus condemns the space-faring Silver Surfer to remain within Earth's atmosphere. The Surfer is trapped on Earth, a stranger in a strange land. As a result of their differences, the Surfer and the Fantastic Four have some brief altercations at first, but they respect each other's honorable characters, and eventually they become each other's most valuable allies and trusted friends.

Years later, in *Fantastic Four* #243–244 (June–July 1982), during writer and artist John Byrne's acclaimed run on the book, the Fantastic Four even demonstrate friendship of a sort toward Galactus. They discover that Galactus is dying, but instead of rejoicing in their deadly enemy's demise, they work with the Avengers to save his life out of a profound belief in the sanctity of all life.

The Black Panther

After meeting a mysterious hidden race and a planet eater and his herald from outer space, Lee and Kirby took on an even more difficult task when they had their heroes cross more earth-bound barriers of culture and race. In the world of fantasy, it is often easier to explore the issues of racial and cultural diversity by telling tales of relationships between earth people and aliens or between dwarves and elves. It can be much more difficult to explore the issues of race and culture directly.

Comic books in America have a shameful history of portraying Africans and African Americans in very offensive ways. As was the case with films and novels of the time, negative stereotypes abounded in comic books of the 1940s, including Timely Comics characters such as Whitewash in *The Young Allies*, whose appearance and actions reinforced offensive stereotypes in an attempt at humor. Even more often, Africans and African Americans were simply ignored in comic books altogether, as though they were not an integral part of life in the United States.

Based on their values and their experiences in World War II, Lee and Kirby began to explore the theme of racial diversity in *Sgt. Fury and His Howling Commandos* #1 (May 1963). The series featured the World War II adventures of a diverse platoon of soldiers. As Lee puts it, "This was probably the first series to feature an Irishman, a Southerner, a Jew, an Italian, and a Black, not to mention, later on, a newcomer who might have been gay."[20] The first several issues made an implicit case for multicultural cooperation simply by showing how the soldiers honored each other. Issue #6 (March 1964) was more explicit in its message. In that story a new soldier, a bigot, is assigned to take an injured Commando's place on a mission. When he does not follow directions and gets trapped, the Commandos risk their lives in order to rescue him. They find him injured and unconscious and in need of a blood transfusion. He awakens to find, to his chagrin, that it is Gabriel Jones, the Commandos' African American bugle player, who has given him life-saving blood. The issue ends with Sergeant Fury saying, "The seeds of prejudice, which takes a lifetime to grow, can't be stamped out overnight, but if we keep trying . . . keep fighting . . . perhaps a day will come when 'Love thy brother' will be more than just an expression we hear in church!"[21] Looking back on those issues, Lee says that it was probably some of the best work that he and Kirby ever did.[22]

In *Fantastic Four* #52 (July 1966) and 53 (August 1966), Lee and Kirby introduced the first black superhero published by any major comic book company. He was the African prince T'Challa, the Black Panther.[23] *Fantastic Four* #52 (July 1966) opens with the Fantastic Four in their New York City headquarters, the Baxter Building, receiving an amazingly technologically advanced flying ship as a gift from the mysterious African chieftain known as the Black Panther. Ben reveals his own stereotypical assumptions about people from Africa when he says, "How does some refugee from a Tarzan movie lay his hands on this kinda gizmo?"[24] The Fantastic Four travel to Wakanda, the imaginary African nation the Black Panther rules, along with Johnny Storm's new best friend and college dormitory roommate, Native American Wyatt Wingfoot. In Wakanda, the Fantastic Four soon learn that, although its citizens wear traditional clothing and respect the traditions of their people, they are much more technologically advanced than the average American. After proving his worth by defeating the Fantastic Four in battle,[25] the Black Panther shares a meal with them. He introduces them to Wakanda's culture and asks them for help in saving his people from the villain Klaw (*Fantastic Four* #53, August 1966). Lee and Kirby present the Black Panther as a character of great dignity, intelligence, and extreme physical conditioning, a far cry from the way Africans had been presented in the past. To bring the reader along, Lee and Kirby used an effective strategy. They have the team's everyman, Ben Grimm, repeatedly make a fool of himself by assuming that he has learned all about African culture and the Panther's background from watching the racist stereotypes in Tarzan movies and reading Bomba the Jungle Boy books.[26] In truth, the racist images of ignorant, savage natives were probably what came to the mind of many comic book readers of the time when they thought of the continent of Africa. In the battle that ensues, Ben and the rest of the Fantastic Four gain great respect for the Black Panther, the people of Wakanda, and Johnny's new friend Wyatt Wingfoot. The Black Panther has continued to be one of the Fantastic Four's best friends. More recently, the Black Panther and his new bride Storm, of the X-Men,[27] even took Sue and Reed's place on the team in order to allow them to take time off to go on a second honeymoon.[28]

Lee and Kirby gave a good deal of attention to their creation of the Black Panther, refining his costume and changing the cover of his first appearance at the last second. They had plans to launch him in his own series but, because of Marvel's limited distribution contract at the time, they had to settle for having him as a recurring character in *Fantastic Four* and soon made him a key member of the Avengers.[29]

Reginald Hudlin, president of entertainment at the BET Network and writer of the 2005 series *The Black Panther* (vol. 4), writes, "Like Sidney Poitier, the Black Panther went a long way towards erasing decades of insulting images in comics. Before him, the best you could hope for was to be ignored altogether."[30] According to Hudlin, that all changed with the Marvel Comics of the 1960s. He writes, "Marvel got it right off the bat. First with Gabe Jones in *Nick Fury and His Howling Commandos*, who didn't have much personality but never did anything wrong—the war comic equivalent to Peanuts' Franklin. But [with] the creation of T'Challa (and special mention to Native American Wyatt Wingfoot, also a cool brother) the game was forever changed."[31]

According to Hudlin, the combination of heritage and progress was just right. "The idea of a black super hero who was a king of a kingdom with incredible wealth and scientific genius that somehow perfectly balanced its own cultural legacy with the best of the Western World . . . who could imagine that but Stan and Jack? To write such a character with *no* superpowers but introducing us by having him defeat the Fantastic Four—in their own book?"[32]During the rest of their run on *The Fantastic Four*, Lee and Kirby continued to weave the Inhumans, Silver Surfer, and Black Panther into their stories as recurring characters, and they have all been featured in their own comic books as well.

Reaching Out

Strangers in the Bible

The charge to love our neighbor is difficult enough when we are called to love our family, our fellow church members, and those who live in our neighborhoods. The task becomes even more difficult when the definition of neighbor is expanded to include people we do not know and who are from other cultures. The commands to love one's neighbors in Leviticus 19 presupposed love for those in need and those from other lands,[33] but there were those in Jesus' day who sought to limit their responsibility. In the parable of the Samaritan, Jesus made it clear that the responsibility to love our neighbors extends beyond our circle of family, friends, and companions.

There was a great deal of religious and ethnic tension between Jews and Samaritans in Jesus' day. Old disagreements regarding religious and cultural practices had simmered to the point that the two groups often despised each other. Both groups condemned the other for worshipping God in a different way than they did. They shared a faith, but practiced it in different ways and from different cultural perspectives. The Gospel of John, for example, tells us that when Jesus asked a Samaritan woman for a drink of water she was shocked. For those unaware of the tensions, the gospel explains "Jews do not share things in common with Samaritans" (Jn. 4:9).

The Gospel of Luke tells the story of how, while they were traveling through the land of the Samaritans, Jesus sent some of his disciples ahead to a village of the Samaritans to make arrangements to stay there. The people there would not welcome them, however, because they knew they were going to proceed to Jerusalem. So Jesus and his disciples had to travel on to another village (Lk. 9:52–53). Anyone who has traveled far and found a "no vacancy" sign at the end of a long day knows how frustrating this can be. In a clear allusion to Elijah's defeat of the prophets of Baal in 1 Kings 18, James and John apparently wanted to use some flame power themselves, and asked Jesus to call down fire from heaven on the Samaritans who had rejected him. Jesus rebuked them, and he and his disciples simply moved on to another village (Lk. 9:54–55).

It is in this context of anger and disdain that Jesus, in the very next chapter of the Gospel of Luke, told the parable of the Samaritan. In Luke 10:29, a lawyer asked Jesus what he must do to inherit eternal life. When Jesus told him that he needed to love God and to love his neighbor as himself, the lawyer tried to give himself some wiggle room by asking, "And who is my neighbor?" Jesus responded by telling the now-familiar story of a man who is robbed, beaten, and left for dead. Two Jewish religious leaders, a priest and a Levite, pass by the injured man without lending aid. But then a Samaritan, a foreigner that Jesus' listeners would not have expected to lend aid to a Jew, happens by and rescues the man, even paying for his care and treatment (Lk. 10:30–35). Jesus then asks the lawyer, "Which of these three, do you think, was a neighbor to the man who fell into the hands of the robbers?" (Lk. 10:36). The lawyer seems to have understood the lesson. He replies, "The one who showed him mercy," and Jesus responds, "Go and do likewise" (Lk. 10:37). Bible scholar Victor Paul Furnish comments on this passage, saying, "For Jesus love is not just an attitude, but a way of life. Love requires the real expenditures of one's time, effort, and resources."[34]

To be fair, the priest and Levite would have been taking a risk in helping the man at the side of the road. If the man had been dead, for example, they could have been disqualified from carrying out some of their religious duties. The Samaritan in the story was engaging in risky behavior as well. He did not know the man who fell victim to the robbers, and he did not know whether he was opening himself up to being robbed himself by stopping and helping the man. He did not know how people would react once he brought the person to receive aid. It would probably have been safer just not to get involved. In the context of the story, however, it is clear that Jesus thinks the Samaritan has done the right thing. The story would have been shocking and offensive to many of those who heard it, because it challenged their religious, social, and ethnic prejudices. Jesus had told a story in which a member of a social group that the listeners despised on religious and ethnic grounds acted in a way that was morally superior to the way their own religious leaders acted. Jesus was calling on his followers to take risks, to step outside their comfort zones, and to care for people who lived outside their own communities.

A pattern emerges in the way Lee and Kirby had the Fantastic Four build relationships with the Inhumans, the Silver Surfer and Galactus, and the Black Panther and people of Wakanda. First of all, the Fantastic Four take a risk and venture outside their comfort zone to meet people who are different from themselves. Then, when the Fantastic Four make their first attempts to communicate with strangers, misunderstandings abound. Still, the Fantastic Four persist in their efforts to communicate. When they do, the two sides tend to perceive each other as enemies at first. They fight, or come near to fighting, each other. Somewhere in the story line, however, a personal meeting occurs. Johnny meets Crystal, Alicia and the Silver Surfer have a conversation, and the Black Panther shares a meal and conversation with the Fantastic Four. They begin to see each other as real people and not simply "the other." Even though they do not fully understand one another, they are willing to take a posture of generosity and help each other. Finally, despite some ongoing tensions, the relationships continue to grow, and they become some of each other's most loyal friends and allies.

The events of these classic Fantastic Four stories presented a great first step in cross-cultural relationships, but there were still ongoing tensions, and they have continued building those relationships over the years. The Fantastic Four learned that the Inhumans, Silver Surfer, and Black Panther are not the same as themselves, under the skin. Race and culture matter. They really do have different values and perspectives from their different experiences of the world, and at times they simply have to agree to disagree and accept the other without attempting to make them conform to their own way of doing things. The Inhumans still do not fully trust the world of humans. The Silver Surfer has continued to have some conflicts with the Fantastic Four, and he continues to be misunderstood and feared by most of humankind. The Fantastic Four and the Black Panther respect each other, but at times they need to communicate better so that they can understand how to show that respect. The heroic thing that the Fantastic Four and these other heroes have done is that they have continued to dialogue with each other despite their differences and some misunderstandings along the way. They have continued to respect each other and have tried to understand each other.

We might ask ourselves whether we have only friends who look like we do, act like we do, and come from the same background as we do. If so, perhaps we should take a cue from the Fantastic Four and be more adventurous and journey into new situations to meet new kinds of people. By looking beyond past impressions and past stereotypes, we can begin to build bridges of understanding. In his December 1967 "Stan's Soapbox," Lee put it well when he wrote, "Always remember—'Love thy neighbor' means EVERYBODY! 'Nuff said!"[35]

Loving Enemies

Another innovation that Stan Lee and Jack Kirby brought to Marvel Comics was that they humanized the villains of their stories. The early stories of the Fantastic Four took the creative step of giving supervillains motivations for their behavior. They do not just try to rob banks to get money or try to rule the world for no apparent reason other than that they are supervillains. In many cases, the villains do not even see themselves as villains. They feel that they are just unlucky or misunderstood. While readers would certainly be rooting for the Fantastic Four to win battles, they often developed a measure of empathy for their enemies as well. Furthermore, the Fantastic Four came to develop relationships with some of their enemies, and some of those enemies even became their friends.

The Mole Man

The motif of creating empathy for the enemy was present from the very beginning of the Marvel Universe in *Fantastic Four* #1 (November 1961). Kirby introduces the villain of the story, the Mole Man, in one small panel in which he looks both frightening and pitiable at the same time. The Mole Man rules an underground kingdom that is populated with the sort of wonderfully imaginative giant monsters that Kirby had been drawing for the past several years. In that first issue, the Mole Man tells the Fantastic Four his story. He explains that people used to mock him for his appearance. He recounts a woman mocking him, saying, "What? Me go out with you? Don't make me laugh!" A potential employer says, "I know you're qualified, but you can't work here! You'd scare our other employees away!" A person on the street mocks him, saying, "Hey, is that your face, or are you wearin' a mask? Haw haw!"[36] Finding no acceptance on the surface world, he decides to leave humankind behind. He travels to find caves that will take him to the center of the earth, reasoning, "Even this loneliness is better than the cruelty of my fellow men!"[37] There, he finds monsters and other creatures that serve him. When he threatens to destroy the surface world, the Fantastic Four seal him and his monsters underground. The reader, however, is left with a bit of sympathy and understanding for the Mole Man.

Years later, in *Fantastic Four* #88–90 (July–September 1969), the Mole Man is still smarting from the humiliation and rejection he had experienced from humankind. Kirby draws him as a pitiful mess of a man, and it is not clear whether readers are meant to pity him or despise him. When he once again rises from his underground dwelling to try to take over the surface world, the Fantastic Four stop him. Before he is captured, he shocks Mr. Fantastic with his mechanized staff, possibly fatally. Sue goes after him, but the Mole Man pleads for mercy. He says, "It was his fault! He tried to seize the staff! I'm not to blame! I've never been to blame! Never! Never!"[38] He screams, "No! No! You've no right to be so angry! All I wanted . . . was justice! Justice for myself . . . and my loyal legions! It was mankind that drove me beneath the surface . . . mankind who feared me and made me an outcast! I just wanted to walk on the surface again . . . to see the dawn come up . . . to feel the warmth of the sun! You can't condemn me for that!"[39] He later adds, "Nobody understands! Nobody ever cares!"[40] In this case, Johnny doesn't buy into the Mole Man's self-pity and does not allow him to play the victim. What the Mole Man is doing, how he is responding to the adversity that he has faced, is unacceptable. Johnny gives him a piece of his mind, saying, "So you had a gripe! Did it ever occur to you that everyone's got a gripe? Nobody exiled you to Subterranea! You went there on your own . . .'cause you couldn't face up to your problems! Well, I've got news for you mister. Ben Grimm had a problem . . . a lot bigger than yours! But he faced it like a man! Even Alicia, a gal not as lucky as you 'cause she's totally blind, managed to take on the world and come up a winner! But you live on hate . . . blaming others for whatever's bugging you. If pity's your bag . . . you won't find it here."[41]

While the Fantastic Four might bear some sympathy and understanding for their enemies, they do not let them get away with their crimes. They may be sympathetic, but they do not believe that their enemies' bad fortune excuses their bad behavior.

Doctor Doom

The Fantastic Four's most famous nemesis, Doctor Doom, first appeared in *Fantastic Four* #5 (July 1962) and became the team's archenemy. In the Fantastic Four films there has not been much time to develop his character beyond making him an evil megalomaniac bent on power. In the comic books, however, readers have learned a great deal about his background and his character.

In *Fantastic Four Annual* #2 (1964), readers learned "The Fantastic Origin of Doctor Doom." The story reveals that Victor Von Doom grew up in a poor gypsy tribe in Europe that was oppressed by a ruthless baron. The baron's men killed his mother when Victor was just an infant. When Doom was a young boy, the baron summoned his father, a gypsy healer, to his castle to save his dying wife. When his father could not save her life, he knew the baron would try to kill him and his son in revenge. Doom's father fled with young Victor into the snow-covered hills surrounding the village, and there his father died trying to save him. After his father's death, Doom discovered that his mother was a sorceress. As he grew into his teen years, he experimented with both science and sorcery. His brilliance as an inventor became legendary, and it won him a scholarship at State U in the United States. There he met Reed Richards who, hearing of their shared interest in science, suggested that they room together. But Von Doom wants privacy, so Reed instead rooms with the school's new football star, Ben Grimm. Von Doom's reckless ambition leads him to conduct a dangerous experiment that damaged his face and his psyche as well. Overcome with a hatred for humankind and irrational jealousy and hatred of Reed Richards in particular, Von Doom left the school, created his famous armor, and set out to become the master of all humankind. His first step was to conquer the country once led by the baron who had caused his parents' deaths. He became the absolute monarch of the Kingdom of Latveria, bringing the people there a peace and prosperity they had never known before. By knowing his background, readers can begin to understand Doom's bitterness and perhaps even admire his accomplishments from such modest beginnings, while still detesting his villainous ways.

Over the years, Doom has developed into a complex man. The people of Latveria seem to adore him and fear him. He brings them peace and prosperity, but he rules them as a tyrant. In an epic story running from *Fantastic Four* #84 (March 1969) through #87 (June 1969), for example, readers learn that Doom has a taste for the finer things in life. He has a master chef prepare a fine meal for his guests (hostages, actually) and plays them a piano concerto of his own composition. He tells them, "I wish only to live with beauty with culture to enjoy the simple pleasures life has to offer."[42] After four issues of battles, he finally has the Fantastic Four within his grasp. Then, when he discovers that one of his underlings has destroyed some priceless works of art, he becomes despondent and simply lets them go.

In 1998, Chris Claremont returned to Marvel to begin a long run on the *Fantastic Four* (vol. 3, #4–32). Claremont took this empathy and understanding of Dr. Doom to a whole new level in a story line in which Reed took on the body and identity of Doom and ruled over Latveria. I asked Claremont about that story line and others.

> RUSSELL DALTON: It was interesting to me, rereading Stan Lee and Jack Kirby's classic run of *Fantastic Four*, issues 40 through 70, that they experienced many new cultures. One of the reasons that led to the Fantastic Four finding victory was they understood and respected other cultures and understood the motivations of those who could be considered their enemies. To jump forward to your run on the *Fantastic Four*, you took that theme exponentially further. You had the Fantastic Four experiencing all sorts of cosmic races and people from different

timelines. You even had Reed literally find out what it is like to live in Doctor Doom's skin for a while.

CHRIS CLAREMONT: And finding that it is a lot more tempting and seductive and dangerous than he ever imagined. That is the nature of heroism. Being brave, from one perspective can be easy. But, how do you take a stand when the thing that you are fighting is an impulse within yourself? The ideal is to look at these as real people. The thing I was frustrated with is that I wanted that to go on for a year or more. I wanted the conflict between Reed and himself, and Reed and Doom, and Sue and both men, to build to a crescendo where you weren't exactly sure how it would turn out or who you should root for. If Reed as Doom is bringing peace to the world, maybe that isn't such a bad thing.[43]

In the film *Fantastic Four: Rise of the Silver Surfer* (2007), in a story line inspired by Stan Lee and Jack Kirby's epic stories from *Fantastic Four* #57–60 (December 1966 through March 1967), Dr. Doom steals the Silver Surfer's surfboard and his almost unlimited cosmic power. In the comic book and the film, it is clear that Doom has brilliantly planned his theft and is headed for world domination. The comic book story makes it clear that it is Doom's arrogance that causes him to fail, along with his personal vendetta against Reed and the rest of the Fantastic Four. In contrast to Doom, Reed, Sue, and other Marvel heroes are usually shown making a distinction between their desire to stop a villain's action and any personal feelings of anger or desire for revenge against the villain. Because these heroes do not feel the need for vengeance or retaliation, they can focus on finding solutions to the problems created by their enemies. Reed makes an effort to understand his enemies and their motivations, and he is therefore better able to anticipate their moves. Because Sue does not dismiss their enemies as simply evil monsters, she is better able to appeal to them to stop fighting and reason things out.

Prince Namor the Sub-Mariner

The benefits of empathizing with one's enemies are perhaps best seen in the Fantastic Four's interactions with Prince Namor the Sub-Mariner, ruler of the undersea Kingdom of Atlantis. Namor was one of Marvel's most famous characters of the 1940s and 1950s, and Stan Lee and Jack Kirby reintroduced him in *Fantastic Four* #4 (March 1962). Along with Dr. Doom, Namor was the Fantastic Four's most commonly recurring enemy, appearing in no less than seven issues in the Fantastic Four's first three years.[44] Namor is portrayed as a proud and noble monarch, enraged by the surface world's actions against his subjects, such as the undersea testing of hydrogen bombs that, unbeknownst to the testers, has devastated Namor's undersea kingdom. Namor is a threat to the surface world, but he is enamored of Sue and invites her to marry him and rule with him over his kingdom. Is he a villain? In *Fantastic Four* #14 (May 1963), Namor is placed under the control of the Puppet Master, who makes Namor kidnap Sue and try to make her his bride. When the Fantastic Four go undersea to rescue her, Namor breaks out of his trance and lets them go. As the Fantastic Four prepare to leave, Sue voices her hope that they will become friends.[45] In *Fantastic Four Annual* #1 (1963), Sue explains, "He isn't bad . . . He's just fighting for what he believes in, the same as we humans are!"[46] In *Fantastic Four* #33 (December 1964), unbeknownst to Namor, the Atlantean Lady Dorma travels to the surface to ask the Fantastic Four to help in defeating Attuma, the powerful leader of a rebel force that is trying to overthrow Namor as ruler of Atlantis. Dorma loves Namor and explains that Attuma would kill Namor and invade the surface world. Namor's pride would never allow him to ask for help, however, so she says that they must keep their help a secret from him. This request must have been a particularly challenging one for Reed. In the past Namor had tried to woo Sue away from Reed on more than one occasion, and he comes across as an arrogant bore who shows disdain for Reed. Reed puts aside any animosity he holds toward Namor, however, and does the right thing. He does not let his personal rivalry with Namor get in the way of the greater cause of keeping the world safe. He is more interested in succeeding in his mission than in gaining personal vengeance by letting Namor fail. The Fantastic Four travel undersea and secretly help Namor quash the rebellion. Namor never even knows that they were there, so they do not get the benefit of his appreciation, but the surface world is spared an invasion by Atlantis.

Since then, the Fantastic Four have repeatedly helped and supported Namor. They strive to negotiate a truce between him and the surface world, rather than quickly resorting to battle. Instead of seeing the conflict as a win-lose situation, they try to find win-win solutions. Instead of demonizing their enemies, they humanize them. As a result, they have held off the threat of Atlantis a number of times, and have won the trust and even the support of Namor, who has served as their ally on more than one occasion. Their efforts have also helped build bridges between Namor and the rest of the surface world, and Namor has served as a member of the superhero teams the Defenders and the Avengers.

"This Man, This Monster"

Fantastic Four #51 (June 1966) is one of the most widely hailed single issues of Marvel comics. In the story, the members of the Fantastic Four do not use their powers in any significant way. Instead, the story focuses on their personalities and their character. The issue tells the story of an unnamed man, a brilliant scientist, who is jealous of Reed Richards' fame and therefore is bent on destroying him, along with the rest of the Fantastic Four. The villain is able to take on the appearance and power of the Thing. He enters the Baxter Building and works side by side with Reed, secretly waiting for the perfect moment to strike. A funny thing happens, however, as he works alongside Reed. He is struck by Reed's humility, his nobility, and his willingness to risk his life to help humankind. When an experiment goes wrong, instead of leaving Reed to die, the unnamed scientist ends up sacrificing his own life to save Reed. As he heads toward his inevitable death, the man reflects on Reed's character and thinks, "As for me, I'm not gonna feel sorry for myself! Not many men get a second chance to make up for the rotten things they've done in their lifetime! I guess I'm luckier than most! I got that chance!"[47]

One of Lee and Kirby's favorite motifs was that of the criminal or villain who changes his ways and makes a heroic sacrifice. The unnamed scientist of *Fantastic Four* #51 joins other early Marvel villains such as Wonder Man in *Avengers* #9 (October 1964) and gangster Slugger Sykes in *The Mighty Thor* #141 (June 1967) as people who are inspired by the nobility and kindness of the heroes to have a change of heart and to sacrifice themselves to save others. As Lee said in his conversation with me, there is a chance for all people, even those who have taken a wrong turn, to redeem themselves.[48]

Jesus' Call to Love Our Enemies

If loving our neighbors, including those who are strangers to us, seems to be a difficult task, then Jesus' words in Matthew 5:38–48 takes the challenge of loving up another notch or two as Jesus calls his followers to love their enemies.

Who are our enemies? For the Fantastic Four, this question was usually easy to answer. Their enemies were the people dressed up in crazy outfits, usually colored green or purple to contrast with the Fantastic Four's own blue jumpsuits. They were the ones who openly voiced their desire to destroy them or take over the world. In Jesus' day people thought of the Romans, who had oppressive authority over them, as their enemies. They also considered people of different faiths and different cultures, such as the Samaritans, as their enemies. For us today, perhaps we think of some person or group of people that we feel has authority over us and who abuses that authority as our enemy. Perhaps it is a group of people from a different faith. We may have more personal enemies. Perhaps he or she is a rival at work or school or a rival in love. Perhaps she or he is someone whom we feel has insulted us or done us wrong in the past. Our enemy could simply be someone whose personality conflicts with our own.

The passage from Jesus' Sermon on the Mount begins, "You have heard that it was said, 'An eye for an eye and a tooth for a tooth.' But I say to you, Do not resist an evildoer. But if anyone strikes you on the right cheek, turn the other also" (Mt. 5:38–39). Of course, this command flies in the face of the whole genre of the superhero story! Superheroes are supposed to resist evildoers! In this regard, the Fantastic Four make lousy role models for turning the other cheek. One of the Thing's favorite catch phrases is "It's Clobberin' Time!" and the Fantastic Four spend more time clobbering and imprisoning their enemies than loving them. One of the most common motifs of the superhero genre is that when villains do something wrong, a hero comes and beats them up. It is sometimes satisfying to our human nature to see that sort of justice meted out.

Does the command to love our enemies mean that we are just to be passive toward evil or injustice, or that we are supposed to let people hit us or physically abuse us? Not really. Bible scholar Warren Carter explains that the passage sometimes translated as "Do not resist an evildoer" is better translated "Do not violently resist an evildoer."[49] According to Carter, this passage does not forbid self-protection or recommend a submissive approach to tyrants. Carter explains that Jesus' command to turn the other cheek does not mean that if someone is punching us in the face, we should just stand there and take it. Instead, it refers to how we respond to an act of public humiliation. One of the most insulting acts of Jesus' day was to strike someone on the cheek with the back of one's hand. Striking someone on the cheek or the other acts mentioned in the passage, such as taking someone's coat or asking them to go a mile, were oppressive demonstrations of power sometimes used by Roman soldiers to flaunt their authority over Jewish people. As Carter puts it, "It expresses the power differential of a superior who disdains an inferior."[50] Jesus' call is not a call to become resigned to oppression or to allow ourselves to become victims of violence. It does, however, call us to resist oppression in nonviolent ways, in ways that apparently have not been learned by most superheroes. When evildoers strike, we are not to retaliate in like fashion.

Like Johnny's defiant response to the Mole Man's excuses, Jesus' words do not mean that we should be naive doormats for every bully or conman who comes our way. In Matthew 10:16, Jesus says, "See, I am sending you out like sheep into the midst of wolves; so be wise as serpents and innocent as doves." We should care about others, but not become pushovers or give in to every sad story we are told. We should have sympathy for the circumstances that helped to lead people down the wrong path but not excuse their bad behavior. We have every right to stop someone from harming us, but we should not wish harm upon them.

Jesus' Sermon on the Mount continues with words that challenge us all. Not only does Jesus prohibit his followers from violently retaliating against those who oppress them and insult them, but he actually asks his followers to love them, saying, "You have heard that it was said, 'You shall love your neighbor and hate your enemy.' But I say to you, Love your enemies and pray for those who persecute you, so that you may be children of your Father in heaven; for he makes his sun rise on the evil and on the good, and sends rain on the righteous and on the unrighteous" (Mt. 5:43–45). While the command to "love your neighbor" is found in Leviticus 19:18, the command to hate your enemy is nowhere to be found in the Hebrew Bible. Apparently that did not prevent some religious people from twisting the Bible's words into a license to hate. Here, Jesus makes it explicit that hate for others has no place in God's realm.

The film *Fantastic Four* (2005), directed by Tim Story, offers a similar sentiment. When Ben first meets Alicia Masters, she helps him gain a new perspective on the God of love. Ben is in a sour mood, understandably feeling sorry for himself. He says, "If there is a god, he hates me." Alicia responds, "She . . . is not so into hate."

But what does it mean, exactly, to love one's enemies? Does it mean that we should let those who do evil have every victory? Does it mean that we always let our enemies win in the interest of politeness? Carter explains, "Love does not . . . mean accommodated 'niceness' without conflict."[51] Carter points out that Jesus challenged the established religious leaders of his day in no uncertain terms. The issue is not whether or not we resist evildoers, but how we are to do it. As Carter explains, "How the community challenges (loving, creative, and active nonviolence) and to what end (the fullness of God's empire) matter enormously."[52]

In the case of Doctor Doom, the Fantastic Four did not sit by and let him take over the world out of affection for him. They did not, however, carry out a personal vendetta to try to harm him, either.

What are some concrete ways in which we can love our enemies? One of the first steps that we can take is to approach them as real people and not just demonize them as monsters or people who are purely evil. While superhero comic books and films such as those of the Fantastic Four do tend to divide the world into heroes and villains, in contrast to many superhero tales, the stories of the Fantastic Four do at least take the important step of humanizing their enemies. While the stories of the Fantastic Four do not present the perfect example of loving enemies, Stan Lee and Jack Kirby at least made an effort to show that the villains were real people with real motivations, and not just monsters. One way we can show such love is by answering Jesus' call to pray for our enemies. By taking time to pray for others, we are forced to stop and see them as real people and not simply objects of our anger and disdain. Social ethicist Stephen Charles Mott suggests that the sort of love commanded in the New Testament "respects the human dignity ascribed to and shared by everyone."[53] He adds, "This involves both a perception of what humanity was meant to be and respect for this potential in every person."[54]

The ancient teaching of the Didache suggests that one benefit of showing love to an enemy is that it may turn them into a friend. Commenting on Jesus' words it says, "Love the ones hating you, and you will not have an enemy" (Didache 1:3). Jesus himself, however, offered no guarantee that our love for others will be returned to us. By taking a gracious approach to the Sub-Mariner, the Fantastic Four were able to win him over as an ally, but this was not the case with Doctor Doom. Loving our enemy does not guarantee they will become our friend. It may, however, help keep us, like the Fantastic Four, focused on our tasks here on Earth rather than putting all our energy into nursing vendettas against others. It may help us focus on finding solutions rather than finding revenge. It may keep us focused on the way of Jesus. Our love may not change our enemies, but it may change us.

How realistic is it to expect us to love our enemies in the real world? Perhaps one of the reasons loving one's enemies seems so unrealistic is because we know too much about our own faulty human nature. Perhaps another reason is that our popular culture repeatedly tells us stories, including those of superheroes, that suggest that the way to confront evildoers is through violence, sending us the message that we are to love our neighbors but hate our enemies and retaliate whenever they do something against us. Jesus called his followers to a different way.

Jesus acknowledged that he was calling his followers to a higher standard than most people follow. This kind of love, the radical, indiscriminate love that Jesus called for, is not for wimps. Many of Jesus' followers were probably taken aback by his call to resist evil in loving and nonviolent ways. Those in authority, including the Romans and their tax collectors, certainly did not play by these rules. How realistic was it to ask them to be nonviolent? In Matthew 5:46–48, Jesus suggests that anyone can love those who love them back. But he is calling his followers to love without restrictions. This kind of loving does not let evildoers "get away with it," as some might fear. Instead, it is a countercultural practice that undermines the petty power plays of the rest of society.[55]

Closing

It is appropriate that this first chapter deals with powers and with love. In order to live heroic lives in the real world, we need to realize that we are empowered with gifts, talents, and fruits to carry out the tasks that are given to us. For Christians, there is no greater task than to love, including loving both those closest to us and those who are not like us, and even finding ways to love those who could be called our enemies. The Fantastic Four are certainly not perfect role models for using our gifts and abilities for good, or for how we should love others. They have, however, committed themselves to using their amazing powers for good, and they have learned to love each other and those from other cultures and even to show love and understanding to some of their enemies. Their stories provide us with the opportunity to reflect on how we can do the same in the real world.

Questions for Reflection

- Of the powers of the members of the Fantastic Four, which power would you most want and why?
- What are your powers? What spiritual gifts have you been given? How can you use these to serve the church?
- What natural talents do you have? How can you use these to serve God and others?
- How have the fruits of the spirit—love, joy, peace, patience, kindness, generosity, faithfulness, gentleness, and self control (Gal. 5:22–23)—helped you live your life as a person of faith?
- Have you committed yourself to using the gifts and abilities you have been given to help do God's work and help others? What are some specific "missions" that you are committed to?
- Real people have different personalities. How do you get along with people who are different from you? What types of personalities are particularly challenging for you to get along with?
- Think about your relationships within your family. Does your family tend to get along or do they bicker quite a bit? Do they do some of both?
- Has there ever been a circumstance in which, looking back, you realize that you were the bad guy and that you were the one in the wrong? Did you rationalize your behavior at the time? Did you feel you had valid motives? How does this help you understand others who have wronged you?

- Can you recall a time when you misunderstood someone from another culture? Did you ever misunderstand someone with a background different from yours and then become friendly later?
- Do you know anyone from another cultural background? We naturally gravitate to people who are like us, but in so doing we often miss out on rich friendships. How can you nurture friendships and relationships with people who are different from you?
- Think about an adversary you have had. Try to think about how life would be if you had to live in their shoes. Does empathizing with them help you understand them, or is it just more frustrating?
- Who are your enemies? What groups of people might be considered to be enemies of the country or group to which you belong? What individuals could be considered to be your enemies?
- How do we resist evil but not hate people who do bad things? How do we behave differently if we love our enemies rather than hate them?
- What are some stories that you have watched or read this week that seem to suggest that the best response to evildoers is to retaliate with violence or to get revenge?
- Have you ever become friends with someone you once might have considered an enemy?
- Can you think of a story you have watched or read that suggests we take Jesus' approach of loving our enemies?
- What are three ways you can think of that you can love your enemy?
- Are there other reflections you have had on the Fantastic Four's comic books, cartoons, or films?

The Amazing Spider-Man

Responsibility and Hard Times

What does Spider-Man have to do with our life of faith? At first glance, it seems downright silly to try to draw lessons for living in the real world from someone who wears red and blue tights and has the proportional strength and abilities of a spider. Yet Spider-Man is the most human of heroes. With the Fantastic Four, Stan Lee and Jack Kirby presented the comic book world with superheroes with distinct personalities. With Spider-Man, Lee and artist and co-plotter Steve Ditko took that innovation to the next level. The stories of Spider-Man offered readers a teenager who faced the same sorts of problems that they faced. In his everyday life as Peter Parker, Spider-Man is just a normal guy who, despite the hard times that come his way, tries to deal with those problems and live his life in a responsible manner. Readers do not fantasize about being Spider-Man as much as they empathize with him and relate to his problems and his insecurities. By reflecting on Spider-man's life and adventures, we can reflect on how we might also live heroic lives, despite all the obstacles that stand in our way and the hard times we must endure.

The Origin of Spider-Man

As was the case with most of Marvel's heroes, Lee began developing the concept of Spider-Man with Jack Kirby. In this case, however, Lee recalled that Kirby's style did not work for his image of Spider-Man. He wrote, "But alas and alack, when I saw the first few pages that Jack had drawn, I realized we had a problem. They were too good. Try as he might, he had been apparently unable to deglamorize Spidey enough. All those years of drawing superheroes must have made it a little too difficult to labor so mightily and come forth with a superloser, or if you will, a supershnook."[1] According to Lee, Steve Ditko's style, on the other hand, was just right. Lee wrote, "Where Jack made his featured characters as heroically handsome as possible, Steve's forte seemed to be depicting the average man in the street."[2]

From the very first page of *Amazing Fantasy* #15 (August 1962), it was clear that Spider-Man would not be a typical hero (Figure 4). On that first page, commonly known as the *splash page* of a comic book, writer Stan Lee and artist Steve Ditko managed to blow away many of the conventions of the comic book superhero. In the background of the scene, looking small and impotent, we see a young teenaged Peter Parker. He is standing apart from the crowd, slump-shouldered and with a sad look on his face. He is clearly a nerd, scrawny, wearing glasses, and holding several schoolbooks. In contrast, in the foreground, looking larger and more powerful, are a number of popular high school kids who are laughing and teasing Peter. When one of the boys suggests they ask Peter to the dance, another says, "That bookworm wouldn't know a cha-cha from a waltz!" A girl mockingly says, "Peter Parker? He's Midtown High's only professional wallflower!"[3] Adding to the drama of the page, Peter's shadow reveals the creepy outline of a giant spider, a spider web, and the powerful silhouette of Spider-Man.

The comic book continues from that page to tell the story of the origin of Spider-Man. Peter's parents died when he was a baby and his kindly Aunt May and Uncle Ben Parker are raising him. Being the science nerd that he is, Peter attends an exhibit on radioactivity at the Science Hall. During the experiment, a tiny spider hangs down from its web and accidentally falls into the path of a radioactive ray. The illustration shows the spider biting Peter, as the narration reads, "Accidentally absorbing a fantastic amount of radioactivity, the dying insect, in sudden shock, bites the nearest living thing, at the split second before life ebbs from its radioactive body!"[4] At first Peter feels a bit woozy, but he soon discovers that he has superstrength, great agility, the ability to climb on walls, and a unique "spider-sense" that warns him of danger, and he even creates web shooters that allow him to shoot webbing from his wrists.[5]

As a normal teenager, Peter does not immediately vow to use his powers to fight evil. Instead, his first reaction is to think about how he might use his new powers to make some money. He hits on the idea of becoming a professional wrestler and a television star. He puts on a makeshift costume, wins a wrestling match, and gets some cash. Later, he creates his famous Spider-Man costume and does tricks on television to gain fame and money. After one of these television performances, a thief comes running through the studio with a policeman giving chase. Peter, still in costume, just stands there and lets the thief get away. The policeman is furious with him. "What's with you, mister? All you hadda do was trip him, or hold him just for a minute!" "Sorry pal!" Peter says, "That's your job! I'm thru being pushed around by anyone! From now on I just look out for number one that means me!" The policeman says, "I oughtta run you in . . . ," and Peter just walks away saying, "Save your breath, buddy! I've got things to do!"[6]

A few days later, Peter comes home to discover that a robber has killed his beloved Uncle Ben. The robber is holed up in an abandoned warehouse and Peter once again dons his Spider-Man costume and goes after the robber. He climbs into the warehouse, climbs up the walls, uses his webbing to disarm the criminal, and uses his superstrength to knock him out cold. Only then does he see that the criminal is the very thief that he had let pass by days before. In most comic books we would

Figure 4. *Amazing Fantasy* #15 (August 1963), page 1; Marvel Comics. Stan Lee script and Steve Ditko art. Ditko constructs the page in a way that highlights Peter Parker's sense of alienation and powerlessness, while Lee's script uses the hip lingo of the day to establish Peter as an unpopular nerd. Copyright ©1963 Marvel Comics, all rights reserved.

expect the hero, after his first successful mission, to smile triumphantly or at least to have a look of grim satisfaction on his face. But on the last page of the story, after he has caught the criminal, Peter takes off his mask and reveals that he is crying. He is distraught. "My fault—All my fault! If only I had stopped him when I could have! But I didn't—and now—Uncle Ben—is dead."[7] Comic book writer and historian Roy Thomas notes, "Up to this point, super heroes didn't cry. But Spider-Man sobs, because he's really only Peter Parker. He's just a kid with problems."[8]

Then in the final panel of the last page of the story, there appear some of the most well-known words in the history of comic books: "And a lean, silent figure slowly fades into the gathering darkness, aware at last that in this world, with great power there must also come—great responsibility!"[9] The words "with great power comes great responsibility" have become Spider-Man's credo through the years, and that of many of his fans as well.

A Normal Guy as a Hero

The success of Spider-Man was partly because he seemed like such an average person. Comic book historian and critic Peter Sanderson writes, "In short, Spider-Man is Everyman as super hero, beset as much by the banal miseries of everyday existence as by the grotesque super-villains who embody the forces arrayed against him. By establishing this dramatic contrast between the lead character's triumphs in battle and his sufferings in his inner life, Spider-Man set the pattern not only for the many Marvel series that followed but also for the entire super hero adventure genre as it evolved at many publishing companies over the next thirty years right through the present day."[10]

In the film *Spider-Man 3* (2007), actor Tobey Maguire as Peter Parker says, "I'm just a nerdy kid from Queens." One of the reasons that Spider-Man fans applauded the casting of Maguire in the role of Peter is precisely because he did not fit the image of the rugged, muscular action hero. While Maguire does not look like the comic book depiction of Peter Parker, fans knew from his roles in films such as *The Ice Storm* (1997), *Pleasantville* (1998), and *Wonder Boys* (2000) that he was well-suited to play a nerdy teenager with real-life problems.

The stories of Spider-Man offer us the opportunity to reflect on the fact that we do not have to fit some preconceived image of the perfect hero in order to fulfill our mission in life. We may think that we are not special, and that may hinder some of us from pursuing the full mission that God has for us. Before Jesus called the twelve disciples to follow him, they did not seem that remarkable either. They had their own limitations and their own foibles. Most of them were fishermen or laborers from Galilee. Some, like Matthew the tax collector, worked jobs that others looked down upon. But Jesus still called them to be his closest disciples, and God used them to accomplish great things. The apostle Paul wrote, "Consider your own call, brothers and sisters: not many of you were wise by human standards, not many were powerful, not many were of noble birth" (1 Cor. 1:26). We may not be famous or wealthy, but we have all been called into God's realm as recipients of God's grace.

We may be tempted to think that because we are not famous or do not fit the image of a "Super-Christian" that we cannot make a difference in the world. Seemingly average people, however, put their faith and passion into action to help others every day. We may not think of ourselves as super, but God has given us the gifts and talents necessary to make a difference. We can all live heroic lives, as long as we have the commitment and the passion to do so.

Hard Luck and Hard Times

A few months after Spider-Man's appearance in *Amazing Fantasy*, sales figures came in for the issue and indicated that the character was a hit. He soon received his own comic book. In *The Amazing Spider-Man* #1 (March 1963), it was soon apparent that Lee and Ditko were not going to start making things easier for Peter. The splash page of the comic book pictures an angry crowd pointing and yelling at Spider-Man, "FREAK! PUBLIC MENACE!" The caption reads, "Sure you've read many stories about many different magazine heroes! But there's never been a story like this one . . . because there's never been a hero like . . . Spider-Man!"[11] The two short stories in the issue establish two enduring themes for Spider-Man: Peter's ongoing struggles with money and the fact that both Peter and Spider-Man are shunned by those around him.[12]

The first scene of the book picks up where the story in *Amazing Fantasy* #15 left off. Peter Parker throws off his costume and cries, "Uncle Ben is dead! And all because I was too late to save him! My Spider-Man costume! I wish there were no such thing!"[13] Far from his powers being a wish fulfillment, Peter from the start thinks of them as a curse and considers giving up his costumed identity.

With his Uncle Ben gone, the family faces money problems. The rent is overdue. For a moment Peter considers robbing. "But no! What am I thinking of! Besides, if I were ever arrested and imprisoned it would break Aunt May's heart."[14] Peter follows Aunt May down the street and sees her pawning her jewelry to get enough money to pay the overdue rent. Peter tries to make some money through show business again, but the bank will not cash the check he receives because it has been made out to "Spider-Man" and he has no identification with that name. To make matters worse, the publisher of the *Daily Bugle*, J. Jonah Jameson, has written stories branding Spider-Man a menace to society. Even after he uses his powers to rescue Jameson's son from certain death, he is still publicly scorned as a villain.

In the first fifty issues of *Amazing Spider-Man*, Peter faces a long laundry list of problems that most heroes had never faced on the pages of their comic books. He has money problems;[15] breaks his arm and has to wear a sling;[16] catches a twenty-four-hour virus;[17] sees a psychiatrist because he is becoming convinced that he may be losing his mind;[18] catches a cold;[19] worries about being drafted into the armed forces and sent to Vietnam;[20] sprains his arm;[21] has a fever that causes him lose a battle;[22] and is constantly worried about his grades in school, his love life, and his elderly Aunt May's health.

The film versions of Spider-Man do an excellent job of carrying out this theme as well. The very first words heard in the first film, *Spider-Man* (2002), set the tone for the character of Peter Parker. His opening narration asks, "Who am I? Are you sure you want to know? The story of my life isn't for the faint of heart. If somebody said it was a happy little tale . . . if somebody told you I was just an average guy, not a care in the world . . . somebody lied." The first film did not end with Peter's problems all solved, either. As *Spider-Man 2* (2004) opens, Peter's responsibilities as Spider-Man have caused him to lose his girlfriend, strained his relationship with his aunt, caused him to lose several jobs, and hurt his grades in school. He even forgets to attend his own birthday party. To make matters worse, since nobody knows of Peter's secret life as a crime fighter, everyone assumes he is just irresponsible and lazy. Hard times seem to be the normal state of Peter's life.

In the early days of his comic book adventures, Peter was prone to responding to these hard times with a private "pity party" or two. For a while, almost every issue seemed to end with Peter alone in his room talking to himself about how difficult his life had become. Perhaps that was not all bad, however. Peter is not in denial. He does not try to pretend that his life is perfect. That he takes a realistic look at his life and admits to himself that he is going through hard times may help him endure them.

One of the very hardest times in Peter Parker's life came on the night Gwen Stacy died. In the comic books, Gwen Stacy was Peter's first great love and one of the few good things in his life. In the film *Spider-Man* (2002), the Green Goblin kidnaps Peter Parker's girlfriend Mary Jane Watson and takes her to a bridge, and Spider-Man is able to rescue her. In the original comic book version of the story told in *Amazing Spider-Man* #121 (June 1973), however, the Green Goblin kidnaps Gwen Stacy and takes her to the bridge.[23] This original version of the story has a much more tragic ending than the film. As Spider-Man arrives, Gwen is unconscious and lying on top of one of the bridge's tall pillars. While Spider-Man and the Green Goblin battle, the Goblin knocks Gwen off the pillar and sends her falling toward the base of the bridge and the water below. Spider-Man shoots his webbing and it catches Gwen before she lands. At first Spider-Man thinks he has saved her, but when he reaches her he realizes that she is already dead. He is distraught, and says, "No! Oh, no, no, no, no . . . don't be dead, Gwen . . . I don't want you to be dead! I saved you, honey don't you see? I saved you."[24] Gwen Stacy's death was one of the most shocking and controversial events in comic book history. For many comic book fans, it marked the end of a more innocent time in comic books.[25]

The 1994 critically acclaimed limited series *Marvels* ended with a retelling of the story of Gwen Stacy's death. In this series, writer Kurt Busiek and painter Alex Ross revisited highlights from the history of Marvel Comics. The story line features photojournalist Phil Sheldon, who builds his career by photographing heroes, or "marvels" as he calls them, and chronicling their adventures with photographs. I asked Busiek about his retelling of the story "The Night that Gwen Stacy Died."

> Russell Dalton: Sometimes things go very wrong in our lives. In *Marvels* you revisited what may have been the worst time in Peter Parker's life, when the Green Goblin killed his girlfriend Gwen Stacy. In your story,

Gwen Stacy's death seems to be presented as the turning point of the Marvel Universe, almost as if it marks the end of the age of the Marvels. What was it about this moment that you thought was so important?

KURT BUSIEK: Again, I have to back into that with history. The reason we ended the story with Gwen is because the whole project began with a bunch of characters Alex wanted to paint, characters and stories he felt were particularly stirring. The earliest of these was the original Human Torch and the latest was Gwen, so we built the story to follow the span between the two of them, so as to get everything in there that Alex wanted to paint.

But in working up a story, there had to be a reason for it—why end with that story? It's a good one, but if it's our climactic moment, what does it say? We were asking the same questions you are. What we settled on was that Phil Sheldon went through an arc of varied reactions to the marvels around him. At first, they're scary. Then they make him wonder if ordinary men are passé. Then he finds his place in the world, is excited and thrilled to be dealing with all this wonder, sees glory and tragedy, and it builds to the point where the Fantastic Four save the world from destruction. At this point, he thinks the marvels are something like angels, here to save us all, and we don't appreciate them (sound familiar?). And the death of Gwen is on the one hand a failure on the part of the marvels—she's the innocent who wasn't saved—but it's also the moment that brings Phil back down to Earth, to realize that the marvels are, after all, human. They may have great powers, but they're still men, still fallible, like the rest of us. This is depressing to him, but it's also an important realization that changes his perspective, and makes him realize that perhaps it's time to pass the torch to a younger hand, to let a fresh perspective chronicle the world. In realizing that the marvels are like him, he realizes too that he's like them, that their struggles may be magnified, but they're all the same kind of struggles.

That's not what the Gwen story is about to Spider-Man, but it's what we used it for in *Marvels*.[26]

From Phil Sheldon's perspective, Gwen Stacy's death underscores the fact that even superheroes like Spider-Man are only human. Their powers are not a magical cure-all that solves every problem. Even with all their power and determination they cannot always save the day.

How does Peter respond to this great loss in the original story? At first, he once again reveals that he is not perfect. This time, however, it is his moral fallibility that is revealed. Peter returns to his apartment to discover that his roommate Harry is losing his mind and really in need of a friend. Harry desperately calls to Peter for help. Peter, however, is more interested in getting revenge on the Green Goblin than helping his friend. Peter thinks to himself, "So now it comes down to it, doesn't it Peter? Do you stay . . . and help your friend? Or do you go find revenge . . . simple, vicious, revenge?

Not much of a contest is there?"[27] As Peter heads for the door, Harry crawls after him, calling out, "Don't leave me Peter . . . I'll be all alone . . . !"[28] Peter makes his choice. He abandons Harry and goes after the Green Goblin with revenge in his heart. When he finds him, the two of them battle. When the Goblin insults Gwen's memory, Spider-Man loses his temper and starts pounding on the Goblin relentlessly. He says, "You took her away! Filthy, worm-eating scum! Good Lord . . . What in the name of heaven am I doing? In another moment I might have killed him! I would have become like him . . . a . . . a . . . murderer."[29] Disgusted with himself, Spider-Man stops punching and is unaware that the Goblin has sent his remote-controlled jet-flyer to soar through the air and stab him in the back. At the last second, however, Spider-Man's spider-sense warns him of the danger. He ducks, and when he does, the flyer impales the Goblin, killing him instead. Looking at his dead enemy, Spider-Man realizes that revenge is not really so sweet. He says, "Funny, I thought seeing the Goblin die would make me feel better about Gwen. Instead, it just makes me feel empty . . . washed out . . . and maybe just a little bit more alone."[30] Not only was this a horrible time for Peter, but also, as fans of both the comic book and films know, the death of the Green Goblin brought Peter a whole new set of problems and hard times.

Some people of faith have the faulty impression that if they devote themselves to God and live right, everything in life is supposed go smoothly for them. They believe that if they are faithful, God will give them a happy life with few or no bumps in the road. As a matter of fact, some Christians almost feel guilty to admit that everything in their lives is not going perfectly well. While there certainly are many benefits to living life the right way, the Bible, the theology of our churches, and our daily experiences all tell us that our faith provides us with no guarantees of an easy life. The book of Job teaches that a righteous person can suffer physical ailments, sorrow and loss, financial ruin, and more. In the Gospels, Jesus repeatedly warns his followers that if they are faithful to him, they will face difficult times. He tells them, "See, I am sending you out like sheep into the midst of wolves" (Mt. 10:16). He warns the crowd that any who followed him would have to carry the cross to be his disciples (Lk. 14:27) and that they would have to be willing to give up everything they had in order to take part in the Reign of God (Lk. 15). Jesus' own life was an example of the hardships that many faithful people are called upon to endure. At the end of his life, he was despised and rejected by many of his followers and suffered one of the most painful and humiliating deaths imaginable. The Christian faith does not guarantee an easy life. In fact, the New Testament seems to promise Christians that the faithful will face trials and tribulations. We are given assurances, however, that we can turn to God to help us through the hard times (Jas. 1:2; 1 Pet. 4:12). Like Peter Parker, we need to live responsibly, not in expectation that it will earn us earthly rewards but because it is the right and responsible thing to do.

Responsibility

Throughout Peter Parker's life, the hard times that he has faced have tempted him to give up his commitment to the creed "With great power comes great responsibility." Sometimes the overwhelming odds that he has faced in battle have made him ready to give up. At other times, the cumulative stress caused by his ongoing efforts to live up to his responsibility made him want to quit being Spider-Man altogether.

In a story told in *Amazing Spider-Man* #31–33 (December 1965–February 1966), Aunt May is dying and Peter feels responsible. In a previous story, Peter had given Aunt May an emergency blood transfusion in order to save her life. Now, however, his irradiated blood appears to be killing her. Peter feels a tremendous responsibility to find a cure for her. He discovers a serum that may heal her, but Doctor Octopus steals the serum and the formula for his own purposes. Peter changes to Spider-Man and strives to get it back. After a battle with Doctor Octopus, Spider-Man finds himself pinned under tons of fallen machinery with the serum lying on the floor just out of reach a few feet away. In a scene that could have taken just a few panels to draw, Ditko takes several pages to show Spider-Man straining to lift the machinery from upon himself. In these pages, Lee's script has Peter reflecting on the nature of responsibility. He says, "Anyone can win a fight . . . when the odds . . . are easy! It's when the going's tough . . . when there seems to be no chance . . . that's when . . . it counts!"[31] With that, in a dramatic full-page illustration, Spider-Man dramatically lifts the burden off his shoulders and is free. He grabs the serum, battles his way through a group of Doctor Octopus's henchmen, completes the cure in a lab, and rushes it to the hospital in time to save his Aunt May. When Peter returns to the hospital wearing his civilian clothes, he is bruised and tired, yet he is smiling. He thinks, "I didn't let you down this time, Aunt May! I didn't fail you!"[32] Spider-Man, however, still gets no credit. As Peter leaves, the doctor thinks, "That Peter Parker certainly is a nice boy! He's sincere—well-mannered—and devoted to his aunt. Too bad there aren't more young men like that. Too bad someone like him can't be an idol for teenagers to imitate . . . instead of some mysterious, unknown thrill-seeker like Spider-Man!"[33]

The story of Peter's quest to find a cure for Aunt May is one of the highlights of Ditko's comic book career. Ditko was the artist for *Amazing Spider-Man* #1 (March 1963) through #38 (August 1966). Actually, as was the case with Jack Kirby, Ditko was more than just an artist on the stories. He played a large part in plotting the adventures as well. Using what would become known as the "Marvel Method," Stan Lee would discuss the basic plot of his stories with the artist. The artist would then draw out the story, often adding subplots and characters, with notes for Lee in the margins of the pages to let him know what was happening. Lee would try to figure out what exactly was going on in the story, and then write the captions, thought balloons, and voice balloons. When working with creative visual storytellers like Kirby and Ditko, Lee often just offered the most basic of plots and waited to see what their creativity would bring.

This working relationship, however, served to uncover some tensions between Ditko's and Lee's ideologies. During his time working on *Amazing Spider-Man*, Ditko was becoming increasingly devoted to a philosophy known as Objectivism, founded by Ayn Rand.[34] Rand, the author of books such as *The Fountainhead*[35] and *Atlas Shrugged*,[36] was an atheist, and she was greatly influenced by her views of American capitalism and individualism. She was opposed to people doing anything out of a sense of altruism, simply for the sake of helping others. According to Rand, the most productive society is one in which people work to realize their own self-interests. She also believed in defending the rights of the elite members of society, those who were the most successful and productive in their own right, rather than in policies that might shift money or resources out of the hands of the successful and redistribute it to the general population or to those in need.[37]

For Lee, however, Peter Parker's sense of responsibility to others, his altruism, was a key aspect of his character. A careful reading of Ditko's last issues on *The Amazing Spider-Man*, however, reveals that Ditko was shifting Peter's approach to others to emphasize his individualism and his sense of responsibility to himself. Some of Peter's hard times came through his seeming inability to get along with the rest of the gang at college. In Ditko's last issues, Peter is seen repeatedly turning his back on Gwen, Flash, Harry, and even his first crush, Betty Brant, all while wearing a superior scowl on his face and giving them a dismissive wave of the hand.[38] The images seemed to convey the message that Peter no longer needed anyone else. He seemed to have recognized that he was better than the others and was becoming an elite, self-sufficient person looking out for his own best interest. When Lee put his scripts onto the art pages, however, he seemed to try to send another message. In *Amazing Spider-Man* #37 (June 1966), for example, Ditko drew Peter insulting Gwen. Her expression shows shock and anger at Peter's rudeness while Peter wears a smug grin on his face as he turns his back to her and walks away. Lee's script, however, has Peter thinking, "Drat that crazy temper of mine! Now I've really put my foot in it!"[39] Ditko abruptly quit working for Marvel after *Amazing Spider-Man* #38 (August 1966). John Romita Sr. took over as the artist starting with issue #39 (September 1966), and readers could immediately notice a shift in the way Peter interacted with others. Rather than showing disdain for others, Peter is seen smiling and actually puts his hand on Harry's shoulder and shows concern for his troubles. Some readers were not pleased by the sudden turnabout. Blake Bell, for example, author of the book *Stranger and Stranger: The World of Steve Ditko*, comments, "The first issue with Romita art—and Lee back in control of the plotting—is one of the outright abominations in Marvel Comics history. In one fell swoop, Lee throws the strip's primary *raison d'etre* out the window and has the entire supporting cast—including Flash Thompson, Harry Osborn and Ned Leeds—deciding they now like Peter Parker, and it's all one big group hug from there."[40] In Bell's view, the unique purpose of *Amazing Spider-Man* was to illustrate Objectivism at work, and the changes made in the book betrayed that purpose.

The abrupt shift in the way Peter related to others, however, can also be seen as a necessary return to the moral principle of responsibility to others that was central to Peter Parker's character. Throughout *Spider-Man*'s earliest issues, it is clear that Peter's own informed self-interest would be best served by quitting his life of fighting crime and just taking care of himself and his Aunt May. In "The End of Spider-Man," from *Amazing Spider-Man* #18 (November 1964), Peter says, "All my problems . . . all my tough breaks . . . are due to being Spider-Man!! If I were just an ordinary Joe, Betty would still be my girl, and all the other worries I've got would just melt away!"[41] Peter throws his costume into the trash and prepares to take the easy path. On the final page, however, he takes the costume out of the trash and puts it back on, saying, "Fate gave me some terrific super-powers, and I realize now that it's my duty to use them . . . without doubt . . . without hesitation . . . and that means Spider-Man is going into action again!"[42]

Lee's and Ditko's philosophy differed on other matters as well. A moral perspective that Lee repeatedly wrote into his stories was that criminals were redeemable and could become productive members of society. In contrast, when writer Dennis O'Neal referred to a character in a Ditko-drawn story as an ex-criminal, Ditko protested. Ditko argued that there was no such thing as an ex-criminal, for once a person commits a crime they are a criminal for life.[43]

Starting in 1995, writer Kurt Busiek worked with artist Pat Oliffe to tell "untold" stories from Spider-Man's earliest years, when Peter Parker was still in high school and had just gained his powers. I asked Busiek about his approach to those stories and Spider-Man's ongoing efforts to do the right thing.

> RUSSELL DALTON: Sometimes we have every intention of doing the right thing and being heroic, but the real world often gets in the way, making us realize that we are just normal people with normal problems, and that realization can stop us from stepping up and trying to help others. In *Untold Tales of Spider-Man* you had the chance to revisit the early days of Peter Parker and Spider-Man, and it seems to me that you focused on this aspect of Spider-Man. He is just this normal, geeky teenager with all of these teenaged problems on top of all the problems created by his superhero identity. But Peter still hangs in there and does the right thing. Is this what you see as the essence of Peter Parker and Spider-Man? As you wrote him, what was it that you felt gave Peter the strength to keep going and fight for what was right, even when it seemed like everything around him was going wrong?
>
> KURT BUSIEK: Spider-Man is thematically and metaphorically an ongoing coming-of-age story, particularly in those early days. Peter Parker is a child thrust into an adult's responsibilities, as both Peter (since he has to provide for Aunt May) and as Spider-Man (since he has to save lives). And he's not yet an adult, so he's still figuring it out. He tries and fails and makes mistakes, and figures out how to do better and fixes things. He's imperfect because he's learning, but he's learning to be better, to be a good man.

At the heart of it, the message of Spider-Man is one of civic duty. The idea that with great power there must also come great responsibility means that with ordinary power there comes ordinary responsibility. We are all a part of society, and if we shirk our responsibilities to society, then things will fall apart. But if we help make our society a better one, things will be better and stronger. That applies to voting, to helping those less fortunate, to not littering, to obeying traffic laws, just as they do to stopping a burglar with your spider-powers. We all have power—perhaps not much, perhaps not superpowers, but we have the power of our citizenship, our role in the world, and thus we have responsibilities. Spider-Man's about that—in his case, he learned a lesson when his Uncle Ben was killed by a criminal he failed to stop, but that's not a lesson about superpowers. Even if Peter hadn't had any powers, the burglar would still have killed Uncle Ben. It wasn't a punishment, it was just a crime. But it was a crime Peter could have stopped. So the message isn't about using one's superpowers to do good or fate will execute your uncle—it's that everyone has uncles and everyone has chances to do good, and if we don't take them, then we've let evil flourish.

Peter does the right thing because he was raised right by his aunt and uncle—and because he strayed from their values and became selfish and unconcerned with others, and learned a lesson about what happens if we're selfish. The charge to live up to one's responsibilities isn't only on him; it's on all of us. Our powers and responsibilities don't involve sticking to walls or fighting guys with mechanical arms, but they're still powers and responsibilities for all that.[44]

While Peter was often tempted to give up his Spider-Man identity, in effect renouncing his civic responsibilities in order to look after himself and his own happiness, on a few memorable occasions he actually did quit, at least for a short while. One of the most iconic scenes of Peter walking away from his Spider-Man responsibilities came in *Amazing Spider-Man* #50 (July 1967), in a story titled "Spider-Man No More!" (Figure 5).

In that issue, Spider-Man is the subject of scathing negative editorials. At the same time, he discovers that while he has been off fighting crime his Aunt May's health has been deteriorating and his grades have been declining. He cannot even find time to go out to a party with Gwen. Finally, he has had enough. He says, "Being Spider-Man has brought me nothing but unhappiness."[45] Marvel writer and comic book historian Roy Thomas describes the next scene, drawn by John Romita and meticulously recreated by director Sam Rami in the film *Spider-Man 2* (2004), as follows: "Impulsively, he begins to tear off his outer clothing. In the next, full-page panel, we see that he has unceremoniously dumped his Spider-Man costume into a convenient trash can and is walking away. That panel has been copied or recreated in one form or another countless times. It was the ultimate image of the renunciation of a secret life, presumably for the good of others."[46]

At first, in both the film and the comic book, Peter is almost giddy to be free of the responsibility of being Spider-Man. In the comic book he says, "I feel like a million bucks! No more worries . . . no more problems. . . . I should'a kissed Spidey off long ago! No more guilt feelings about Aunt May . . . and I'll have plenty of time to study tonight! Yep, this is the life, all right! I never had it so good before!"[47] In the

Figure 5. *Amazing Spider-Man* #50 (July 1967), page 8; Marvel Comics. Stan Lee script and John Romita Sr. art. Romita uses a full page to add weight to a powerful scene. Peter tosses away his Spider-Man costume as though it were simply a piece of trash and turns his back and walks away from his great responsibility. Copyright ©1967 Marvel Comics, all rights reserved.

film, Peter walks down the street with a silly grin on his face while the cheerful song "Raindrops Keep Falling on My Head" plays in the background. But throughout the rest of the issue and the rest of the film, Peter realizes how many needy people will suffer if crime is allowed to run rampant in his neighborhood. As he declares in the comic book, "I can never renounce my Spider-Man identity! I can never fail to use the powers which a mysterious destiny has seen fit to give me! No matter how unbearable the burden may be . . . no matter how great my personal sacrifice, I can never permit one innocent being to come to harm . . . because Spider-Man failed to act . . . and I swear that I never will!"[48]

What motivates Peter to use his power to make a difference in the world? It is a sense of responsibility. He is not motivated by the fame his powers will bring him. He is not motivated to do it because he believes that it will necessarily make him personally happier and more fulfilled. He is not motivated by a sense of revenge, as are many superheroes who feel the need somehow to get back at criminals like the one who killed a loved one. He is not even primarily motivated by guilt.[49] In *Amazing Spider-Man Annual* #1 (June 1964), another issue in which Peter temporarily quits being Spider-Man, Peter realizes that he has lost his powers because he has dwelled too long on his guilt over his Uncle Ben's death. Instead, by the end of the story, he takes up the responsibility to be Spider-Man and face the Sinister Six. It is this motivating sense of responsibility to use his powers for the good of all people that helps Peter endure all the hard times and still do what he needs to do.

Responsibility is a good motivation for us to live our own heroic lives as well. If our good works are motivated by a desire for fame, we may soon begin to do things that will bring us acclaim rather than doing what is right. When we do not get the recognition we feel we deserve, we may soon quit our task. If we are motivated by revenge or anger at others whom we perceive as evil, then we can end up going on self-righteous crusades and hurting others. If we are motivated by guilt, we can become paralyzed in our efforts. Furthermore, if we are dwelling on our guilt, it means that we have not truly embraced the grace and forgiveness that God offers to us. If we are instead motivated by a strong, healthy sense of responsibility, then we can carry on and use the powers that we have been given, even when the going gets tough.

Because the New Testament writers knew that their readers would face many hard times, they often spoke of the need to endure through those hard times. The apostle Paul encouraged the Christians in Galatia to continue in their good work by writing, "So let us not grow weary in doing what is right, for we will reap at harvest time, if we do not give up. So then, whenever we have an opportunity, let us work for the good of all, and especially for those of the family of faith" (Gal. 6:9–10). The author of the book of Hebrews may have had an Olympic race in mind when challenging believers to "run with perseverance the race that is set before us" (Heb. 12:1). In the same way, some early churches were commended for the way they endured in carrying out their responsibilities to God under the most difficult of circumstances (Rev. 2:2, 2:19). A strong sense of responsibility helps us to carry on, even when the going gets tough.

The film *Spider-Man 2* (2004) brought out another aspect of our civic responsibility. We are all called to do what is right in order to be a role model and an inspiration to others. In the film, Aunt May tells Peter that a young neighbor boy, Henry, wants to be Spider-Man when he grows up. Peter asks her why. Aunt May responds, "He knows a hero when he sees one. Too few characters out there, flying around like that saving old girls like me. And Lord knows, kids like Henry need a hero. Courageous, self-sacrificing people, setting examples for all of us. Everybody loves a hero."

Spider-Man's strong sense of responsibility may have influenced at least one famous fan. President Barack Obama has said that he read and collected Spider-Man comic books while growing up. As a young man he exercised his sense of civic responsibility by working as a community organizer, and in his 2009 Inaugural Address he called U.S. citizens to a "New Era of Responsibility." Some commentators have speculated that Obama may have developed his interest in the virtue of responsibility, at least in part, through reading Spider-Man comic books. *Amazing Spider-Man* #583 (March 2009) featured a special "back-up story" in which Spider-Man meets Obama and prevents the Chameleon, a villainous master of disguise, from taking his place at the inauguration. Along with being a fun way to recognize the inauguration of an acknowledged Spider-Man fan, it was a savvy marketing ploy by Marvel as well. The variant cover that featured Obama received a great deal of publicity and became one of the best-selling comic books in years.

While I served as a pastor in Branford, Connecticut, I learned a great deal about civic responsibility from a group of women who served at the Community Soup Cellar housed in the basement of our church. They faithfully arrived for their shifts and carried out their work with grace and kindness. Like the fictional Peter Parker, they received no money and little fame or recognition for their work. Like Peter, they even received some criticism, not from our guests, but from some in the community who thought we were somehow encouraging people to be poor by offering them one hot meal a day! Many of these women were part of a generation that helped the United States endure the Great Depression and World War II precisely because they had such a strong sense of civic responsibility. They served in the Soup Cellar in order to help their neighbors, not in order to receive their own reward. They had a sense that it was their duty. If you had asked these women, none of them would have claimed to have great power. But they did. I saw that power firsthand in their ability to rustle up a tasty chicken and rice casserole and to serve it with graciousness and compassion. They used those powers responsibly, and as a result many lives were touched and many lives were changed, not only because of the nutritious meals that were served, but also because of the friendship, encouragement, and counsel these women gave so generously to our guests.

We are called to recognize that we are part of a greater community and that we have responsibilities to it. We all have gifts and abilities that can be put to use. There are many ways for us to look beyond our own interests and serve those around us. Part of being a responsible person is figuring out how we can use the abilities we have been given to help others. Another part of living responsibly is to continue to carry out our duties even when we face hard times. When we face hard times we may be ready to quit. It may seem easier just to look after our own interests. It is not only those who have been bitten by radioactive spiders who need to learn the lesson that with great power comes great responsibility.

Facing Our Dark Side

Marvel's heroes are not always presented as perfect people representing a heroic ideal. Some characters, such as the Incredible Hulk and the Sub-Mariner, seem to vacillate between being heroes and being villains. Spider-Man is usually presented as a pillar of virtue, but even he has had times (such as when he almost killed the Green Goblin) when he had to face the fact that he was not perfect. As human beings, we cannot count on ourselves to be morally perfect. Sometimes external forces in our lives can serve to bring out some of our most unpleasant internal characteristics.

The Alien Symbiote

An interesting chapter in Spider-Man's life is the saga of his black costume. In *Secret Wars* #8 (December 1984), Spider-Man is trapped on an alien world and mysteriously receives a black costume. It is an amazing costume that has the ability to ooze onto him whenever he wants to wear it. It also gives him more strength and agility. In the months that follow, however, readers discover that while Peter thought he was sleeping in his bed at night, the black costume would slip onto him and have him swing around the city all night. The costume became more and more attached to Peter and began to resist Peter's efforts to take it off. In *Amazing Spider-Man* #258 (November 1985), Peter finally takes the costume to Reed Richards for analysis and they discover that the black costume is actually a living thing. It is an alien symbiote. Peter is shocked and a bit repulsed. He rejects the alien symbiote in favor of his classic red and blue costume, and the Fantastic Four hold the creature for further study. Later, the alien symbiote escapes and, in *Amazing Spider-Man* #300 (May 1988), Peter discovers that it has bonded with a personal rival of his named Eddie Brock. Brock is a reporter whose big story turned out to be inaccurate. Peter revealed the story to be untrue and, in the process, humiliated Brock and ruined his career. The alien symbiote and Brock both have reasons to be angry with Peter. When the symbiote finds Brock, he senses a kindred spirit and merges with him. Together they become Venom, a larger, more violent version of Spider-Man who has become one of Spider-Man's most dangerous enemies.

The 1994 television series *Spider-Man: The Animated Series* retold the story but introduced an interesting new twist. In the three-episode "The Alien Costume Saga," the costume not only makes Peter stronger, but it also makes him increasingly angry, aggressive, and violent. He starts to enjoy hurting criminals. In episode 8,

Spider-Man says to the villain, the Shocker, "I'm going to tear you limb from limb!" The Shocker panics and says, "You can't do this! You're supposed to be the good guy!" Spider-Man replies, "Why not? I've got the power!" He starts to attack the helpless Shocker but stops when he remembers Uncle Ben's words, "With great power comes great responsibility." When Peter discovers the costume is alive and is trying to take over his actions, he gets rid of it. The film *Spider-Man 3* (2007) explored this story line as well.

It is interesting to note, however, that Peter begins to exhibit some unpleasant characteristics even before the alien costume finds him for the first time in the park. We see, for example, that Peter is already being insensitive to Mary Jane's needs. He becomes enamored of Spider-Man's celebrity status and, as Spider-Man, kisses the beautiful Gwen Stacy at a public event, not stopping to think about how that will make Mary Jane feel. Even before he gets the suit, when Peter hears that a criminal named Flint Marko is the one who shot his Uncle Ben, Peter wants revenge. He's rude to Mary Jane when she offers him advice and angrily tells her, "I don't need your help."

Viewers know that Peter Parker is usually one of the nicest people you would ever want to meet, but after the alien symbiote bonds with him, we see a very ugly side of Peter come to the fore. The alien symbiote serves to bring out these already-present negative characteristics—his ego, his self-centeredness, his desire for revenge, and even more. He is especially consumed with a desire to get revenge on Marko, who has become the supervillain Sandman. When Marko appears to die in their battle, Peter proudly tells Aunt May, "Spider-Man killed him." Aunt May is shaken by the news. She says, "I don't understand. Spider-Man doesn't kill people." She adds that Uncle Ben would not want them living one second with revenge in their hearts. "It's like a poison. It can take you over. Before you know it, it turns us into something ugly." Peter begins to realize that the black costume, which serves as a metaphor for his already present self-centeredness, anger, and desire for revenge, is turning him into something ugly. Aunt May helps him gain perspective on the sinfulness of his own life, and he begins to change by getting rid of the alien costume that has been nurturing the negative aspects of his personality. Near the end of the film, Peter says, "Whatever comes our way, whatever battle we have raging inside us, we always have a choice . . . It's the choices that make us who we are, and we can always choose to do what's right."

We may not have an alien symbiote crawling over our bodies to draw out our sinful side, but there are any number of influences that may be drawing out the worst rather than the best in us. We may have certain friends and acquaintances who are always negative and bring out negativity in us as well. Some movies and television programs endorse a flippant, mean-spirited response to anyone who annoys us. Other shows portray people who get angry and get revenge as though they were being heroic. Certain radio and television news commentary shows mock those on the opposite side of the political spectrum and try to convince listeners that anyone who disagrees with them is an idiot or an immoral demon. These shows are designed to get our blood boiling and to indulge unpleasant sides of our personalities. Sometimes something chemical that we consume can bring out our worst characteristics. Drinking too much caffeine, whether it is in coffee, soda, or energy drinks, or drinking too much alcohol can change us into someone whom we barely recognize. We would do well to ask ourselves what people and what things there may be in our lives that are drawing out our sinful side. Instead, we can immerse ourselves in prayer and meditation and surround ourselves with good people who will help bring out the best of who we are. As Philippians 4:8 puts it, "Finally, beloved, whatever is true, whatever is honorable, whatever is just, whatever is pure, whatever is pleasing, whatever is commendable, if there is any excellence and if there is anything worthy of praise, think about these things."

None of us are perfect. We all need God's grace. As Paul writes, "For there is no distinction, since all have sinned and fall short of the glory of God" (Rom. 3:22–23). The book of Ephesians suggests, "For by grace you have been saved through faith, and this is not your own doing; it is the gift of God" (Eph. 2:8). Many Sunday school lessons, children's Bibles, and Bible videos seem to try their best to portray biblical characters as perfect role models of morality. The stories of the Bible itself, however, seem to go out of their way to show that even the so-called heroes of our faith, whether it be Jacob, Moses, David, or Paul, were capable of committing terrible, sinful acts.

The Gospel of Luke tells us that Jesus told a certain parable "to some who trusted in themselves that they were righteous and regarded others with contempt" (Lk. 18:9). In the parable, a Pharisee and a tax collector go to the temple to pray. Pharisees were respected by people of faith, while tax collectors were looked upon with disdain for working with the Romans to take people's money. The Pharisee in the parable is feeling pretty good about himself and thanks God that "I am not like other people: thieves, rogues, adulterers, or even like this tax collector" (Lk. 18:11). In contrast, the tax collector prays, "God, be merciful to me, a sinner!" (Lk. 18:13). Jesus taught that it was the tax collector who went home justified on that day. The parable was Jesus' call for us to recognize our own sinfulness and to recognize God's grace to us. Those of us who think we get the message need to be careful, however, that we do not begin to pray, "Thank you, God, that I am not like that Pharisee."

Intellectually, we may believe that we are all sinners in need of God's grace, but it can be a helpful discipline to step back and take inventory of our lives. We can look back and realize that some behavior that we may have thought was justified at the time was questionable at best or downright bad at the worst. We may realize that we treated someone cruelly or that what we convinced ourselves was a moral gray area seems pretty dark from the perspective of time. The goal of such an inventory should not be just to make ourselves feel guilty but to prompt us to ask for forgiveness and have a clearer picture of our actions as we move into the future.

Taking such an inventory can help us live a heroic life in several ways. It can help us realize our own capacity for sin. It can keep us humble, reminding us not to think of ourselves more highly than we ought and not to think of ourselves as better than other people. It also helps us to be more grateful for God's grace toward us. Grace is not something we earn by being more virtuous than others; it is God's unwarranted mercy toward us, and we can thank God for it.

Recognizing our own capacity for sinfulness also helps us be more forgiving of others. We might recognize that "there, but for the grace of God, go I." In *Spider-Man 3*, viewers learn a bit about Marko's background. As played by Thomas Haden Church, Flint Marko becomes a tragic figure. He starts to get involved in robberies when he becomes desperate for money to pay for a lifesaving surgery for his daughter. After a botched robbery, things get out of control. As Marko puts it, "I'm not a bad person. Just had bad luck." Later, Peter discovers that the gun in Marko's hand went off by accident when he shot Uncle Ben, and Marko is truly remorseful for what had happened. Peter realizes he almost killed this man and says, "I've done terrible things, too." Peter then does a very heroic thing, and says to Marko the powerful words, "I forgive you." Moments later, Peter is on the receiving end of grace and forgiveness. Before Peter's friend Harry Osborne dies, he forgives Peter for the cruel things that Peter has said and done to him.

Finally, recognizing our own sinfulness helps us to stay on our toes spiritually. If we know that we ourselves, not just other people, are capable of evil, then we will be diligent in our spiritual lives. It is human nature to rationalize the bad things we do, to indulge our worst tendencies and try to portray them as something noble and heroic. People rarely recognize themselves as villains, even when they are in the midst of harming someone else. People who cheat on their spouse or partner sometimes say that they were only being true to love. People who become selfish, greedy, and insensitive to the concerns of others sometimes say that they are merely learning to love themselves. Some Christians launch vicious crusades against a person or group and justify it by saying that they were boldly standing up for what is right and true. By recognizing our own potential for sinfulness, we are better able to acknowledge that not all of our actions are heroic.

It is very tempting to try to justify some of the worse aspects of our character, such as the desire for revenge or disdain for others, as being heroic. In *Spider-Man 3* (2007), viewers recognize Venom as a villain. He is everything that Spider-Man at his best is not. He is vicious and brutal and wishes to harm others. There are some people, however, who are drawn to his strength and violence. Ironically, he became such a popular villain among some comic book readers that, throughout the 1990s, he was given several of his own limited series, with titles such as *Venom: Lethal Protector* (1993), *Venom: License to Kill* (1997), and *Venom: Sinner Takes All* (1995), in which he is depicted as the hero of the book. The same thing happened with a former Spider-Man villain named the Punisher. The Punisher is a vigilante who is driven to kill gangsters and criminals out of a sense of revenge against those who killed his family. He was introduced as a misguided villain whom Spider-Man naturally had to stop. In the late 1980s and early 1990s, however, the Punisher became one of Marvel's most popular heroes. It may be part of human nature to be drawn to anger and violence, as well as to feel that as long as it is our violence and done for the sake of our side, for our vengeance, then it is acceptable. The more heroic act, however, is throwing off these aspects of our nature and clinging to that which is good.

Back in Black

In the 2007 story line "Back in Black," which ran through several comic books featuring Spider-Man, it was not an alien symbiote but horrendous circumstances that brought out Peter Parker's dark side. After getting rid of the alien symbiote, Peter Parker wore a normal black costume of similar design for a time. He eventually gave up the costume because he came to believe that Spider-Man was not meant to look like a grim and gritty vigilante, and the costume did not present the right image.

Amazing Spider-Man #539–543 (2007) tell the story of how Peter once again put on the black costume. With Spider-Man's secret identity exposed to the world, someone sends an assassin to shoot Peter Parker. The bullet finds Peter's elderly Aunt May instead. Peter rushes her to the hospital, where she is in critical condition. The doctor does not expect her to survive. In *Amazing Spider-Man* #539 (2007), writer J. Michael Stracynski and artist Ron Garney show Peter Parker on the run and angry. Instead of staying and lending support to his Aunt May and his wife Mary Jane, Peter says he is leaving "to do what I do best when I really put my mind to it, MJ. I'm going to hurt someone."[50] Peter decides that he is not going to be his normal self and that he is not going to follow his normal standards. He says, "No jokes. No punches pulled. As of tonight, no one gets away. No one threatens my family. No one."[51] To find out who shot the bullet, Spider-Man finds some low-level thugs and beats them bloody. He takes one and breaks the bones in his hand. At the end of the issue he explains that he had gotten rid of the black costume because he thought it sent the wrong message. Now, however, he seems to want to send that very message. He says, "The rules don't apply anymore. That the gloves are off. That I won't stop, can't BE stopped, until I find the people responsible for shooting May. I WILL find them. And when I do . . . I'm going to kill them."[52]

In *Amazing Spider-Man* #542 (2007), Peter faces the Kingpin, whom he discovers is the person ultimately responsible for hiring the assassin who shot Aunt May. The Kingpin is in prison, and Spider-Man breaks into the prison in order to confront him face-to-face. He tells the Kingpin, "What this suit stands for, what it means . . . is something you can never understand. It represents a promise about all the things I said I would do . . . and all the things I said I would never do . . . all the lines I said I would never cross because doing so would destroy everything this suit stands for. I'm not here to kill you." Then, Spider-Man takes off the mask and shirt of his Spider-Man costume, revealing the face and body of Peter Parker, and he says, "I am." He proceeds to beat the Kingpin bloody. He leaves him humiliated and says that he will come back and kill him the moment that Aunt May dies (which, thankfully, she never does).

One gets the sense that readers are supposed to see Peter's actions as noble. He gets his violent revenge yet shows some restraint in not murdering the Kingpin, at least not until he can rationalize it as taking an eye for an eye. But in the story Peter admits that he is violating the standards and the responsibility that make him who he is. Stories of revenge may be emotionally satisfying for some comic book readers, but from the point of view of Christian faith, they are not something that should be lifted up and admired.

In the story, Peter Parker somehow thinks he is excusing his actions and doing something noble by taking off his costume. I remember a college student who told me one night that he was planning to go into a seedy establishment intending to do some unsavory things. He made a point of telling me that before he went into the building, he stopped to change out of the Christian T-shirt he was wearing. It was clear that he felt he had done something noble by changing his clothes and thought I would be impressed that he had done so. I really was not. We cannot change our moral standards just by changing our clothing. Even in the worst of times, we are always wearing our faith. The apostle Paul writes, "The night is far gone, the day is near. Let us then lay aside the works of darkness and put on the armor of light; let us live honorably as in the day, not in reveling and drunkenness, not in debauchery and licentiousness, not in quarreling and jealousy. Instead, put on the Lord Jesus Christ, and make no provision for the flesh, to gratify its desires" (Rom. 13:12–14). Even someone as nice as Peter Parker has to acknowledge that he has a dark side. When he is able to recognize this, he is able to stop the damage he is doing to others and to his own soul. When he tries to rationalize his sinful side, however, he is simply discarding his core values as if they were worn-out pieces of clothing.

Closing

At the end of the film *Spider-Man* (2002), Peter Parker says in a voiceover, "Whatever life holds in store for me, I will never forget these words: With great power comes great responsibility. This is my gift, my curse. Who am I? I'm Spider-Man." With these words, Peter has completely embraced his powers, his calling, and his identity, even though he knows it will cost him dearly. As director Sam Rami says in his DVD commentary on the film, "I really feel that he has matured and grown into the person his uncle thought he could be."

What does the future hold for us? Do we acknowledge the power we have to make a difference in the world? Do we acknowledge the responsibility that comes with that power? Do we see that power and responsibility as a blessing or a curse? Who are we? We are not Spider-Man, but if we accept the responsibility, we can use the abilities we have been given through good times and bad times to live truly heroic lives.

Questions for Reflection
- Have you ever felt that you were not special enough to make a difference?
- What have been some of your hardest times?
- What are some of the ongoing challenges that you face in your everyday life?

- Some people carry a great deal of guilt when their lives are not perfectly happy, because they have the misperception that a Christian's life is supposed to be perfect. How does it help you to know that people of faith are not immune from hard times? How does it help you knowing that God is there to help us through the hard times?
- If you had a friend who was becoming disillusioned about his or her faith because things were not going well for them, how might you help them?
- What gifts and abilities have you been given? What is your responsibility to use those gifts and abilities for the rest of your community and the rest of the world?
- Can you recall a time when you were tempted to give up on a responsibility you were carrying out? What tempted you to quit? If you did quit, what happened? If you carried on, what is it that helped you carry on?
- If an alien symbiote were to latch onto you and draw out the negative parts of your personality, what do you think are the things it might draw out of you first? What can you do to help prevent those parts of you from coming out in destructive ways?
- What people or things in your life bring out the worst in you? How might you avoid them or avoid their negative influences?
- What other insights, if any, have you had as you read or watched Spider-Man's adventures?

The Incredible Hulk

Controlling Our Anger

When brilliant scientist Bruce Banner gets angry, he transforms into the mean green monster known as the Incredible Hulk. The Hulk has become one of the most easily identifiable fantasy characters in popular culture. People today know him through comic books, cartoons, the 1978–82 television series *The Incredible Hulk* starring Bill Bixby, and recent films and video games.

The Hulk certainly is popular, but is he a superhero or a supervillain? The anger that fuels the Hulk's strength is often used to fend off threats to his friends and those in need. At other times, however, his anger leads to destruction, pain, and sorrow.

The image of a huge, angry, violent green monster presents comic book readers and filmgoers with a vivid image of the visceral power of our own anger. Does our anger make us stronger? Does it motivate us to stand up against injustice? Or does our anger make us lose control? Is it destructive? As it explores the stories of the Incredible Hulk, this chapter will reflect on our own ambivalent relationship with anger.

The Origin of the Incredible Hulk

The Incredible Hulk #1 (May 1962) appeared on newsstands while Marvel was still primarily publishing stories about monsters and aliens. As with the first two issues of *The Fantastic Four* that appeared around the same time, Stan Lee and Jack Kirby seemed to be hedging their bets by keeping one foot in the monster genre. The cover of *The Incredible Hulk* #1 asked the question "Is he man or monster or . . . is he both?" Stan Lee says he was inspired by the Boris Karloff version of *Frankenstein* (1931), based on the novel by Mary Shelley, and Robert Louis Stevenson's novel *The Strange Case of Dr. Jekyll and Mr. Hyde*. When watching the Karloff film, Lee says, he always felt that the monster was not really a bad guy. He was just misunderstood.[1]

The first issue tells the story of a wimpy scientist who has a heroic streak. Bruce Banner is a civilian scientist working for the military. On the day the military is testing the gamma bomb that Banner has developed, teenager Rick Jones goes out onto the testing grounds on a dare. Banner tells his assistant Igor (who, with a name like Igor, naturally turns out to be a communist spy) to stop the countdown while he goes to remove the pesky teenager. Instead, Igor lets the countdown continue. Out on the testing area, Banner realizes the danger they face. He throws young Rick Jones to the safety of a protective trench but is not able to get to safety himself. The bomb explodes and floods Banner's body with gamma radiation. Incredibly, Banner is not killed. At first the blast seems to have had no effect at all. Only later does an amazing metamorphosis take place, and puny Dr. Bruce Banner is transformed into the muscle-bound Incredible Hulk.

The series took a while to find its bearings, including changes in the Hulk's coloring, changes in the cause of his transformations, and changes in his personality. In the first issue, the Hulk was colored gray. Lee soon discovered, however, that the gray ink used in comic book production was inconsistent. Sometimes the Hulk looked very dark, almost black, and at other times he was light gray. So starting with the second issue, and without any explanation, the Hulk was given his now-famous green color. At first Banner transformed into the Hulk only when the sun went down. Then, for a few issues, Banner controlled his own transformations in his hidden lab with a blast of gamma rays when the Hulk was needed. The Hulk's personality also changed. He went from being an angry, gangster-like character to being a tough-talking but fairly intelligent hero. Perhaps because of this lack of consistency in character, the Hulk's first series was cancelled after only six issues.

In the year that followed, the Hulk showed up in other Marvel Comics, usually as the ultimate adversary for Marvel's other heroes. His appearances were so popular that he was given his own ongoing series in 1964, as part of the *Tales to Astonish* anthology comic book series. Eventually, the Hulk received his own title again, and the series seemed to settle on the convention of a highly intelligent Banner who, when he is angry, transforms into a large, green, childlike Hulk. Along the way, the Hulk also gained his own set of villains. Perhaps the best known were two other gamma-irradiated green characters, Samuel Sterns, the superintelligent Leader, and Emil Blonsky, the superstrong Abomination. Anger became a central part of the Hulk's identity. Banner's transformations occurred when he became angry and, as every Hulk fan knows, the madder Hulk gets, the stronger he gets.

In the years that have followed, the Hulk has been through a variety of incarnations in his comic book adventures, including that of the big, green, childlike Hulk; a smarter, meaner, gray Hulk; a Hulk with Bruce Banner's intelligence; and an angry green warrior Hulk.

Anger Issues

In *The Incredible Hulk* comic book series and the television show of the same name, the story lines often followed a similar pattern. Dr. Banner would be pushed too far by some bad guys. His pulse rate would rise, his skin would turn green, his body would begin to grow, his clothes would rip open, and the Hulk would emerge to defeat the bad guys and save the day. At first glance, this may seem like a dream come true. There may be a bit of wish fulfillment that is responsible for the Hulk's popularity. There are times when some of us get angry and may wish that we could "Hulk out" and simply smash our problems away. If that is our wish, however, then perhaps we should be careful what we wish for. In these stories the Hulk often reacts like a child throwing a tantrum. When he is confused or frustrated, he lashes out. After his "Hulkisodes," Dr. Banner often regrets the destruction of property the Hulk has caused and worries about the people he has placed in danger. Often, Banner and the Hulk are left without any friends and hounded by the army, superheroes, and villains alike. These stories play like a melodramatic tragedy, and fans are more often left feeling sorry for the Hulk than wishing they could be like the Hulk.

From 1968 to 1975, the Hulk's adventures were drawn by artist Herb Trimpe. One memorable image from that time is Trimpe's cover to *The Incredible Hulk* #130 (August 1970; Figure 6), which depicts the terror of being confronted with a frightening side of oneself. It is the shocking image of the menacing figure of the Hulk poised to grab Bruce Banner. The Hulk is saying, "This is the end, Banner . . . your end!" Bruce Banner is clearly terrified, putting his hands out in front of himself in a futile attempt to ward off the Hulk. He says, "Stop Hulk, stop! You don't understand . . . you're me!" The two cover captions read, "A nightmare come true! Bruce Banner at the mercy of the Hulk" and "If I kill you, I die!" In the story, written by Roy Thomas, a scientist tries to cure Banner by shooting him with radiation from a device known as the Gammatron. The Gammatron isolates the part of Banner that is the Hulk from the rest of his body. The expectation is that the Hulk's radiation will then just fade away. Instead, the Hulk survives as a separate being. He sees Bruce and says, "You must be Bruce Banner . . . the one Hulk hates most of all!"[2] The Hulk tries to smash Banner and as he chases him through the city, destroys everything that gets in his way. Wherever Bruce tries to hide, the Hulk is mysteriously drawn to him. Banner eventually realizes, "Even though we're two entities now, the Hulk's still a part of me . . . and I of him!"[3] In the very next issue, a frail-looking Banner risks his life by running up to the muscle-bound Hulk and grabbing his hand so that the two of them could be shot with the Gammatron together and once again merge into one being. Banner has realized that this angry, destructive creature is an undeniable part of who he is.

Trimpe worked with a variety of writers during his time drawing *The Incredible Hulk*, including Lee, Thomas, and others. I asked Trimpe about his depiction of the Hulk.

> RUSSELL DALTON: When most people today think about the Hulk, they think about this strong, angry character. But as I read *Incredible Hulk* every month while I was growing up, during your run on it, I think I was most struck by his vulnerability. He seemed like a misunderstood child who just wanted to make friends or to be left alone. Your illustrations really

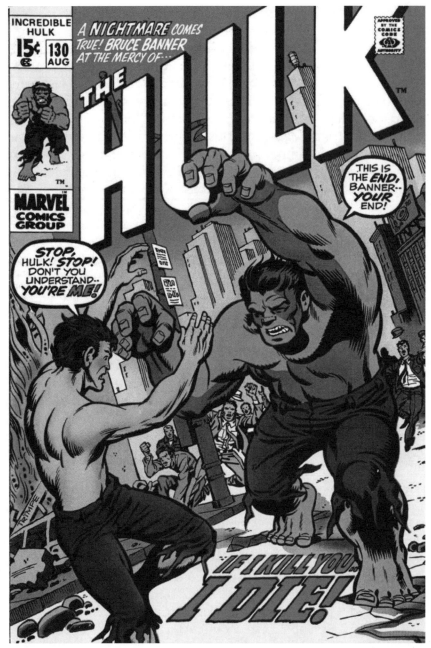

Figure 6. *The Incredible Hulk* #130 (August 1970), cover; Marvel Comics. Herb
Trimpe art and Roy Thomas script. Trimpe dramatically portrays the terror of
being confronted by a powerful and dangerous side of oneself. Trimpe's framing
of the scene allows readers to see the look of terror on Bruce Banner's face, while
still allowing readers to share Banner's view of the threatening figure of the Hulk.

called the reader into a kind of empathy with the character. Do you recall your thoughts on trying to depict that? Was that one of your goals?

HERB TRIMPE: That's right. Basically that's it. The writers understood it. I don't know when that occurred. I think when Kirby developed the character along with Stan, they put some of that in it. And I picked [*The Incredible Hulk*] up from [the previous artist] Marie Severin and I identified with that strongly . . . I understood what it was like to be torn between two personalities, especially since, as a kid, I suffered from anxiety attacks, which in those days were very debilitating. I'm talking about the real ones. It's not just being nervous about something. That's not an anxiety attack. It usually affects you very strongly, physically and mentally, to the point where you think you're coming apart at the seams basically. So I kinda knew what transformation meant, in that sense. And we had a lot of freedom in drawing the stories because we weren't working from full scripts. That was Stan Lee's way. And I think the writers, especially Roy Thomas, understood that.

    The character, as I've told people, is not essentially a violent character. And I can't stand these new versions of the Hulk that show him completely enraged constantly. That's not the character, you know what I mean?

DALTON: Yes, it seemed as though you tried to draw the stories in a way that made the readers empathize with the Hulk. Anger was a part of the character, as you portrayed Bruce Banner and the Hulk, but you seemed to convey that there was more than just anger to the character.

TRIMPE: Well, there was a fear factor involved here. I mean, can you imagine being a human who would be subject to this sort of thing . . . For instance, the Hulk became angry when he was attacked. When the Hulk was left alone [he was fine]. But he was kind to animals and he was kind to children and he was kind to anyone who he did not perceive a threat from. Now sometimes he perceived threats when they weren't actually happening, so there was an element of paranoia in there that really grew out of constantly being bombarded by people who hated him and thought that he was this huge threat.[4]

In many of the stories Trimpe drew, the Hulk would find friends such as Mogul, Jarella, or Cracker Jack Jackson, only to tragically lose them by the story's end. I told Trimpe how poignant these stories were and how they moved me when I read them as a boy. He responded by explaining to me that he never felt that he was a great artist, especially compared to the other artists in Marvel's "bullpen" at the time. As he put it, "I mean, I was coming in with Gene Colon, John Romita, Jack Kirby, John Buscema. I mean these people were icons. They were all extremely accomplished illustrators and painters. They drew very, very well." As a matter of fact, he said, Stan Lee would say to him, "Trimpe, when are you going to learn to draw!" But Trimpe felt that his strength was in putting together panels of illustrations that would help to tell moving stories. As he puts it, "When I came on at Marvel I was hired primarily, I think, for my storytelling. I was a very good storyteller and a pretty good writer I think, to this day."[5]

The ability to draw people into empathizing with a large, green, raging monster was also a key to the popularity of the 1978 television series *The Incredible Hulk*. Actors Bill Bixby and Lou Ferrigno portrayed their characters in a way that made viewers care about Dr. Banner and the Hulk. They were not bad people. Banner was a victim of his deep-seated rage, and the Hulk was misunderstood. They were able to do some good on their travels, but their anger also caused problems. When Banner lost control and became the Hulk, the Hulk's rampages caused sorrow and destruction for themselves and others. As Bill Bixby's character David Banner says in the pilot episode, "Mr. McGee, don't make me angry. You wouldn't like me when I'm angry."

In this incarnation of the Hulk, the Hulk's childlike tantrums often got Banner into trouble. Young children sometimes get mad and hit people when they do not get their way or do not know how to ask for what they want. But as adults we know that anger and violence rarely, if ever, solve our problems. We know that we can't make our problems go away just by lashing out when we get angry. Bruce Banner often feels guilty when he reverts to his human form and sees the carnage he has caused as the Hulk, and we often regret the trouble we cause when we let our anger control our words and our actions.

Feelings of anger often come when we feel threatened, confused, or misunderstood. Life begins to overwhelm us and we want to lose control and lash out. Not only the Hulk but also many of today's much more human-looking action-movie heroes solve their problems in a very unrealistic and overly simplistic way. It seems that the movies are trying to say that if the hero only gets mad enough at the bad guys and then really lets loose and goes off on them, then all the hero's problems will be solved. But in the real world, when we let our anger control us, we do not look powerful but merely immature and undisciplined. The image we take away from the childlike Hulk is not one of power and respect but of the wanton damage that has been left behind.

Another incarnation of the Hulk brought out another, meaner aspect of anger. Writer Al Milgrom reintroduced the grey Hulk from the very first issue in *The Incredible Hulk* #324 (October 1986), and a couple of years later, writer Peter David gave the gray Hulk an extended series of stories starting with #347 (September 1988). This Hulk was a more canny, tough-talking character who took on the name Joe Fixit and worked as hired muscle for a Las Vegas "businessman." He was not very nice and not that big on morals. He clearly enjoyed feeling powerful and intimidating others. He usually vented his anger on very bad Las Vegas gangsters or supervillains, so readers did not seem to mind.

Sometimes our anger is like this. When things are not going well in our lives, we can get comfortable with a brooding and angry mindset and begin to lack remorse for what we do out of anger. We wear our anger as a suit of armor, deluding ourselves into thinking it makes us powerful and invulnerable. At times our anger makes us feel entitled to our bad behavior. We feel angry and mean and we simply abdicate any moral responsibility for our words or actions. We may rationalize acting out of anger by saying, "Well I'm sorry, but I'm mad!" as though that justifies our mean-spiritedness.

Whether our anger comes from childlike frustration or a mean-spirited power trip, when we act out of anger, we can cause all sorts of problems. With harsh words or vengeful actions, we take a bad situation and make it worse. In today's era of instant e-mail, Facebook posts, texting, and tweeting, even a temporary fit of rage can destroy someone's reputation (including our own) if we are not disciplined in choosing our words. The results of such fits of anger have ranged from hurt feelings to job loss and even suicide. The Bible warns us against the danger anger can bring. Bible scholar Kathleen A. Farmer notes that the issue of anger is dealt with repeatedly in the book of Proverbs. She writes that according to Proverbs, "A hot temper is considered a serious character flaw. Anger can be habit-forming (19:19), and people with quick tempers act foolishly and stir up strife (14:17, 29; 15:18; 26:21; 29:22). Only fools give 'full vent' to their anger: the wise person 'quietly holds it back' (29:11)."[6] The words disciple and discipline come from the same root, so we should not be surprised to find that if we are to be faithful disciples, we must learn to practice discipline and self-control.

According to the opening narration to the television series *The Incredible Hulk*, Banner was on a quest to "find a way to control the raging spirit that dwells within him." In order to live out a heroic life, we must learn to do the same.

Acknowledging Our Anger

How can we control our anger? Perhaps the first step is to acknowledge that we have anger. This can sometimes be difficult for people of faith, because many of us have the misconception that anger is a sin, in and of itself. Everyone feels anger, though, and it is essential that we recognize it and acknowledge it.

One of the highlights of Peter David's unprecedented twelve-year stint as the writer of *The Incredible Hulk* came in the landmark story "Honey, I Shrunk the Hulk" in *The Incredible Hulk* #377 (January 1991). In the story, Bruce Banner is diagnosed with multiple personality disorder and has a counseling session with superpowered psychiatrist Doctor Leonard Samson. With Bruce under hypnosis, Samson talks with the childlike green Hulk, the mean gray Hulk, and a frightened and passive Bruce Banner. In a bit of backstory introduced earlier by writer Bill Mantlo and later explored in the Ang Lee film *Hulk* (2003), readers discovered that Bruce's father was an angry and abusive man who killed Bruce's mother in a fit of rage. Bruce wanted to be sure that he did not grow up to be like his father and therefore learned to suppress his feelings. His inability to acknowledge his anger and express it in healthy and appropriate ways, however, is revealed to be one of the factors that created the Hulk. Since Bruce suppressed his anger, it stayed bottled up inside him until it was unleashed in a monstrous form by the gamma rays that flooded his body. Through Doc Sampson's helpful therapy, Banner and the two Hulks acknowledge the source of their anger and pain, and they transform once again. This time, they become integrated into a larger, savvy, highly intelligent, and very powerful new Hulk. The series makes clear that it was not only the Hulks who had been the problem but also the fact that Bruce had not learned to deal with his emotions in healthy ways. This new integrated Hulk became one of the most well-adjusted and most effective incarnations of the Hulk in the series' history.

The sources of our anger may or may not be as traumatic as Bruce Banner's, and we do not undergo an incredible physical transformation when we learn to deal with it. Still, learning to acknowledge our anger is an important step in living a faithful life.

For people of faith, one of the obstacles to acknowledging our anger is that many of us have been taught that all anger is sinful. Pastoral theology and pastoral care scholar Andrew D. Lester has written a great deal about anger. He writes about how, unfortunately, many children are taught that any feelings of anger are bad and that they should suppress them right away. He writes,

> In many families if a child dares to get angry with a brother or a sister, what does the child hear? "Shame on you!" Or "You shouldn't feel that way about your sister." Or "It's not nice to fight with your brother!" And if a child dares to get angry with a parent, she will hear, "Don't talk that way to me!" and perhaps be punished. Parents find it difficult to focus on "why" a child is angry, because they often believe that the anger itself is unacceptable. So many of us grew up hiding our anger behind plastic smiles, which leads to dishonest communication about emotions.[7]

According to Lester, "Scripture is clear . . . that when anger does lead to suffering, it *is not because anger itself is automatically bad*, but because the anger is either unnecessary or expressed harmfully. Like any aspect of life, the capacity for anger can be co-opted by sin and evil."[8] People of faith have often had an ambiguous relationship with emotions. The Psalms, however, affirm a wide variety of emotions, including joy, sorrow, peacefulness, fear, and anger, as emotions given by God. The Psalmists felt free to express those emotions to God. Psalm 4:4, for example, tells us, "In your anger, do not sin." It does not tell us that we should not feel angry, for anger is a God-given emotion that we all have. The key is to learn to acknowledge our anger and express it in appropriate ways.

According to the gospels, Jesus does not appear to have denied his feelings. He was no shrinking violet, as Bruce Banner has often been portrayed. Jesus called the hypocritical religious leaders of his day a brood of vipers (Mt. 12:34) and white-washed tombs full of everything unclean (Mt. 23:27). When some legalists did not want him to heal a man on the Sabbath, the gospel says, "He looked at them with anger; he was grieved at the hardness of their heart and said to the man, 'Stretch out your hand.' He stretched it out, and his hand was restored" (Mk. 3:1–5). When those in charge of the temple had used people's desire to worship God as an opportunity to exploit them and turn a profit, he overturned the money changers' tables, made a whip, and drove them out of the temple (Jn. 2:13–16). Jesus was angry at the injustice he saw. Jesus did not go around in uncontrolled fits of rage, smashing bad guys, as the Hulk did. Instead, he often turned the other cheek and taught love for one's enemies. The gospels, however, do not portray Jesus as a man out of touch with his feelings or one who suppressed his feelings of anger.

I worked my way through seminary as a therapist and religious issues consultant in a residential substance-abuse rehabilitation center. In the course of their therapy, many of the residents would request a session with me to talk about issues of God, forgiveness, and guilt. They would talk about the horrendous things that parents, relatives, former boyfriends or girlfriends, or others had done to them. It was sometimes painful to hear all that they had gone through. While substance abuse is never the answer, I gained some insight on why they would self-medicate to avoid their feelings and numb their pain. Many of them would immediately follow up their stories by saying something like, "Oh, but I'm not mad at them, Russ. I'm not angry with anyone because it's a sin to be angry." They were often surprised when I would respond by saying, "Really? Because I would be very angry! I would think that you would be mad about it and I think that God would be very angry about it as well!" Once I was able to explain to them that the feeling of anger itself, and even expressing that anger, was not automatically a sin, a heavy burden seemed to be lifted off them. I often heard back from those clients' primary counselors that my sessions with those clients were turning points in their therapy. They could not move on until they had dealt honestly with their feelings of anger and felt they had permission to feel that anger. Doing so lessened their need to self-medicate in order to escape or mask their feelings. Whatever the issues that we face in our lives, acknowledging our feelings of anger is an important step to take.

If we do not deal with our anger, it can hurt both us and those around us. When we deny our anger and keep it stuffed inside, it can poison our souls. Instead of evaluating the sources of our anger, we can fall into a pattern of turning it inward, where it can turn into depression, or venting it outward toward people around us who do not deserve to be the recipients of our anger. By acknowledging our anger, we can begin to learn to respond to it in appropriate ways. Once we acknowledge our anger, we can begin to work on controlling it.

Controlling Anger

The film *The Incredible Hulk* (2008), directed by Louis Leterrier and starring Edward Norton and Liv Tyler, opens with Bruce Banner living in Brazil. He is working with a coach who is teaching him breathing and meditation techniques to help control his anger. The man playing his coach is actually Rickson Gracie, a Brazilian jujitsu master. Gracie's character tells Bruce, "Fear no good. So emotion and control." He adds, "The best way to control your anger is to control your body." Bruce is learning helpful anger management techniques. We discover that Bruce also wears a watch-type device that monitors his heart rate.

While we may not have a breathing coach or wear a heart-rate monitor, we can pay attention to our body's signals. As Lester writes, "How do you know you're angry? Your body lets you know first: perhaps your fists clench, face flushes, nostrils flair, jaw muscles tense, teeth grind, blood pressure goes up, and you break into a 'cold' sweat. The second clue is usually a spontaneous action, or at least the thought of acting in some way, perhaps yelling, slapping a table, shaking a fist, or slamming a door."[9] Lester suggests that once we recognize that we are angry, it is important to acknowledge it to ourselves and to others instead of becoming defensive and denying that we are angry. Once we acknowledge our anger, we can take a moment to calm our bodies through deep breathing, meditation, exercise, or even taking a moment to listen to music. Whatever techniques we use, once we calm our bodies, we are better able to evaluate the sources of our anger. If we feel that the cause of our anger is valid, we are now calm enough to respond directly and honestly to it in an appropriate way.[10] Lester also makes it clear that sometimes, if we have ongoing issues with anger, it is best to seek a counselor to help us work through our anger.[11]

Anger as an Ally?

As many problems as the Hulk causes, there are many times that he acts heroically and saves the day. When he, his friends, or other innocent people are threatened, his anger is directed at the threat and good comes from it. Can any good come from our anger?

A number of books have been written by scholars and professors of pastoral care that, while outlining the dangers of inappropriately expressing our anger, look at the positives that can come from our anger. These books, including Lester's *Anger: Discovering Your Spiritual Ally,*[12] Doris Moreland Jones's *God's Gift of Anger,*[13] and Carroll Saussy's *The Gift of Anger: A Call to Faithful Action,*[14] all look at the ways that appropriate responses to feelings of anger can actually help guide us in our spiritual lives.

Lester describes anger as a God-given emotion that can help us recognize when we are being threatened. This can include physical or psychological threats, such as threats to our self-esteem, our relationships, our future hopes and dreams, and our values.[15] Our feelings of anger can help us recognize when we are being threatened, and once we identify that threat, it can give us the strength and energy to respond.

As way of illustration, once my wife Lisa and I were out for a walk in a quiet neighborhood with our baby in the stroller, our toddler toddling beside us, and our dog on a leash. Suddenly, a teenager in a red sports car came around the corner going at least twice the speed limit, with his motor roaring, stereo blasting, and tires squealing. He was barreling right toward us, obviously oblivious to anything on the road in front of him. My wife, usually known for her gentle spirit, immediately went into momma-bear mode. She screamed, "Slow down!" I had never heard her be so loud. She was more than loud enough for the driver to hear her above the din of his car, for he immediately put on the brakes and slowed down to below the speed limit. When he drove by us, I sneaked a look at his face. The poor guy was scared, not sure where that mighty roar had come from. My wife perceived a threat, and she used her anger as an impetus to protect her children from that threat.

Lester goes on to say that anger can even be our spiritual friend. For one thing, by being like the Psalmists and expressing our anger toward God, we can have a more healthy and honest relationship with God.[16] Also, through the life of faith, we can reflect on the things that should be making us angry as well as how we should express our anger appropriately. Lester uses Jesus as an example: "Most Christians think of Jesus as a model for living a faithful, God-centered life. Doesn't Jesus' example demand that we take a more ethical responsibility with our anger, more action on behalf of those who are victimized? Most of the time we live in circumstances that call for conventional politeness and political correctness. But our weak faith, fear of anger, and lack of courage often hinder us when we should confront evil in the world as Jesus did."[17] The Bible repeatedly speaks of God's own anger at injustice and oppression. As Lester notes, "From a Christian perspective *NOT being angry at evil, injustice, and suffering is sinful.*"[18]

In some stories, Bruce Banner Hulks out at very appropriate times. Evil is afoot and needs to be stopped. At these times, the Hulk truly is a hero. In the same way, there are times when our valid feelings of anger can serve to motivate us to do what is right. We should be clear, however, that uncontrolled anger is almost always a destructive force.

Avoiding Indulging Anger

In the film *Hulk* (2003), directed by Ang Lee and starring Eric Bana and Jennifer Connelly, Dr. Banner tells Betty, "You know what scares me the most? Is that when it happens, when it comes over me and I totally lose control, I like it."

We can come to like the feeling of being angry too much. Anger gives us a physical rush and a sense of strength. There is a real danger that we can become intoxicated by and addicted to anger, and that should scare us. While we should acknowledge our anger, control it, and express it in appropriate ways, we should not indulge it.

Our popular culture is increasingly indulging our anger with stories of aggression and violence. Action movies often celebrate the moment when a hero gets angry and wipes out the enemy. News programs on both ends of the political spectrum often end their episodes with some outrageous, extreme example of the other side's views, trying to enrage their audience. Politicians and preachers alike sometimes try to tap into people's sense of outrage. Anger sells, and our popular culture today not only indulges in anger but also at times celebrates unchecked rage and violence.

While this chapter strives to use the stories of the Hulk as a way to reflect on how we might wisely deal with our anger, we should not delude ourselves. Many of the stories of the Hulk are examples of our culture's infatuation with anger and violence.

In *The Incredible Hulk* #92–105 (2005–7), writer Greg Pak tells the story "Planet Hulk," in which the Hulk is tricked and sent off in a rocket to another planet because his anger and power threatened the Earth. He lands on the wrong planet, a planet whose ruler, the Red King, outlaws the practice of ancient religions and forces aliens into gladiator battles in an arena for his entertainment. The Hulk keeps winning the brutal matches, and eventually leads a revolt and becomes the new ruler of the planet. The story line allows the Hulk to be a brutal and savage gladiator. He has to fight or die, at first in the arena and then in the war that follows.

The story line that followed in 2007, "World War Hulk," was a "crossover event" that took place in many of Marvel's titles. The Hulk and his small band of warriors return to Earth to wreak violent revenge upon Marvel's superheroes, who he wrongly assumes are responsible for the destruction of his planet. In his anger, he tries to smash every hero whom he feels has betrayed him. There is a lesson that can be learned from the story. As is often the case when we respond in anger, the Hulk discovers that he does not know the whole story and has jumped to the wrong conclusions. The heroes of Earth are not the ones to blame. As a result, people are hurt, one of the Hulk's best friends dies, and the earth is nearly destroyed. In the end, Bruce remembers who he truly is and does his best to atone for his sins.

While there are lessons such as these that we can reflect upon while reading these stories, many readers will simply become enamored of the image of an angry, aggressive Hulk who is powerful and looks really tough as he smashes his enemies. In *The Incredible Hulk* vol. 2, #1 (January 2008), writer Jeph Loeb and artist Ed McGuiness introduced a new character, the villainous Red Hulk (or Rulk), who embodies the murderous rage and power of the Hulk. He is a mean and vicious Hulk who does not mind killing people. While he is intended to be a foil for the real Hulk, part of the character's appeal to his fans is his unrestrained savagery.

The sights and sounds of film can go beyond the static pictures of comic books to provide viewers with an even more visceral experience of unchecked aggression. In the film *Incredible Hulk* (2008), there is a scene in which the Hulk has ripped a police car in two and is using the two halves of the car to "wail" on the Abomination, smashing him into the pavement. The scene is incredibly brutal and disturbing. The DVD of the film contains a commentary by director Louis Leterrier and actor Tim Roth, who played Emil Bronsky, the character who turns into the Abomination. In their commentary on the scene, Roth begins to laugh, perhaps because he is embarrassed at the scene's brutality or because he is just surprised at its ridiculously over-the-top violence. In response to Roth's laughter, Leterrier explains that he got the idea for that part of the scene from the video game "The Incredible Hulk: Ultimate Destruction," in which players can grab different items such as police cars and use them as weapons. Roth laughs in response. Leterrier tries to justify the scene, saying, "This actually was fun. This is actually funny." Roth just laughs again and Leterrier defensively says, "Well, it's fun." A bit later, when the Hulk and the Abomination are whipping each other and choking each other with a giant chain, Leterrier admits to being amazed that the Motion Picture Association of America gave the film only a PG-13 rating. He says, "That's so brutal. The MPAA was very nice to us! [*laughs*]." Roth replies, "It should be though. It's what kids want, though." Leterrier then returns to describing what is happening on the screen, saying, "He's putting his finger in his eye! He's tearing his bone out and stabbing him with it. It's like crazy!"

It is disturbing that so many people find indulging in anger and violence to be a fun pastime. Video games such as those featuring the Hulk allow players to smash things or shoot things and to be rewarded for destruction. The rationale seems to be the faulty assumption that our monster is better than their monster, our anger is more justified than their anger, and our violence is better than their violence.

Ephesians tells us, "Be angry but do not sin; do not let the sun go down on your anger, and do not make room for the devil" (Eph. 4:26–27). By reading too many angry and violent stories, watching too many angry and violent films, and playing too many violent video games, we are in danger of normalizing anger and violence. Perhaps we are making room for anger to take a deep hold in our spirits. Perhaps we should avoid indulging in stories of anger and aggressive violence, even if that might mean avoiding some of the stories of Marvel superheroes.

Conclusion

In the middle of the film *The Incredible Hulk* (2008), Bruce tells Betty, "I don't want to control it. I want to get rid of it." We may wish to simplify our lives by simply getting rid of our anger, but we could not do it even if we wanted to. Anger is part of being human. We all feel anger and, at times, that can be a good thing. Being in tune with our feelings of anger allows us to recognize threats to our own safety and well-being as well as threats to the well-being of others. We can use our anger to motivate us to protect those whom we care about. We can use our anger as Jesus did, to motivate us to speak up and act to end suffering and injustice. At the same time, we must recognize that anger can be a dangerous thing. By the end of the film, it seems that Bruce has changed his mind. He sits in a yoga pose and his eyes go green. The audience with which I saw the film began to cheer. We presume that Bruce was no longer trying to get rid of the Hulk but trying to use him for good. But anger can be an unpredictable ally. When Edward Norton's Bruce Banner looks up at the camera and smiles that smile, eyes all green, perhaps we should still feel a bit uncomfortable.

Questions for Reflection

- Which version of the Hulk do you enjoy the most: the comic book, the cartoons, the Bill Bixby and Lou Ferrigno television series, the Ang Lee *Hulk* film, *The Incredible Hulk* film, or something else? What do you think it is about that version that makes you enjoy it the most?
- If you have read the comic book, which incarnation of the Hulk do you find the most interesting: the childlike Hulk of the early days, the tough-talking grey Hulk, the Hulk with Bruce Banner's intelligence, or another Hulk?
- Have you ever felt hounded and/or misunderstood like the Hulk?
- Have you ever wished that you could "Hulk out" and smash away your problems?

- Has your anger ever gotten you into trouble?
- Has your anger ever helped you by helping you identify things that needed to be changed?
- Have you ever been taught that feelings such as anger or sadness were, in and of themselves, a sin? How does it help you to understand that emotions are created by God and not inherently good or bad?
- Describe a time when you were angry but did not sin (Eph. 4:26–27).
- Have feelings of anger ever helped you to take a positive step in your life?
- What do you find are the most helpful ways for you to control your anger? Put another way, what are your own personal best anger-management techniques?
- Are there stories of Marvel heroes that, as much as you enjoy them, perhaps are not a positive influence on you? Are there stories of the Hulk that indulge your feelings of anger? Are there other films, songs, books, or games you can think of that indulge in anger and violence?
- What other insights or reflections have you had while reading or watching stories of the Hulk?

4

The Uncanny X-Men

Dealing with Discrimination and Diversity

The X-Men are a group of people who were born as mutants, with strange mutant powers that manifest during their teenage years. Because of this, many people fear and hate them. Still, the X-Men have sworn to protect the very people who are prejudiced against them. They do this by banding together into a group that is truly diverse. While the Fantastic Four and the Avengers have diverse personalities among their members, the X-Men have had more ethnic, racial, and gender diversity than any other superhero team.

What would you do if you were mistrusted, feared, and even hated simply because of the way you were born? As we reflect on the X-Men's adventures, we can reflect on the ways in which our churches and community organizations can confront prejudice, offer a sanctuary to those who need acceptance, and become diverse, multicultural communities that band together to confront evil as well.

The Origin of the X-Men

According to Stan Lee, one reason he wrote a book about a group of mutants is that he was having difficulty coming up with new origins for his heroes. Instead of having them bitten by radioactive bugs or bombarded with radiation in order to gain their powers, it would be easier, he figured, just to have them born that way.[1] He originally wanted to call the comic book *The Mutants*, but publisher Martin Goodman was concerned that customers would not know what the word meant. Lee countered by suggesting the name *The X-Men*, even though he knew that no one would know what an "X-Man" was either. To Lee's surprise, Goodman approved the name, and it stuck.[2]

X-Men #1 (September 1963), with a script by Stan Lee and artwork by Jack Kirby, opened with Professor Charles Xavier, headmaster of a private school in New York's Westchester County, putting his teenage students through their paces. These were no ordinary students, however. They were mutants, each with his or her own unique power. The dashing, wealthy teenager known as the Angel has wings and can fly.

Iceman, the youngest member of the group, can cover his body with ice and can create shields and weapons out of snow and ice. The Beast, who looks like a brute but is the intellectual of the group, has great acrobatic skills. Cyclops, the group's grim student leader, shoots optic blasts from his eyes. Charles Xavier, code-named Professor X, is no ordinary headmaster either. He is confined to a wheelchair and has tremendous mental powers, including the ability to communicate with his students telepathically. As the story opens, the teenage boys are excited to be welcoming a female student to their school. Her name is Jean Grey, code-named Marvel Girl, and she has telekinetic powers. Professor Xavier explains their mission to her, saying, "Jean, there are many mutants walking the earth and more are born each year! Not all of them want to help mankind! Some hate the human race, and wish to destroy it! Some feel that the mutants should be the real rulers of the earth! It is our job to protect mankind from those . . . from the evil mutants!"[3]

One such evil mutant is Magneto, an incredibly powerful master of magnetism, who feels that mutants are superior to normal humans and therefore should rule the world. Later in the issue, Magneto declares, "The human race no longer deserves dominion over the planet Earth! The day of the mutants is upon us! The first phase of my plan shall be to show my power . . . to make homo sapiens bow to homo superior!"[4] By the story's end, Professor Xavier's young students face their first true test. They successfully defend some of the U.S. armed forces against an attack by Magneto. Magneto would return many times, however, and serve as the primary foil to Professor Xavier and the X-Men.

Facing Prejudice

The issue of prejudice has become a central theme of the X-Men mythos. Lee, in a story with art layouts by Kirby and finished art by Jay Gavin, first highlighted the issue in *X-Men* #14 (November 1965). In that issue, a famous anthropologist, Dr. Boliver Trask, declares that mutants are a hidden threat that will soon take over the world. He whips the nation into antimutant hysteria. Soon, television shows begin to discuss the "mutant problem" and newspaper headlines read "Mutant Menace." Trask unleashes a group of giant robotic creatures known as the Sentinals that he has created to destroy all mutants. To Trask's surprise, however, the Sentinels instead decide to take over the earth themselves. Over the next several issues, as the young X-Men heroically fight to protect humankind, Trask realizes the error of his ways. In *X-Men* #16 (January 1966), Trask sabotages the headquarters he used to create the Sentinels, causing it to collapse on top of the Sentinels as well as himself. By doing so, Trask heroically sacrifices his own life in order to destroy the threat of the Sentinels. As the story ends, the caption reads, "Dr. Bolivar Trask, whose last earthly sacrifice brought the work of a lifetime crashing down about him . . . whose last earthly lesson proved to be: Beware the fanatic! Too often his cure is deadlier by far than the evil he denounces!"[5]

In "Monsters Among Us," in *Marvels*, book 2 (1994), writer Kurt Busiek and painter Alex Ross retold the story of *X-Men* #14 (November 1965) from the point of view of photojournalist Phil Sheldon and a little mutant girl named Maggie. Ross's painted art effectively depicts the chaos and hatred of an angry mob as well as the imposing threat of the Sentinels. Busiek portrays Sheldon as a good man, but even Sheldon begins to get caught up in the antimutant hysteria. Meanwhile, unbeknownst to Sheldon, his daughters have discovered Maggie, who is on the run and hiding from the angry mobs. Maggie has a round head and huge eyes, clearly marking her as a mutant. Sheldon's daughters befriend her and hide her in the family's basement. Maggie explains to the girls that her father was fired from his job for having a mutant child and that her mother just cried all the time. The stress of having a mutant daughter had become too much for her parents, so they just abandoned her. Sheldon soon discovers that his daughters have been hiding Maggie and is moved by their courage and compassion. He is ashamed of the prejudice that was growing in his heart. Aware of the chaos that is growing outside the house, Maggie sneaks away and leaves the Sheldons' home to avoid putting the family in danger. The family and readers are left wondering whether Maggie will be safe or whether she will be found and attacked by a mob.

In the same issue, Busiek and Ross juxtapose this story with that of the wedding of Reed Richards and Sue Storm, which is portrayed as the celebrity social event of the year. When I asked Busiek why he chose to retell those two stories, he explained that, for one thing, his study of comic book continuity suggested that the two events were happening at the same time. He went on to explain a deeper purpose for retelling the two stories.

> BUSIEK: I needed to tell those stories because those are two important strains in Marvel history—some of the heroes are loved, some are hated, and it doesn't seem like there's that much difference between them, so why do they get treated differently? In exploring that, the idea of Phil and his family briefly sheltering a mutant child was a way to make it personal to him, a way to make him confront his own prejudice and see it collapse in the face of a scared little girl who needed help.[6]

In *X-Men* #57–59 (June–August 1969), writer Roy Thomas and artist Neal Adams returned to the Sentinels and the issue of prejudice. This time it is Boliver Trask's son, Larry Trask, who blames the X-Men for his father's death and warns people about the "Mutant Menace."[7]

Marvel writers and artists have continued to use mutants as a metaphor for groups who are disenfranchised and discriminated against in our society. Joe Casey, who retold the story of how Professor Xavier first recruited young, frightened mutants into his school in the 1999 miniseries *X-Men: Children of the Atom*, explained, "[T]he metaphors contained within the X-Men concept should be obvious. In fact, they're meant to be obvious. Mutants are different. Mutants are hated and feared. Mutants are a minority. Mutants are discriminated against because of what they are. Sound familiar? Apply the mutant metaphor to any disenfranchised group, any minority, anyone who feels alone . . . and it works. To me, that makes it an extremely potent metaphor. It's the main reason I wanted to write this story."[8]

In Chris Claremont's seventeen years (1975–1991) as the writer of the *Uncanny X-Men*, he repeatedly used the X-Men to explore the themes of prejudice and discrimination. According to Claremont, "Mutants in the Marvel Universe have always stood as a metaphor for the underclass, the outsiders, they represent the ultimate minority."[9] Claremont explained that, as an immigrant himself, part of the perspective that he brought to the title was to show that the X-Men were "strangers trying to fit into a neighborhood that doesn't always want them."[10] Many of Claremont's stories highlighted the different reactions that mutants had to the discrimination they faced. Some mutants tried to hide who they were in order to avoid conflict. Others became angry and belligerent toward the rest of the world. Magneto, a child of the Holocaust, took the perspective that since mutants were superior, in his estimation, they should rule the world, or at least be allowed to establish their own homeland. Professor Xavier and the X-Men spoke out against the discrimination against mutants but also sought to live in peace with the very humans who feared and hated them.

In these stories, the X-Men often have the opportunity to fight against prejudice in violent ways by using their fists and their mutant powers to blast away the Sentinels and other forces of prejudice. The battle against bigotry in the real world is not so simple. Even as Stan Lee was writing stories in which his heroes fought the forces of bigotry, he acknowledged that in the real world, we cannot fight it in the same way superheroes do. Prejudice and bigotry were the most common themes of all the topics that Lee addressed in his monthly "Stan's Soapbox." In November 1968, he wrote, "Let's lay it right on the line. Bigotry and racism are among the deadliest social ills plaguing the world today. But, unlike a team of costumed supervillains, they can't be halted with a punch in the snoot, or a zap from a ray gun. The only way to destroy them is to expose them—to reveal them for the insidious evils they really are."[11] He added, "Sooner or later, we must learn to judge each other on our own merits . . . For then, and only then, will we be truly worthy of the concept that man was created in the image of God—a God who calls us ALL—His children. Pax et Justitia, Stan."[12]

For people of faith, Lee's suggestion seems like a good starting point. Bigotry can be exposed through education and by building bridges of understanding. While people of faith cannot simply target superpowered villains, they can raise public awareness of discrimination where they see it and work through political channels to insure equality and to fight discriminatory practices and laws.

The Danger of the Mutant Metaphor

The X-Men writers who have used mutants as a metaphor for oppressed and marginalized groups in society have done so with good intentions, telling stories intended to increase comic book readers' and movie viewers' consciousness of the dangers of discrimination and bigotry. Still, there are dangers inherent in the mutant metaphor.[13]

In *Astonishing X-Men* #1–6 (2004–2005), for example, writer Joss Whedon and artist Joe Cassaday told a story in which a company discovers a cure for being a mutant. The story line was adapted for part of the film *X-Men: The Last Stand* (2006). The character of Rogue considers her powers to be a curse. Her power is that she absorbs the memories, strength, and powers of anyone she touches directly with her skin. This means not only that she cannot physically touch anyone she cares about but also that she is a threat to them if she even accidentally touches them. She can unintentionally absorb so much of their strength that she could kill them. In the story, some mutants protest the whole idea of a cure as offensive, while other mutants line up to receive it. In the film version of the story, upon hearing about the cure, Rogue asks, "Is it true? Can they cure us?" The X-Man Storm responds, "There is nothing to cure." At the end of the film, Rogue chooses to receive the cure and loses her powers.

The story line is an intriguing one and raises many questions for reflection. It is the sort of story that can, however, perpetuate the very perspective that bigots have used to justify discrimination and their own feelings of superiority over others. Members of the dominant group in a culture tend to suggest that their group is the norm, while minorities or other marginalized groups are aberrations from that norm that must be fixed, cured, or changed. By comparing different groups to the X-Men, some comic book readers and movie viewers may subconsciously get the impression that the members of these groups are indeed mutants or aberrations. While some readers and viewers may then be inspired to feel sympathy for these individuals or to act charitably toward them, they may also on some level assume that they are the normal ones and look down on others as being as aberrations who need our help.

In contrast, some X-Men writers, including Chris Claremont, have told stories that make a point of suggesting that the X-Men are not really mutations but simply a part of the diversity of the human race. Claremont asks the rhetorical question, "Are we all, in some manner or shape or form, children of God? Or are some of us perhaps more beloved than others?"[14] As the story he is introducing makes clear, Claremont wants readers to realize that all people, in all their wide diversity, are indeed created by God and beloved of God.

The Danger of Religion as a Source of Intolerance

Chris Claremont's acclaimed 1982 graphic novel *X-Men: God Loves, Man Kills*, created with artist Brent Anderson, served as the basis of the film *X2: X-Men United* (2003). In both the graphic novel and film versions of the story, a man named William Stryker sees mutants as a threat and whips up fear and hatred against them (Figure 7). He hates mutants for what they are and how they were born and feels they have no right to exist. So he launches a crusade to kill them all and, by using a delusional Professor Xavier and the Cerebro machine, he almost succeeds.

One significant difference between the graphic novel and the film is that in the film Stryker is a military man, a colonel, while in the original graphic novel

Figure 7. *X-Men: God Loves, Man Kills* (1982), page 57; Marvel Comics. Chris Claremont writer and Brent Eric Anderson art. Claremont and Anderson have Rev. Stryker fan the flames of prejudice and intolerance by spouting scripture. Stryker argues that the hateful acts he inspires are not his responsibility since he is just "an instrument of the Lord." Copyright ©1982 Marvel Comics, all rights reserved.

Stryker is a Christian minister and the head of a worldwide television ministry known as the Stryker Crusade. Claremont does not take the easy approach and depict Stryker simply as a hypocritical televangelist. Instead, Stryker is depicted as someone who is sincere in his beliefs and who consistently lives out those beliefs. Stryker continually quotes scripture texts that he interprets in ways that justify his hatred of mutants. His sin is not that he is secretly corrupt or a fraud but that he has distorted the message of his faith to justify his hatred and persecution of others.

In 2003, Claremont wrote a sequel of sorts to *God Loves, Man Kills* in *X-treme X-Men* #25–30. The story again shows that Stryker is sincere in his beliefs. In an often-repeated motif of Marvel Comics, the story demonstrates that even someone as misguided as Stryker is redeemable. In the end, Stryker surprises the X-Men by sacrificing his own life to save someone who was once his enemy. As one X-Man put it, "Stryker was wrong . . . He wasn't evil."[15]

I asked Claremont about these stories, his background and preparation for writing them, and the themes of prejudice and intolerance in the X-Men.

CHRIS CLAREMONT: In a way, the heartbreak of it is, those themes [prejudice and acceptance], sadly, are no less valid today than they were in 1974. We thought there were times we crossed a milestone—that things were getting better. But things don't seem to get any better. We thought we stepped away from the chaos and stupidity of my parents' generation. Instead, we discovered history is harder to break free of than we suspected. People ask me why I continue to do it. It is because I keep trying until I get it right. That, and getting paid by the word, which is why I babble incessantly!

RUSSELL DALTON: I just recently reread *God Loves, Man Kills*. It seems to me that the issue of religious intolerance is more relevant now than ever.

CLAREMONT: My youngest son just read it for the first time. He was very sad.

DALTON: In your introduction to the new premier classic edition of *God Loves, Man Kills*, you mention that you read the Bible through several times in preparation for writing the book, and you reference concepts such as Manichaeism, which has been considered a heresy by the Christian church. It seems that you are quite a lay theologian. I wonder if you have had any theological education or formal training or have done extensive reading in theology.

CLAREMONT: My grandparents, on my father's side, were Church of England. My great-great-great-great grandfather on my mother's side was, I think, a Grand Rabbi. Out of that, both of my parents gave the impression they had to be dragged kicking and screaming into the church for my wedding. They were young socialists in England. My original academic training was in political theory. Don't ask me how I went from political theory to acting to writing comic books. I haven't the faintest idea. It just seemed the logical thing to do.

The year before I wrote *God Loves*, we had it on the docket for quite some time before I had to get it ready to publish in a rush. We had to fill in some space in the publication schedule. I had spent time reading the Bible and watching just about every Sunday morning televangelist and ministry that I could get my hands on. That was pre-cable. Just to see what people were talking about, how they were talking about [it], and to get a sense of the environment I was going to write about.

DALTON: At one point in the story, you make the point that some fundamentalist and evangelical ministers are opposing Reverend Striker and his crusade. Was that an intentional plan to make it clear that you were not writing *God Loves, Man Kills* as anti-Christian diatribe? That it is really about religious intolerance?

CLAREMONT: It is actually more than that, even. The whole point, the intent of *God Loves*, which I made clearer in the sequel, is that Striker is not an evil man. He does not see himself as evil. He sees himself as a man of faith, of deep and passionate faith, fulfilling what he sees as God's will. To me, as a writer, what I came away [with] from reading the Good Book was a sense that to proclaim yourself the executor of God's will, that [you alone are] fulfilling God's will, to me anyway, is a measure of arrogance. The conflict in the book between that attitude and what is actually there, is a difference between presenting the option to people and forcing them to accept it. The essence of the book is that here is a set of ideals, here is a choice, and every person must make that choice. Imposing it [on others] changes the whole nature of the situation.[16]

Claremont's stories of Reverend Stryker's crusade against the X-Men are not simplistic antireligious attacks that suggest all ministers are hypocrites or all religion is evil. Instead, they are cautionary tales that warn us of the danger we face when we become too certain that we know the mind of God or that we speak for God. When we do so, we can begin to use our faith and the Bible in twisted ways in order to justify hate and discrimination. Although Stryker had no superpowers of his own, he was one of the greatest threats that the X-Men ever faced due to his ability to appeal to people's faith and rally them to give in to their fear and hatred for those who are different. Stryker twisted the Christian religion and used it to allow people to feel that they were the only true children of God and that they were justified in discriminating against others.

One way that our communities of faith can confront prejudice and discrimination is to make sure that we ourselves are not guilty of committing acts of discrimination and intolerance in the name of God. Unfortunately, a great deal of prejudice and persecution has been perpetrated in the name of Christianity and other faiths. Philosopher René Girard has described the phenomenon in which members of a society express their pent-up violent emotions by uniting against a common victim or scapegoat. Instead of hating each other or hurting each other, they find an individual or a group that they can agree to hate and blame for all that is wrong in their society. Girard traces this phenomenon throughout human history and throughout the world, through oppression and massacres and executions. He points to the crucifixion of Jesus Christ as a powerful critique of this process of scapegoating. Jesus is seen as the completely innocent victim who is made into a scapegoat by the people of his time. His crucifixion is a travesty that calls into question the whole process of trying to justify oneself by targeting a scapegoat. Girard suggests that it is the voice of Satan that urges people to unite against a common victim or scapegoat.[17]

Unfortunately, there is a shameful history of Christian groups that have scapegoated various minority groups with the same sort of fear and hatred as Reverend Stryker did with the X-Men, from discrimination against Roman Catholics in the United States, to the genocide of six million European Jews during World War II by the Nazi Party, to the lynching and terrorizing of African Americans by the Ku Klux Klan and other Christians, to more recent attempts by some Christian groups to blame immigrants or gay and lesbian people for many of the country's problems. Of course, other Christians have taken the lead in defending and supporting the rights of marginalized and victimized groups and fought against policies and laws that discriminate against them.

In the 2001 book *Unchristian: What a New Generation Really Thinks about Christianity . . . and Why It Matters*, David Kinnaman, president of the Barna Group, and Gabe Lyons, founder of Fermi Project, report the troubling results of research funded by Fermi Project and conducted by the Barna Group. The researchers presented sixteen- to twenty-nine-year-olds with twenty words or phrases, including ten favorable and ten unfavorable ones, and had them indicate which words and phrases describe present-day Christianity. Of those words and phrases, "antihomosexual" and "judgmental" were the two most commonly identified with present-day Christianity by Christian and non-Christian respondents alike, outranking other unfavorable phrases such as "hypocritical," "old-fashioned," and "not accepting of other faiths," and far outranking favorable phrases such as "friendly" and "consistently shows love for other people," especially among those who did not regularly attend a Christian church.[18]

If the Barna Group's research is accurate, Christians who embrace an ethic of love and inclusion have a great deal of work to do to wrest the image of Christianity away from those who are more focused on judging and blaming others than on loving them. Groups like the Nazi Party, the Ku Klux Klan, and al-Qaeda share a view that everyone should look, act, think, and believe as they do, and others should not be tolerated. Christians, on the other hand, are called to love their neighbors, including those of different ethnicities, from different cultures, and with different beliefs (Lk. 10:25–37).

Becoming an Inclusive, Diverse Community

One effective way that the X-Men have confronted prejudice is through the process of becoming a diverse, multinational, multicultural, and inclusive community that reflects the diversity of God's creation. One reason for the team's cultural diversity seems to have been the result of an abandoned marketing strategy. By 1970, sales of the original X-Men's comic book adventures had stalled, and despite some innovative stories by writer Roy Thomas and artist Neil Adams, Marvel stopped publishing new X-Men stories and began publishing only reprints of their earlier adventures. In 1975, however, a new team of X-Men was introduced that soon became the stars of the top-selling comic book in the country. According to Thomas, who by then was serving as Marvel's editor, it was an abandoned marketing scheme that served as the catalyst for creating the new team. Marvel's new president, Al Landau, headed up Trans World Features Syndicate, which licensed American publications around the world. Landau wondered whether Marvel could come up with an international group of heroes and then market them in each hero's home country.[19] The idea behind the marketing plan apparently got lost in translation, because writer Len Wein and artist Dave Cockrum ended up populating their new X-Men team with heroes from a variety of nations including the Soviet Union and Kenya, countries that certainly did not show promise for much in the way of comic book sales. Still, with a strange serendipity, the international group of heroes was an immediate hit with fans.

In *Giant Size X-Men* #1 (May 1975), Wein and Cockrum had Professor Xavier leave his school in Westchester, New York, and travel around the world. He recruits Nightcrawler in Winzeldorf, Germany; Wolverine in Quebec, Canada; Storm in the Serengeti Plain in southwestern Kenya; Sunfire in Osaka, Japan; Colossus in Lake Baikal, Siberia, in the Soviet Union; Thunderbird on an Apache reservation in Camp Verde, Arizona; and Banshee in Nashville, Tennessee, although he is originally from Ireland. The new members of the team struggle to get along and do not always understand each other's words or actions, but they eventually learn to work together.

Another distinctive characteristic of the X-Men has been the role women have played on the team. Unlike some depictions of women in past superhero comic books, the female members of the X-Men do not just tag along as pretty faces or girlfriends. Women are full-fledged members of the team and have often served as the team's leaders. This may not seem that radical today, but in the realm of superhero comic books, dominated by male creators and male readers, this type of equality had been rare. When I asked Claremont about this aspect of his stories, he suggested that his portrayal of women as leaders and full participants in the group helped his X-Men stories better reflect the real world and helped boost sales of the comic book as well.

> RUSSELL DALTON: You seem to highlight the role of women in your comics. For all the great innovations brought about by the writers of the Silver Age of Marvel Comics, one thing that they didn't do well was to write good, strong women. That is something you did with Storm, Jean Grey, and Kitty Pryde. Is that something you did intentionally, as a corrective to the stories of the past, or were you simply trying to write genuine, interesting characters?

CHRIS CLAREMONT: It wasn't a corrective, but [women are] half the human race. Why shortchange the audience? If you are going to do an X-Person who is a female, why should that person be any less interesting, conflicted, honorable, or butt-headed than the guys? If you up the ante for one gender, the other gender has to rise to meet them. You end up with the best of both worlds. If Kitty is really cool, then you have to up the ante with Logan to match her. If you have a really neat Storm, you need a really neat Nightcrawler to get her attention. The readers will look at this and think they are both cool.

DALTON: I wonder if you have heard from women readers about what those characters have meant to them.

CLAREMONT: The unique thing about the X-Men in the original heyday, when we were averaging 400,000 to 500,000 copies an issue, is that a significant number [of the readers] were women. That never happened before and it hasn't happened since. To me, that seemed like it should be a no-brainer. You don't ignore that portion of the audience. It is part of the reason the X-Men were so socially ecumenical. We were open to everyone. We didn't care what continent, culture, race, or background they came from . . . If having an African hero or a Mexican hero or heroine intrigues a wider spectrum of audience, go for it. At least, as a writer you might learn something and find something neat to play with.[20]

According to the gospels, Jesus made women, Gentiles, and even Samaritans the heroes of his stories. He proclaimed the good news that all are accepted into God's realm. The Gospel of Luke especially highlights Jesus' efforts to include people who were often excluded by the rest of society. He raised eyebrows and tempers by welcoming Gentiles, Samaritans, tax collectors, and other "sinners" into the Realm of God, all people whom many religious groups of his day excluded. Rather than judging and excluding a tax collector like Zacchaeus, for example, Jesus went to his house and broke bread with him even before Zacchaeus promised to change his ways (Lk. 19:1–10).

Paul saw the wide-ranging, revolutionary implications of Jesus' gospel. He proclaimed that we are renewed in Christ and that "in that renewal there is no longer Greek and Jew, circumcised and uncircumcised, barbarian, Scythian, slave and free; but Christ is all and in all!" (Col. 3:11). New Testament scholar Jennifer Berenson comments on that verse, "In the church human distinctions associated with ethnicity and socioeconomic status are meaningless."[21] The similar verse "There is no longer Jew or Greek, slave or free; there is no longer male or female; for you are all one in Christ Jesus" (Gal. 3:28) adds the idea that Christ tears down barriers and distinctions between genders as well.[22]

The early Church struggled with this concept of radical inclusiveness at first. Early churches had been excluding Gentiles from their communities, and according to Acts 10, God gave the apostle Peter a vision of how inclusive this community should be. Upon seeing that Gentiles as well as Jews had received the Holy Spirit, Peter is amazed and says, "Can anyone withhold the water for baptizing these people who have received the Holy Spirit?" (Acts 10:47). Michaela Buzzese notes, "In Peter's incredulity, we glimpse how very difficult it was for the first disciples to 'get' the radical inclusiveness that is God's reign, encompassing even strangers, enemies, and the unclean. Lest we are tempted to feel superior in the face of such ignorance, we need only recall the fact that, to this day, many Christian churches still deny gays and lesbians and women full access to all of God's sacraments—a painful reminder that we don't get the radical inclusiveness that is God's reign, either."[23] The inclusive nature of the early church movement may be one of the reasons for its success. Since the church transcended race, gender, class, and social status, it appealed to everyone and could use its members' diverse strengths even within local communities of faith. In Christ, the church was strong because of, not despite of, its diversity.

The book of Acts makes it clear that from the very beginning, on the day of Pentecost, the church included people from many different nations who spoke many different languages (Acts 2:9–11). If today's Christians were to walk into a first-century church, they would probably be struck by how radically diverse it would seem compared to many churches today. If churches today could reflect that diversity, it would be a significant way to combat prejudice and discrimination in our society. In a public interview at Western Michigan University in 1963, the Reverend Martin Luther King Jr. said,

> We must face the fact that in America, the church is still the most segregated major institution in America. At 11:00 on Sunday morning when we stand and sing that Christ has no east or west, we stand at the most segregated hour in this nation. This is tragic. Nobody of honesty can overlook this. Now, I'm sure that if the church had taken a stronger stand all along, we wouldn't have many of the problems that we have. The first way that the church can repent, the first way that it can move out into the arena of social reform is to remove the yoke of segregation from its own body.[24]

Unfortunately, many churches today are taking approaches to their outreach and their ministries that, intentionally or unintentionally, lead to more uniformity in their congregations rather than to more diversity. Some churches have adopted church growth strategies that target one specific demographic group and then design all their programs and worship events to meet the needs of the kind of people that are already attending the church. This approach does not follow the gospel's call to enter into an inclusive community, and it also has some practical problems. As our wider culture grows increasingly diverse, younger generations of people are finding it strange and uninviting to walk into homogeneous congregations where everyone seems to look and act the same. Also, as many businesses and community organizations know, by having a diverse workforce and leadership team they are better able to understand the needs of their communities and the world around them. When we are around only those people who have the same background we do, we begin to assume that our way is the only way to approach a problem. Diversity brings with it new ideas and new approaches and enriches our congregation.

Diversity can enrich our personal lives as well. Friends from different racial, social, and cultural backgrounds can expose us to new perspectives on the world and enrich our lives immensely. These friendships may not come naturally or easily, but we can benefit from stepping outside our comfort zones and making new friendships with people who may be different from us in some ways.

Another way in which Claremont wanted his characters to be diverse and reflect reality was to give some of them specific faiths, something that was quite rare at the time and is still rare in comic books today. Kurt Wagner, also known as Nightcrawler, is portrayed as a devout Roman Catholic, while Kitty Pryde is portrayed as a practicing Jew. Claremont explained to me that one of his goals in exploring his characters' faiths is to give readers a window into other belief systems and through that to help readers gain some understanding and empathy for those who may have different beliefs than they do.[25]

In the film *X2: X-Men United* (2003), Kurt Wagner's faith is unfortunately portrayed as a disturbing aspect of his character. While the film does show Kurt saying the Lord's Prayer and drawing on his faith for courage to survive his trials, it also depicts him as being overburdened with feelings of guilt. He admits to carving painful tattoos on his body as a sort of penance for his sins. By contrast, in the comic books, Kurt's faith has usually been portrayed as a source of serenity and as his motivation for loving and forgiving those who have persecuted him. A memorable episode of the 1995 cartoon series *X-Men: The Animated Series*, titled simply "Nightcrawler," shows the rest of the X-Men traveling to Germany and hearing about a demon who has been seen around a local monastery. The demon turns out to be the mutant Nightcrawler, a member of the community who is loved and accepted by most of the monks there but feared and hated by those in the local community because of his powers and monstrous demon-like appearance. Despite the hatred shown toward him and his betrayal by one of the monks, Nightcrawler is able to forgive those who persecuted him. Wolverine is depicted in the episode as having no use for faith or organized religion. By the episode's end, however, Kurt's faith has had a profound impact on Wolverine and, for the first time in years, Wolverine enters a church to pray.[26]

In the 2002 four-issue miniseries *Nightcrawler,* volume 2, by writer Chris Kipiniac and artist Matthew Smith, Kurt leaves the X-Men for a time to study for the priesthood. The series has a mature story line that deals with issues for older readers, such as drug use and human trafficking. Kurt starts off thinking that the transition from X-Man to priest will be a smooth one. "The difference isn't huge," he says. "We wear uniforms, tackle injustice, dutifully follow our leader."[27] But soon Kurt is tempted to resort to violence to try to solve the problems that people in his parish face. The priest who is Kurt's mentor says to him, "Punching is all well and good for stopping alien invasions or whatever you're used to with the X-Men, but no matter how many traffickers you catch, or crooks, or pirates or whatever else . . . there's always going to be more . . . If you think you can save humanity, Kurt, you are setting yourself up for a fall."[28] The priest's point is that communities of faith fight their battles in ways inherently different from the way superheroes do. By the end of the miniseries, Kurt recognizes that his efforts to beat up the criminals responsible for the pain and suffering he sees have not helped anyone. He realizes, to his regret, that he does not have enough patience to work in small steps or to support people where they are in their lives. So he regretfully decides that he is more suited to be a member of the X-Men than to be a priest, and he returns to the team.

Kitty Pryde's Jewish faith sustains her through several trying times. In *Uncanny X-Men* #159 (July 1982), Kitty first tries using a cross to repel the vampire Dracula. Since she adheres to the Jewish faith, however, it does not work for her. So instead she uses the Star of David on her necklace, and it holds off Dracula. It is interesting to note that at the end of the X-Men's second encounter with William Stryker in *Extreme X-Men* #30 (2003), Kitty takes a very different approach than does Nightcrawler. Tired of having to hurt and even perhaps kill others in battles, Kitty chooses to leave the X-Men and try to change the world by running for the position of alderman in a local election. She decides that it is better for her to try to change the world by performing her civic duty than by wearing a costume. As she explains to Wolverine and Storm, "Keeping the peace is important. That's what YOU do. But so is making sure we have a community, a country worth preserving."[29] The issue closes by citing the end of Psalm 23: "For surely goodness and mercy shall follow me all the days of my life. And I will dwell in the house of the Lord forever."

In these stories, Nightcrawler and Kitty Pryde both realize that beating up villains is not the only way, and indeed not the best way, to effect change in our world. Both characters, however, eventually go back to fighting supervillains with the X-Men. Part of the reason for their return may be the commercial implications of having a popular hero relegated to such relatively mundane work. One wonders whether these heroes might have stayed with their alternate vocations for longer if the work of the ministry or the work of a civil servant were as visually exciting to readers as battling costumed villains.

Wolverine: Virtue, Vice, and a Vicious Nature

Wolverine is the most popular member of the X-Men. The character was originally created by writer Len Wein and art director John Romita Sr., and first appeared on the last page of *Incredible Hulk* #180 (October 1974), drawn by artist Herb Trimpe. Wolverine's first full appearance was in the next issue, *Incredible Hulk* #181 (November 1974), where he is revealed to be a superhero working for the Canadian government. In *Giant-Size X-Men* #1 (May 1975), Wolverine quits that assignment to join Professor Xavier's new X-Men. In that issue, the Wolverine is depicted as a violent fighter with a bad attitude who gets on the nerves of the other X-Men.

The Wolverine's powers include enhanced physical abilities, a healing power that allows him to recover from almost any wound, and retractable razor-sharp claws that come out of the backs of his hands. These claws, along with the rest of his skeleton, are covered with adamantium, a nearly indestructible metal in the Marvel universe. The Wolverine's adamantium-covered skeleton and healing power make him nearly indestructible, although they leave him vulnerable to injury and pain. The Wolverine is a vicious fighter with a hair-trigger temper and a problem with authority. He constantly has to fight to control his more animalistic instincts.

There may be a bit of wish fulfillment fantasy behind the Wolverine's popularity. As Claremont has said, "Wolverine is what every adolescent wants to be. Strong, sure of himself, a sense of honor, a strong moral code. I know what's right, I know what's wrong. I won't take any bull from anybody, and I have the moxy, ability, and strength of character and body to pull it off."[30]

The character was developed further in Claremont and artist Frank Miller's 1982 miniseries *Wolverine*. In the series, Logan (Wolverine) is in Japan and he takes on the role of a samurai, choosing self-control and discipline over his baser animal instincts. Claremont says that some people complained that after the series Wolverine was never again going to be "the wild man psycho butcher he used to be."[31] The first line of the miniseries still sums up the character. He says, "I'm Wolverine. I'm the best there is at what I do, but what I do isn't very nice."[32] Through the years Wolverine has continued to struggle with his animalistic nature, but the results have not always been successful or admirable.

The film *X-Men* (2000) shows the complexity of the character. On the one hand, Wolverine is belligerent, rude to those who would help him, and very violent. On the other hand, he is willing to sacrifice his life in order to save Rogue. Wolverine's mutant ability to heal himself generally makes him invulnerable to most threats on his life. In order to save Rogue's life, he is willing to let her absorb his healing power to the point that it nearly sucks the life away from him.

X2: X-Men United (2003) illustrates another side of Wolverine and at the same time illustrates just how far the sights and sounds of film can lead viewers to accept the unacceptable. In the film, viewers are led to think of William Stryker and his mysterious troops as pure evil, and Wolverine as the man who is tough enough and brutal enough to adopt whatever means are necessary to do what is right. So when a group of Stryker's soldiers, under orders to invade Professor Xavier's school for the sake of national security, shoot some of the young students with tranquilizing darts, Wolverine responds by brandishing his long razor-sharp claws and stabbing at least ten of the soldiers through the chest and into the heart, presumably killing them. If viewers were to stop and think about it, they might be inclined to think that this is a gross overreaction on Wolverine's part. These U.S. soldiers are carrying out orders, completing a mission they were told is in the nation's best interest, and they are not using lethal force. Unlike the vast majority of superheroes in superhero stories, however, Wolverine uses his claws to impale and kill his enemies. Observing these actions objectively, most people of faith would be appalled by Wolverine's actions. The sights and sounds of the film, however, lead many viewers to watch uncritically and to cheer for Wolverine and hope that he kills more soldiers. Viewers can get caught up in the action of the moment and feel that Wolverine is nobly protecting the children and that the soldiers must be stopped at any cost and by any means. Such an attitude is, of course, perpetuated by many action films.

The film *X-Men Origins: Wolverine* (2009) opened to generally poor reviews, with New York Daily News film critic Joe Neumaier calling it a "slice-and-dice superhero fiasco."[33] The film, however, gave many Wolverine fans just what they wanted. The film contains many violent battle scenes including a decapitation, yet it somehow earned only a PG-13 rating. In the film, Logan meets an older farming couple who show him grace and mercy by taking him in and showing him hospitality when he is lost and in need of help. Logan's enemies find the couple and kill them in order to get to Logan. When Logan gets the upper hand over his enemies, he remembers the male farmer's kind words to him. He told Logan that he had a choice in his life—he does not have to be a killing machine. For a moment, it seems that Logan is going to restrain himself and just walk away, content that he has defeated his enemies. At the last minute, however, he opts for revenge instead. He uses his claws to create a spark that starts a fire and blows up his enemies' helicopter with them in it, killing them. As he walks away from the explosion, the camera captures Logan in what is sometimes referred to in the film industry as a "hero shot." The camera looks up at the actor, making him look strong and powerful, as he strides purposely toward the camera. The use of this shot seems to suggest that in killing his enemies Logan is a hero, a strong man who does what needs to be done and gets his revenge. Those who follow the way of Jesus, however, a way of forgiveness and mercy, may reflect on Logan's action and recognize it as the unfortunate and immoral act of a tortured soul.

As Claremont wrote them, the rest of the team have mixed opinions on being the Wolverine's teammates. In *X-Men* #148 (August 1981), the Angel, one of the founding members of the X-Men, is angry that Wolverine has been so vicious in battle. The Angel quits the group, saying that he does not want to be on the same team as someone so violent. After he is gone, Storm tells Professor Xavier that she takes a different perspective. "I, too, abhor Wolverine's violent nature. But he is not an X-Man because of his perfect, sterling character. It's because of his potential for good. Our duty as X-Men is to help him achieve that potential. To deny Wolverine would be to deny our true reason for being. Why does Angel not understand that?" The professor replies, "He does, Storm, but he wonders if the goal is worth the cost. I must confess that occasionally, so do I."[34]

Years later, the New Avengers would face the same question. In *New Avengers* #6 (2005), Iron Man and Captain America argue over whether or not they should offer Wolverine membership on their new team. Iron Man argues to Captain America that Wolverine is the missing ingredient that will make their team effective. Captain America replies, "Tony, he's a murderer."[35] Iron Man counters by suggesting that a murderer is just what the team needs. He says, "He's a samurai warrior. After . . . what we know happened here today we can't afford not to have him. We're going to need someone to go to that place that we can't. And you know exactly what I mean."[36] In so doing, Iron Man betrays the long-held standards and values of the Avengers and argues that the ends justify the means.

As our churches and community organizations work together with other groups and individuals for a common cause, we are sometimes faced with a similar dilemma. While we do not expect everyone to be perfect, is there ever a limit to our posture of inclusion and cooperation? Are there times when such alliances tempt us to compromise the very values that bind the rest of our groups together?

A Sanctuary, a School, and a Mission Center

Part of the reason for the X-Men's great appeal to teenage readers and viewers can be found in their stories of alienation and acceptance. Bryan Singer, who directed the films *X-Men* (2000) and *X2: X-Men United* (2003), says, "Every young person—whether you're in a minority or not—any young person, at some point in their life, feels different. They feel strange, like they don't belong. And they dream of going to a special place where they could be taken care of and loved for who or whatever they are."[37]

In the film *X-Men* (2000), there is a powerful scene in which Wolverine is introduced to Professor Xavier's School for Gifted Youngsters. Wolverine asks, "What is this place?" Professor Xavier explains that it is a school and a sanctuary of sorts for mutants. He explains that Cyclops, Storm, and Jean Grey were among his first students. He says, "I protected them, taught them to control their powers, and in time, teach others to do the same." He goes on to explain that he recruits teenage mutants to come to his school, where, instead of being persecuted, they are "learning, being accepted, not feared." Ultimately, Xavier explains, they are trained to use their powers to help protect humankind and save the world around them.

The scene depicts a hopeful image of what a church can be for teenagers. As psychologist David Elkind explains in his book *All Grown Up and No Place to Go*,[38] contemporary American society does not really know what to do with teenagers. Teenagers are often left with a sense that they are resented for being adolescents and feel that they do not really belong anywhere. Like Professor Xavier's school, church can be a place where teenagers are welcomed and loved for who they are. It can be a place where they can be taught to use their newly manifesting mental and physical powers effectively for the cause of what is right and good, as they come to feel that they do belong. Teenagers are very idealistic, and a church can be a place that helps them put that idealism to work in mission and ministry for a cause that is greater than themselves.

One of the churches where I served as a pastor did an excellent job of this. The church had had a small youth ministry that served the teenage members of the families in the church. These teenagers were mainly good kids who often came to church looking and acting like miniature versions of the adults in the congregation. Our new youth ministry began to reach out and welcome teenagers from a wide variety of backgrounds and life experiences. Many of them had made mistakes in the past and really needed a place where they could feel they belonged. These teenagers did not come to church wearing the clothes or adopting the attitude of traditional churchgoers. As a matter of fact, some came with chips on their shoulders and almost dared us to love and accept them. After some initial shock, our congregation was able to look past its image of what a teenage churchgoer should look like and recognize that these were teenagers who needed a church family. As a result of this attitude of hospitality, the congregation grew in numbers and in its reputation as a community that cared for others. The members of the church worked together to help these teenagers learn to use their gifts and abilities to help others. Many of the teenagers came to love the church and became essential members of it. They supported our work with their talents and brought new insights and contagious passion to our work together.

The church can be a home away from home for teenagers, and of course it can be a place where all those who have been marginalized can find a home. Despite his gruff exterior, Wolverine is certainly someone who needs a sanctuary. As he tells Rogue late in the film *X-Men* (2000), "There's not many people out there who understand what you're going through. But I think this guy Xavier is one of them. He seems to genuinely want to help you. And that's a rare thing for people like us."

Churches and community organizations can be sanctuaries for all those who need a place where they are safe and where they are loved and accepted for who they are. Indeed, many churches in the United States and across the world have embraced the mission of providing sanctuary to those who are in need of political asylum from other countries. The church can also be a school, giving people a sense of self-worth by teaching them to use whatever gifts and abilities they may have for the cause of what is right. And the church can be a mission center that finds ways to help people help others and make the world a better place. Through these means, our churches and community organizations can confront prejudice and other problems in our society.

Questions for Reflection

- Who is your favorite member of the X-Men and why?
- Which X-Man's power do you wish you had? How would you use that power?
- Have you ever feared or looked down upon a group or individual who was different from you and later realized that you were wrong to do so? If so, what helped you realize that you were wrong? Were you able to establish a new way of acting toward that group or individual?
- Describe a time when you have heard the Bible or faith used as a rationale for discriminating against others.
- How are you similar to the majority of people in your church? How are you similar to the majority of the people in your workplace? How are

you different from the majority of people in your church? How are you different from the majority of people in your workplace?

- Do you have any friends who are of a different race or different cultural background than you are? If you are part of the dominant group in our society, how does knowing people who are a part of groups that have traditionally been marginalized and oppressed help you understand the struggles they face? If you are part of a traditionally marginalized or oppressed group in our society, how does knowing people who are part of the dominant group in our society help you understand the nature of prejudice and discrimination?

- How can you and your church or community organization fight discrimination in your local area? What do you think are some concrete steps you could take to raise public awareness? What political avenues are open to you?

- Is your community of faith multicultural or homogeneous? What might you be doing consciously or unconsciously that may not be welcoming to others?

- Nightcrawler and Kitty Pryde have both struggled to reconcile their lives as superheroes with their lives of faith. From the perspective of our faith, how do we approach social issues differently than superhero groups do?

- There is often conflict between Wolverine and the rest of the X-Men over his violent approach to stopping their enemies. How do you handle it when a member of your group starts to use tactics that you feel violate your group's standards?

- Is your church a place where a diverse group of people are welcomed? Does it show hospitality even to those who are different and marginalized by society? If so, how does it do this? If not, why do you think it does not? How could you help your church become more welcoming?

- Can you think of other insights you have gained from other X-Men stories that have not been discussed in this chapter?

The Invincible Iron Man

Being a Good Steward

Young Tony Stark is a man who seems to have everything. He is rich, handsome, brilliant, a known ladies' man, and he has a creative and rewarding profession. Stark's life is aimless, however, until he has a change of heart and commits to using the resources at his disposal for the cause of good. As he takes on the identity of Iron Man, Stark attempts to change from a man who selfishly squanders all he has been given on his own pleasure and amusement to one who uses his resources and his very life to help others. Tony Stark's change of heart offers us the opportunity to reflect on our own stewardship of what God has given us. How are we using our money, our mind and talents, our relationships, and our health to glorify God and serve others?

The Origin of Iron Man

In *Tales of Suspense* #39 (March 1963), in place of one of the series' usual stories of giant monsters from outer space, Marvel introduced its readers to Iron Man. After Stan Lee plotted out the origin tale and Jack Kirby designed the original Iron Man armor, they handed over the task of scripting to Lee's brother Larry Lieber and the penciling chores to Don Heck. That first issue told the story of the origin of Iron Man. The story has been retold many times over the years—for example, *Iron Man* #1 (1968); #122 (1979); vol. 3, #5 (2006); and the film *Iron Man* (2008)—but the story has remained remarkably unchanged.Suave millionaire weapons manufacturer Tony Stark takes a field trip to Vietnam to demonstrate how his new weapons technology can help in the war effort (for the 2008 film, the setting is changed from Vietnam to Kunar Province, Afghanistan). Unfortunately, Stark trips over a booby trap, leaving a deadly piece of shrapnel in his chest that begins to work its way toward his heart. He is captured by a communist guerilla chief and, in what appear to be his dying days, he is forced to make weapons for him. Instead, along with a fellow prisoner, the famous South Vietnamese Professor Yinsen, Stark secretly constructs an iron suit fitted with weapons and a magnetic chestplate that prevents the shrapnel from moving toward his heart and killing him. At a crucial moment, Yinsen distracts the guerilla soldiers, drawing their gunfire and sacrificing his life to allow Tony's armor time to power up and to give him time to escape. In the film, Yinsen's dying words to Tony are "Don't waste it. Don't waste your life." Those words haunt Tony. Because of Yinsen's selfless sacrifice, Tony realizes that he must use his great resources, including the Iron Man armor that allows him to fly, shoot repulsor rays, and much more, for the good of all people.[1] Tony understands his calling, his purpose on Earth. When he returns to the United States, he tells his assistant, Pepper, "I shouldn't be alive, unless it was for a reason. I'm not crazy, Pepper, I just finally know what I have to do. I know in my heart that it's right." Although his physical heart is now weakened, in other ways his heart is stronger than ever before.

The example of another's noble act had a great impact on Tony and helped many others indirectly through Tony's later actions. While we may not be asked to give up our lives in a manner as dramatic as Yinsen's sacrifice, our smaller acts of sacrifice may inspire others. For those who hold to the Christian faith, Jesus' self-sacrifice inspires us to generous living. According to the Gospel of John, Jesus said, "This is my commandment, that you love one another as I have loved you. No one has greater love than this, to lay down one's life for one's friends" (Jn. 15:12–13).

Stewardship

After living an irresponsible life and seeing another person make such a noble sacrifice for his sake, Tony Stark had to come face to face with the question of how he was going to live the rest of his life. He had to determine how he was going to use the blessings he had been given, including his money, his time and talents, his relationships, and his life. In the world of Marvel comics, this meant that as Iron Man he would use all of his resources to make the world a better place. He would repeatedly put on his suit of armor to combat all manner of domestic, foreign, and alien villains to prevent them from taking over America and the world. While Tony Stark retained the outward appearance of a businessman, he also, as Iron Man, secretly took on responsibility for keeping the world safe.

Award-winning writer Kurt Busiek had one of the most memorable recent runs on *Iron Man*. I asked him about Tony Stark's sense of responsibility:

> RUSSELL DALTON: In writing the character of Tony Stark and his alter ego Iron Man, both in the *Avengers* and in Iron Man's own comic book, it seems as though you and past writers have highlighted Iron Man's strong sense of responsibility. But Tony Stark has not always lived very responsibly. He has had to overcome his own alcoholism and, as you highlighted in your run on the book, Tony has not always been wise in choosing the women he dates. What do you think is the key to the character of Tony Stark? He is intelligent, attractive, and wealthy and could easily live a playboy lifestyle. Yet in the *Avengers* and in *Iron Man*, he continues to strive to do the responsible thing. Why is that?

KURT BUSIEK: I wrote Tony Stark as an American aristocrat, a man whose wealth and power came from the success of his business, so he was where he was due to the support of his workers and customers. And he felt a real sense of *noblesse oblige*, that having lifted him into a position of great power, he should protect them—both out of gratitude and out of enlightened self-interest. He does lead a playboy lifestyle, to a degree, but he tempers it with an awareness of what makes that lifestyle possible, and that many people depend on him, and he in turn depends on them.

I'm not sure all that many other writers would put it the same way, but that's how I saw the character. He's a rarity in comics in that he doesn't have a strong, motivating moment that drives him to fight evil—like, say, Bruce Wayne witnessing the murder of his parents, or Spider-Man and the death of Uncle Ben. Tony Stark built himself superpowers in order to save his own life, not because of a moral conversion. And then there he was, stuck in the chestplate (since early on he needed it to keep his injured heart beating), and he ran a big company that seemed constantly under attack, so he defended it. He was a hero of opportunity more than a hero of choice. But still, he acted as Iron Man even when his business wasn't in peril, and he funded the Avengers and so on.

So my take on that was that he had kind of a Rockefellerian sense of obligation to take care of the world, because the world had been making his life very comfortable, and he should return the favor.[2]

Most of us are not in the same position as Tony Stark, who has an abundance of resources to use to help others. Still, like Stark, we can take the opportunity to use our money, our time and talents, our relationships, and our health to make the world a better place.

Stewardship of Money

After his adventure overseas and Yinsen's sacrifice, Tony Stark begins to use his money differently. He pours much of his resources into developing better Iron Man armor. Later, he would use his fortune to pay for the Avengers Mansion and cover the Avengers' operational expenses. In a contemporary twist, in *Iron Man* vol. 3, #1 (1998), Busiek had Stark create the Maria Stark Foundation, named after his mother, in order to finance a number of charities and renovation projects.

We have a strange relationship with money in the real world. On the one hand, our culture often idolizes money and possessions, making them the measure of a person's worth. It is not uncommon to hear "he's done very well for himself" or "she's become quite successful" solely in reference to how much money the person has made. On the other hand, perhaps because money is valued so highly, money is almost a taboo subject in polite company. It is, for example, considered bad form to ask someone how much money she or he makes.[3]

Jesus did not have such qualms about talking about money. In his book, *Generous People*, Eugene Grimm writes, "If we were to strike the comments of Jesus about money, we would reduce his teaching by more than one-third. Sixteen of Jesus' approximately thirty-eight parables deal with money. One of every seven verses in the first three Gospels in some way deals with money. In fact, Jesus spoke about money more than about any other single subject, except the kingdom of God itself. Perhaps this was because Jesus understood how money itself can become a god."[4] Mark 10:17–22 tells the story of a young man who asked Jesus what he must do to inherit eternal life. After some discussion, Jesus told him that there was only one thing that he lacked. He had to sell everything he had and give the proceeds to the poor. The gospel tells us, "When he heard this, he was shocked and went away grieving, for he had many possessions" (Mk. 10:22). This is the point at which many Christian writers would quickly reassure their readers, most of whom are many times wealthier than those who were listening to Jesus, that the story is not really about money and possessions but more about having a generous attitude. Jesus' story, however, is very much about money and possessions. Jesus does not chide the young man for unwarranted spiritual pride or ask him to check his attitude. Nothing in the story suggests that Jesus was lying or being deceptive when he suggested that he wanted the man to give his wealth away. Our spiritual life is about more than money, but money certainly is a big part of it. As 1 Timothy 6:10 warns us, "The love of money is the root of all kinds of evil."

The biblical term *stewardship* refers to the task of managing someone's money and resources. As used in the context of Christian practice, it refers to understanding that everything we have, including our very lives, belongs to God. We serve as stewards for God, managing what we have been given in order to best live a life pleasing to God.

Mark Allan Powell writes, "When we are faithful stewards, 1) we acquire our money in God-pleasing ways; 2) we regard our money in God-pleasing ways; 3) we manage our money in God-pleasing ways; and, 4) we spend our money in God-pleasing ways."[5] We are called to the wise use of money, and this is not as simple as giving our money away to our church or other charities. As Powell writes, "The Bible also teaches, for instance, that we ought not give religious institutions money that is needed for the care of dependent family members (Mark 7:9–13; 1 Timothy 5:8)."[6] Contrary to the popular interpretation, Jesus never said that we should be like the widow and give our last coin away. Instead, reading the story in its context (Mk. 12:38–13:2), we see that Jesus was protesting against a corrupt religious institution that was making widows and others destitute because of its policies and demands.[7] We are to use the money with which we have been blessed wisely.

We all have times in which we feel that we struggle financially. Still, it is important for those of us who live in the Western world today to realize that we live in a time and place of incredible affluence. We are very rich compared to our sisters and brothers who struggle to find enough food to eat each day, whether within our own country or in the rest of the world. Most of us could get by on much less and, therefore, we are challenged to be generous in our giving.

As a young student pastor with little discretionary income and relatively few expenses other than seminary tuition, I used to try to downplay the offering when I was in charge of that part of the worship service. I thought that it was unseemly to focus too much on something as private as how one handles one's money and so I would find myself rushing through the offertory. When I graduated from seminary, however, and had a real income and real monthly bills, I began to realize that the offertory is a very real, very concrete act of worship and not one that should be minimized or rushed. The offerings that are collected at churches can do much good in our communities and in our world. I was not doing anyone any favors by giving the offering short shrift in the service.

According to the Gospel of Matthew, Jesus urged his followers to keep their priorities straight: "Do not store up for yourselves treasures on earth, where moth and rust consume and where thieves break in and steal; but store up for yourselves treasures in heaven, where neither moth nor rust consumes and where thieves do not break in and steal. For where your treasure is, there your heart will be also" (Mt. 6:19–21). Jesus concluded that we need to make a choice, saying, "You cannot serve God and wealth" (Mt. 6:24).

In our materialistic culture, we are constantly bombarded with messages telling us what we need to purchase. In this environment, there is a very real danger of becoming convinced that our vocation in life is to be consumers. We are in danger of letting our possessions possess us. Collecting comic books may be one aspect of that force at work. It can be an enjoyable hobby, but it may be a helpful exercise to take an inventory of our superhero collections. We may be surprised to realize how much money and time we have spent collecting comic books, DVDs, action figures, deluxe editions, and other memorabilia of Marvel Comics. Though there is nothing wrong with having a hobby or a collection, we may want to ask ourselves if we truly need all these things. Might some of that time and money we spend collecting Marvel comics be better spent on doing and supporting God's work? Instead of spending our time and money storing up a superhero collection, perhaps we can spend more time and money storing up treasures in heaven.

Also, while we may not be millionaires like Tony Stark, most of us do have many possessions. We have apartments, homes, automobiles, entertainment systems, and more. If we have an attitude of generosity we can see that all good gifts around us come from God, and we can share those gifts with others for God's good purposes. When I was a pastor, I took a group from our church on a mission trip to the Dominican Republic. Though many members of our church could not go on the trip themselves, many of them loaned us tools and other supplies and supported us with their money. When our youth group grew in size, a number of people offered to let us use their station wagons or vans when we took our teenagers on social outings. One couple in our church had a lakeside cabin in Maine, and every summer they let our youth group invade their second home. These people took the attitude that what was theirs was God's, and even if they did not go on these trips themselves, they used their resources to take part in our work. They were being generous stewards of the resources God had given them.

Stewardship of Time and Talents

In the film *Iron Man* (2008), Tony Stark is shocked to discover that the weapons he invented and produced for the U.S. military are in the hands of terrorists and are being used to kill innocent people. Yinsen tells Tony, "Look. What you just saw. That is your legacy, Stark. Your life's work, in the hands of those murderers."

Tony is confronted with questions of not only how he will use his money but also how he will use his engineering skill and how he will live out his vocation in the future. In the past, he simply did his job but took no responsibility for how his work was being used. Now, he takes a look at his legacy. He asks himself what he is leaving behind for the world.

When Tony returns from Afghanistan, he calls a press conference and announces, "I realized that I had more to offer this world than just making things that blow up." He decides to shut down his weapons manufacturing operations, at least until he can get a handle on how the weapons are being used. He says, "I'm being responsible. That's a new direction for me . . . for the company."

Busiek and artist Sean Chen explored a similar story line in *Iron Man* vol. 3, #1 (1998), having Tony create a new company, Stark Solutions, designed to find answers to some of the world's most pressing problems. Through his work in this new company, and by devoting his time and talent to increasing his Iron Man armor capabilities, Tony is striving to use his engineering genius not simply for his own enrichment, but to make the world a better place.

Deciding to use our time and talents in the best way possible sometimes means that we change the jobs we do for forty or more hours a week. This does not necessarily mean that we enter into full-time ministry or do full-time charity work, but it may mean that we find a way to work for a company that is doing more good than harm in the world. It may also mean that we choose our careers based on how much good we can do through our work rather than on how much money we can make. It may mean doing our jobs in a new way, the best way possible, to leave a lasting legacy. Sometimes it may mean changing the way we use the hours we have been given outside the workplace, to spend more of our evenings and weekends serving in ministries of our churches or volunteering at soup kitchens, working with Habitat for Humanity, volunteering with Big Brother and Big Sisters of America, or working with some other charitable group. It may mean taking a more hands-on role in raising our children and striving to be the best parents we can be. Our challenge is to make the most of the time and the talents we have been given. We only have one life on this earth, and even if we do not get shrapnel in the chest as a wakeup call, we can still make an inventory of our life and determine whether we are living it in the best possible way.

In Matthew 25:14–30, Jesus tells the parable of a man who went on a journey and left his servants a great deal of money, measured out in units known as "talents." A talent was a large unit of weight and represented a great deal of money at the time, evoking the same general impression that "a million dollars" would evoke today. According to Matthew, "to one he gave five talents, to another two, to another one, to each according to his ability. Then he went away" (Mt. 25:15). The servant who had five talents traded them and gained five more. The servant with two talents invested them and made two more. We are told, however, that "the one who had received the one talent went off and dug a hole in the ground and hid his master's money" (Mt. 25:18). When the master returned, the servants who traded and invested the money were greatly rewarded. He told them "well done" and "enter into the joy of your master" (Mt. 25:21, 23). The servant who buried his one talent tried to make the excuse that he buried his talent because he was afraid of wasting what he had been given, but the master replied, "You wicked and lazy slave!" (Mt. 25:26). The word for talent in the original Greek language used in the New Testament is the root for the word "talent" in the English language today, and the parable probably has both the stewardship of money and abilities in mind. The master in the parable had left his servants with a task to do and great resources to use to carry out that task. The unfaithful servant's failure is that he did not even attempt to use what he had been given. God has left us here on earth with tasks to carry out as well. Even if we do not feel that we have as many talents as others do, the talents that we do have are precious and valuable resources, not to be hidden away or squandered. Whether it is our money and material resources or our spiritual gifts and talents, we are left with the task of using them to further God's work on earth.

Stewardship of Our Relationships

The film *Iron Man* (2008) shows Tony Stark having a romantic liaison with a beautiful reporter whom he does not even like and whose name he does not even bother to remember. Later in the film, a soldier is impressed that Tony has dated all the cover models for a year's worth of men's magazines. On the one hand, these scenes could be taken as an indication that Tony is living an irresponsible life. On the other hand, one cannot help but wonder if these scenes are also designed to give viewers the impression that Tony is really cool. The romantic encounter with a very beautiful woman is made to look very glamorous, and Tony's smirk seems to indicate that he is in control. If the point of the scene is to reveal a character flaw and how it is unwise to be a womanizer then it is filmed in a way that does not make the point very clear to the audience.

Love is a wonderful thing, and relationships can be great, but it is also true that infatuation can turn our head around and get us moving on the wrong path. A recurring theme in Iron Man through the years has been Tony Stark's relationship problems. He has a habit of getting involved with the wrong kind of women.

In *Tales of Suspense* #53 (May 1964), after the beautiful Black Widow has already been exposed as a communist spy, she calls to schedule a meeting with Stark under the pretense of apologizing for trying to kill him in an earlier adventure. Her real plan, however, is to steal a top-secret antigravity ray that Stark has invented. She is confident that Stark will agree to the meeting for, as she puts it, "Anthony Stark was interested in me before. Like most Americans, he is sympathetic and therefore weak!"[8] She meets with him, flirts, apologizes for trying to harm him, and begins to cry. To make her feel better, and to try to impress this beautiful woman, Tony puts on a silly grin and takes out the antigravity ray. The caption informs us, "And so it seems that Tony Stark, brilliant scientist and man of action, isn't the first to be taken in by a pair of limpid eyes."[9] Predictably, the Black Widow shoots Tony with some paralyzing gas from her purse and grabs the weapon. As she leaves she thinks, "It was almost too easy!"[10] The whole scene is quite comical. Sometimes we can look back at past relationships and have to ask ourselves, "What were we thinking?" It is difficult to do, but sometimes it helps to try to gain a realistic perspective on a relationship while we are in the midst of it.

Tony's misadventure with the Black Widow is only the first of many such episodes in his life that reveal that he has a knack for getting involved with femmes fatales who turn out to be up to no good.[11] Tony is rich, handsome, and suave. Despite being the most eligible bachelor in the Marvel universe, he continually has problems in his love life.

Stories of femmes fatales and Black Widows can reinforce a harmful negative stereotype of women as schemers who try to destroy men. On the other hand, these stories can serve as cautionary tales for both women and men who do not use common sense when it comes to their relationships. First Corinthians 13 is a chapter that we often read at weddings, but it contains great wisdom for what true love means in all our relationships. These ancient words of wisdom continue to speak to us today about the nature of true love: "Love is patient; love is kind; love is not envious or boastful or arrogant or rude. It does not insist on its own way; it is not irritable or resentful; it does not rejoice in wrongdoing, but rejoices in the truth. It bears all things, believes all things, hopes all things, endures all things" (1 Cor. 13:4–7).

How are we managing our hearts? We would do well to take an inventory of our relationships, whether they are romantic relationships or friendships, and ask whether they are relationships that build us up or drag us down. Are they relationships that bring us closer to God or further away from God and God's ways? Love is a powerful force, and infatuation and the desire to be loved can make us do things we never thought we would ever do. Proverbs 31 advises us that an ideal partner is someone who has integrity, is a capable and diligent worker, is generous to those in need, and is one who has a good reputation. Such a person can be trusted. We would do well to heed this advice as we think of our relationships and, of course, as we strive to be the kind of person described in Proverbs 31 ourselves.

Stewardship of Our Health and Well-Being

In *Iron Man* #120–128 (March–November 1979), writers David Michelinie and Bob Layton and artist John Romita Jr. embarked on a story line that would come to be known as "Demon in the Bottle." The story was quite controversial at the time, as it presented the hero Tony Stark as an alcoholic (Figure 8). In his introduction to the premiere hardcover reprint of the story, Michelinie explained that he was not trying to come up with a relevant or edgy story line. As he took over the writing chores of the book, he was struck at the pressures Tony was under from his work, the government, and his girlfriend. So he and Bob Layton asked themselves how a real person might respond to those pressures. The answer they explored was alcoholism. "We showed the effects of his addiction on his health, his business, and his personal life as he swam ever deeper into a hundred-proof pit. And yes, we got our share of flack for it."[12] The story unfolds gradually over months. In *Iron Man* #120 (March 1979), Tony orders a fourth martini while on a plane. He rationalizes it by saying that he is drinking for two men, Iron Man and himself. The martinis dull his reflexes in battle, but he cannot admit to himself that his drinking is contributing to his problems. Over the next several issues, Tony's friends begin to notice that he is drinking too much. When they try to help, he turns on them and alienates the very people who are trying to help him. In *Iron Man* #127 (October 1979), Tony's longtime butler, Jarvis, has had enough and resigns. Like many in the throes of addiction, Tony blames everyone else and everything else for his problems and refuses to take responsibility for his own actions or to acknowledge that his drinking is a problem. In fact, in *Iron Man* #128 (November 1979), Tony argues that alcohol does not dull the senses but rather makes things clearer. Finally, after hitting rock bottom in many areas of his life, Tony realizes that he is an alcoholic and that he needs help. Tony works his way into sobriety and seeks to make reparations to the people he harmed through his drinking.

A possible weakness of the story line is the fact that Tony's descent into alcoholism, so well developed over nine months of issues, is resolved in a one-page montage showing him giving up alcohol. Some readers were concerned that this trivialized the effort necessary for recovery, for in the real world it takes months and even years to attain sobriety and then it takes a lifetime of effort, a lifetime in recovery, to stay sober.

Perhaps because of this, writer Denny O'Neal revisited Tony's struggle with alcoholism two and a half years later in *Iron Man* #161 (August 1982) and the issues that followed. Tony starts drinking again and it costs him his company and his fortune. In *Iron Man* #169 (April 1983), his friend and colleague Jim "Rhodey" Rhodes is forced to take over for Tony as Iron Man because Tony is too drunk to do the job. Rhodey would continue in the role of Iron Man for the next two and a half years while Tony got his life back on track. In *Iron Man* #200 (November 1985), in a story that inspired scenes in the *Iron Man* film, Obadiah Stane has manipulated his way into taking control of Tony's company, developed a larger, more powerful

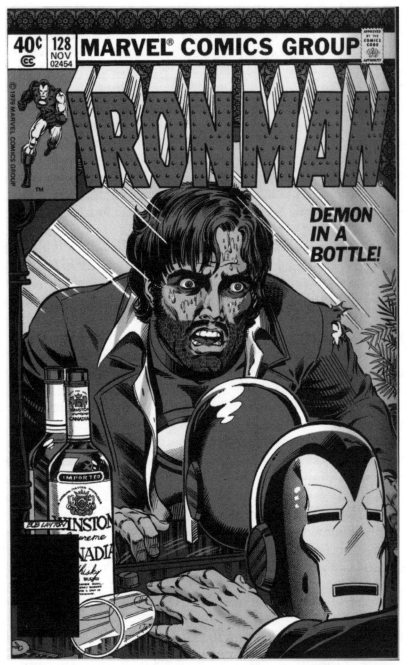

Figure 8. *Iron Man* #128 (November 1979), cover; Marvel Comics. David Michelinie writer, John Romita Jr. and Bob Layton artists. This cover shocked many comic book fans, as it graphically depicted a hero looking far less than heroic. Tony Stark, who had won so many battles as Iron Man, was falling victim to his own addiction to alcohol. Copyright ©1979 Marvel Comics, all rights reserved.

suit of armor, and kidnapped a baby. When Rhodey is injured, it is up to Tony to reclaim the mantle of Iron Man, battle Stane in his larger armor, and rescue the child. Later, Tony develops another suit of armor for Rhodey, who now fights crime as War Machine.

Tony Stark has, for the most part, been on the wagon since then. I asked Kurt Busiek about the way he had Tony play another role in a story line involving alcoholism.

> DALTON: You did not feature Tony Stark drinking in your run on *Iron Man,* but you did tell the story of Carol Danvers, who is the superhero Warbird, and her struggle with alcohol in a long story line that ran through both *Iron Man* and *The Avengers.* What were your goals for that story line?
>
> BUSIEK: We didn't want to ignore Tony's alcoholism, but at the same time we didn't want to just have him fall off the wagon and struggle with it— that'd just be a rerun. So what's the next step, for a recovering alcoholic? In many cases, you pass on what you've learned by helping others. So we wanted to have Tony become an AA sponsor to another alcoholic—and given that he stars in a superhero comic, it made the most sense to me to have him become a sponsor to another alcoholic superhero.
>
> We didn't get all the way to [Tony becoming a sponsor], but we were able to explore both Tony's struggle and Carol's by having her deal with issues he'd had to deal with, and him understanding what she'd been through and helping her through it.[13]

The story line culminated in *Iron Man* vol. 3, #25 (February 2000), with Carol finally admitting that she has a problem. She and Tony go to an Alcoholics Anonymous meeting, where she stands up and says those crucial, life-changing words, "Hello, my name is Carol . . . and I am an alcoholic."[14]

When we think about living out our vocation and our mission in life, one of the very specific things that prevents people from doing so is substance use and abuse. If we do not remain clean and sober, we cannot be of help to anyone, including ourselves. Substance abuse is a significant problem in our country and it is everyone's problem. Many of us have known someone who has died or been injured in an automobile accident caused by an impaired driver. In 2007, an estimated 12,998 people died in alcohol-related traffic crashes in the United States alone.[15] The fact that these fatalities get less media attention than a single case of poisoning or a single plane crash reveals how much we have come to take alcohol abuse for granted.

But drunk-driving accidents are just one result of our problems with substance abuse. According to the American Correctional Association, over half the inmates in U.S. prisons were under the influence of alcohol or drugs at the time of their current offense.[16] Many lives and many families are torn apart by substance abuse and many lives are lost. As people of faith, we should support the work of organizations such as Mothers Against Drunk Driving (MADD) to help create and enforce laws that prevent people from driving while impaired. We can also support the creation and funding of residential and outpatient substance-abuse rehabilitation programs because, unfortunately, those who have the clarity to realize that they need help sometimes cannot find it. There are often not enough openings available in these programs to meet the need. Our churches can work to ensure that those who need help to recover from alcoholism and drug abuse have programs and space available to them so that they can take this important step toward recovery.

While I was working as a counselor at a residential substance abuse rehabilitation center, I saw first-hand that recovering from an addiction is not as simple as making a wise decision or having enough will power. One truly does need to have support and draw upon a higher power. One of the strongest bits of advice our residents tried to give to others was to tell them not to begin abusing substances in the first place. Whether it is alcohol, illegal drugs, or prescription drugs, once someone gets headed down the road of abuse it is a very difficult road to recovery. I have gained a great deal of respect for those who are living in recovery, living one day at a time and staying clean and sober.

There are many helpful organizations, support groups, and treatment facilities designed to help those struggling with substance abuse, including Alcoholics Anonymous, Narcotics Anonymous, and Al-Anon for friends and family whose lives are affected by someone's substance abuse. All of these organizations have Web sites with a great deal of helpful information.[17]

Bob Layton and David Michelinie received an award from an alcohol abuse foundation for their realistic portrayal of alcoholism in Iron Man's "Demon in a Bottle" story. Some fans at the time thought it unseemly that the story should depict a hero like Tony Stark with such a weakness. Michelinie did not see it that way. He writes, "As Bob and I always envisioned him, Tony Stark, when stripped of everything nonessential, is a man of innate nobility."[18] That nobility and strength was depicted in his recovery. "And when he landed at the bottom of that bottle, and found the unbeatable demon that was his own weakness, he faced it, he fought it, and he drove it back into the darkest corner of his soul. And if there's a better definition of 'hero,' I don't know it."[19] He says that if readers take anything from the story "we hope it's this simple awareness: we can all be heroes. It's just a matter of choice."[20]

Not everyone struggles with substance abuse. There are other ways, however, in which we are called to be good stewards of our health. Whether our struggle is with being overweight, underweight, out of shape, or other health concerns, we would do well to do what is in our control to keep our bodies healthy as we offer ourselves in the service of God.

Closing

A favorite recurring scene for many fans of Iron Man comes when Tony Stark puts on his Iron Man armor. According to Ephesians, Christians are encouraged to "take up the whole armor of God, so that you may be able to withstand on that evil day, and having done everything, to stand firm" (Eph. 6:13). These pieces of armor include the belt of truth, breastplate of righteousness, shield of faith, helmet of salvation, and sword of the Spirit, which is the word of God (Eph. 6:14–17). Some Christians, especially those who are going through challenging times, have found it helpful to read this passage each morning and to envision clothing themselves in this armor. By staying immersed in thoughts of God and the ways of God, they are protected from the temptations that come their way. Perhaps we can think of how we are using each of these not just as protection for ourselves but to help others.

In the comic book, Tony devises the alibi that Iron Man is his bodyguard in order to explain why they are often seen in the same place and why Tony disappears and Iron Man appears whenever there is danger. In the film *Iron Man* (2008), however, Tony Stark makes a different choice. An agent of S.H.I.E.L.D. instructs Tony to use the alibi that Iron Man is his bodyguard. At the press conference at the end of the film, Tony starts to toe that company line, but suddenly changes his mind. He says to the press, "I'm just not the hero type. Clearly. With this laundry list of character defects, all the mistakes I've made—largely public. The truth is . . . I am Iron Man." In so doing, Tony embraces his identity as a hero.

We may not own a suit of superpowered armor, but we are still called to be good stewards of what we do have. We can still live a heroic life by using all that we have been given to the glory of God.

Questions for Reflection

- In what ways could you use your money better to serve God and others?
- Are there ways you can think of that you are misusing or wasting money that could better be used to help those in need and support good ministries?
- What talent has God given you that you are either not using or misusing? Brainstorm several ways that you could use the mind and talents that God has given you for good causes.
- What physical resources, such as a home, automobile, computer, or money, do you have? How can you use these to do God's work and help others?
- Have you ever been in a relationship that was unhealthy for you? Have you ever thought of a relationship in terms of whether or not it makes you a better person?
- Have you, or do you know of someone else, who has struggled with addiction? What do you believe are the most common misconceptions about addiction? What steps can you take to help yourself or someone else toward recovery?
- In what ways do you struggle in your stewardship of the body that God has given you? What steps could you take to be healthier?
- If you were to live your life totally for the will of God, living your entire life striving to do what is right, how would your life change?

The Mighty Thor

Living between Heaven and Earth

What do we have in common with a Norse thunder god with long blond hair and an enchanted hammer? Not much, it seems, at least at first glance. In Marvel's version of the myth, when frail Doctor Donald Blake pounds his cane on the floor he transforms into the Mighty Thor. This dual nature, however, creates tensions in his life to which we might relate. Is Thor's primary loyalty to the heavenly realm of Asgard or to the planet Earth? Does he see himself primarily as an immortal prince of Asgard engaged in epic adventures or as a human being with his own important work to do here on Earth? Does he carry himself with the pride and nobility befitting a god of thunder or the proper humility of someone who knows that others are as special as he is? Thor's struggles with these tensions offer us the opportunity to reflect on how we must work through similar tensions in our own lives.

The Origin of the Mighty Thor

After creating heroes such as the Fantastic Four, the Hulk, and Spider-Man, Stan Lee says that Marvel did not know how to top what they had already done. Lee writes, "The only one who could top the heroes we already had would be Super-God, but I didn't think the world was quite ready for that concept yet."[1] Instead, after hearing someone refer to Marvel Comics as twentieth-century mythology, Lee and Jack Kirby hit on the idea of updating a character from Norse mythology.

The Mighty Thor debuted in *Journey into Mystery* #83 (August 1962), with a plot provided by Lee, art by Kirby, and a script written by Lee's younger brother Larry Lieber. The origin tale introduces Donald Blake, a frail doctor who walks with the aid of a cane. Blake is vacationing on the coast of Norway. While he is there, he sees a group of giant Stone Men who had been sent from the planet Saturn to prepare for an invasion of Earth. Blake runs into a cave to hide and there discovers an ancient cane. When he accidentally strikes the cane against a rock it is transformed into the enchanted hammer Mjolnir and Blake is transformed into the Mighty Thor, Norse god of thunder. He soon discovers that as Thor he has tremendous strength, the power to create storms, and, by tossing his hammer and immediately grabbing onto its leather strap, the ability to soar through the air.[2] Thor uses these powers to chase off the Stone Men of Saturn and stop the invasion.

With Lee and Kirby busy with different projects, Lee handed off the early issues of Thor's adventures to Lieber and a variety of artists. Those early issues introduced Thor's evil brother, Loki, and his father, Odin, but more often the stories showed Thor battling a variety of conventional costumed villains on Earth.

In Between Heaven and Earth

With *Journey into Mystery* #97 (October 1963), Lee took over the scripting of Thor's adventures, and with issue #101 (February 1964), Kirby began his long run as the artist. The two creators soon hit their stride. Lee began to have Thor speak in a version of old English he drew from his reading of Shakespeare and the King James Version of the Bible, such as when he tells the Super Skrull, "Hast thou so soon forgot?? 'Tis the god of thunder who doth oppose thee! 'Tis Mighty Thor . . . at whose behest the storm doth erupt . . . the lightning doth flash . . . the heavens themselves reveal their awesome majesty! SO BE IT!"[3] Lee apparently felt that such verbiage was befitting the nobility of a modern-day Norse god. The stories soon began to explore Thor's life in Asgard, the home of the Norse gods, and his relationship with his father Odin, the All-Father and ruler of Asgard. Thor would spin his hammer and be transported to the Rainbow Bridge that led to the heavenly realm of Asgard, where he had epic adventures with friends and foes drawn from the world of Norse mythology.

Lee and Kirby intentionally balanced Thor's adventures between those set in Asgard and those set on Earth, or as Asgardians called it, Midgard. Thor himself began to struggle to fulfill his duties both as a prince of the realm of Asgard and as the protector of Earth. He also sought to balance his love for his immortal father Odin in Asgard with his love for Don Blake's mortal nurse, Jane Foster. At the same time, he tried to balance the time he devoted to fighting epic battles as Thor with the time he spent fighting seemingly more mundane battles as Doctor Donald Blake. Lee says he created the character with such dilemmas in mind: "I wanted Blake to be a surgeon because of the dramatic possibilities it would later present. I could envision themes where Thor is needed in Asgard but Dr. Blake is needed on Earth to perform a critical operation (which none but he can perform, natch). Oh, the suspense, the tension, the choice that must be made."[4] One example of just such a scenario came in *Journey into Mystery* #108 (September 1964). Dr. Don Blake is in the middle of a surgery to save the life of Dr. Strange when Odin summons Thor to Asgard. Blake cannot interrupt the surgery to respond and Odin, being quite a jealous god in those days, is furious and later refuses to respond to Thor's plea for help.

A few years later, in *The Mighty Thor* #137–140 (February–May 1967), Thor fights off an army of Trolls that is invading Asgard. It is a grand and glorious victory. During the celebration that follows, however, Thor quickly asks Odin's permission to return to Earth, the land that he loves and is sworn to protect. Arriving on Earth, he soon transforms into Don Blake and reflects on the good he does there. He looks in a mirror and says, "My face is the face of a scholar . . . a healer . . . a dedicated man of peace! And yet, even as Mighty Thor has dedicated his life to fighting evil, so have I dedicated mine to fighting the ills and ailments that afflict mankind!"[5]

Thor is devoted to both Asgard and Earth. *The Mighty Thor* #143 (August 1967) opens with Thor slurping a soda at a soda joint. People gather around him, asking him to describe his home in Asgard. Thor replies, "How can I describe that which is beyond the ken of mortal understanding?"[6] Still, he gives it a try, describing Heimdall guarding the Rainbow Bridge. When it comes to Asgard itself, however, he says, "But, for the fabled realm itself, there are no words . . . there is no way . . . it is truly beyond description!"[7] While those in the soda shop are not given a description of Asgard, readers of the comic are treated to pictures of Jack Kirby's wildly imaginative architecture of the golden realm of Asgard. While Thor obviously loves Asgard, a few pages later he changes to Don Blake and says, "For, to a doctor, the life of one sickly man is as important as the fate of thousands."[8] As he helps a patient he thinks, "The joy in his eyes . . . in his heart! Even the life of a thunder god can offer no greater satisfaction than this! For I have helped a fellow man!"[9]

A poignant example of this dynamic is seen in *The Mighty Thor* #171 (December 1969), a story Lee wrote in the wake of the 1968 assassinations of civil rights leaders Martin Luther King Jr. and Robert F. Kennedy. In the story, a fictional character named Pedro Luis Lopez is shot and is clinging to life. Thor says, "I have heard of this man Lopez! He is among the most dedicated . . . the most beloved of all those who crusade for civil rights!"[10] Thor desperately wants to be of assistance but realizes his strength and powers are no help at all. As he pounds his hammer on the ground and transforms into his human form, he says, "What now is needed is not the power of a warrior god, but the medical skill of Dr. Donald Blake!"[11] While Blake performs surgery on Lopez, the villain the Wrecker escapes captivity and goes on a destructive rampage through New York, which shakes the very foundation of the hospital where the surgery is taking place. Blake leaves the surgery room, secretly transforms back into Thor, captures the Wrecker, and then returns in time to complete the surgery successfully. The story likely represents a bit of wish-fulfillment fantasy for Lee, Kirby, and their readers. In the real world they knew that good men had died, but at least in the comic books they could save the life of a civil rights hero.

Christians also struggle to balance their lives on Earth with the glories that await them in heaven. We do not have drawings by Kirby of the glories of heaven, but the Bible does offer us a variety of images, including John's apocalyptic vision of the City of God, with streets of gold and gates of pearl (Rev. 21:21). None of the books of the Bible, however, provide readers with a detailed description of the afterlife. Some passages suggest that it is not like life in this world (e.g., Jn. 18:36; Heb. 9:11, 24; and 1 Cor. 15:50). While Jesus took the issue of marriage here on Earth quite seriously (e.g., Mk. 10:11), according to Matthew he said that in heaven people will not be married (Mt. 22:30). Jesus then goes on to make the point that God is not the God of the dead, but the God of the living (Mt. 22:32). Although the Bible does not give a full description of heaven or the life to come, many Christians believe in heaven as a place of peace, joy, and contentment where God is worshipped.

We cannot travel a rainbow bridge to heaven whenever we please, but some Christians can be tempted to stay in heaven, at least in their minds. Some people of faith get so caught up in spiritual things that they forget to live on earth. Those who do so can lose sight of the responsibility that they have to live out their faith on earth. They may drive from a meeting at church and go straight to a Christian bookstore while listening to a Christian radio station and talking with Christian friends. Nothing is wrong with that, unless they forget that they are also called to be the light of the world and salt of the earth. We do not want to get so caught up in the spiritual matters of the heavenly realm that we forget to live a faithful life on earth.

The hope of heaven is never meant to be a reason to neglect what is happening on earth. Instead, it is offered as a motivation for being persistent in our service to God. In the First Letter to the Thessalonians, the church at Thessalonica was encouraged to keep their hope in the resurrection alive. From reading the Second Letter to the Thessalonians, however, some commentators have speculated that members of the church may have been quitting their jobs and just sitting around thinking about Christ's return. Whether that was the cause of their lethargy or not, they were ignoring their work on Earth and, in response, the epistle tells them that they should stop being idle and get back to work (2 Thess. 3:6–10).

While our eternal life has already begun, our hope in what is to come should motivate us to work for God's purposes today and to combat real earthly problems such as hunger, illness, and injustice. Like Thor, our belief in the glories of a heavenly realm should inspire us to be even more committed to the work we have to do on earth. To do otherwise would be to prove Karl Marx right; our religion really does become the opium of the people, preventing us from working to change the world.[12]

At times, Christians can allow a strong sense of the spiritual life and their hopes of the future to paralyze them from acting when action is necessary. In the early days of World War II, as Nazi tyranny was spreading throughout Europe, many American Christians shied away from acting to stop it and resisted getting involved in the war. In his essay "The Christian Faith in the World Crisis," theologian Reinhold Niebuhr noted that many Christians hesitated to act because they had a utopian hope that all war could be prevented if only Christians would refuse to become involved in war. By doing so, they hoped to build a utopian future governed by the principles of love and justice. Niebuhr acknowledged that the Christian faith had an important role in building such a future but came to another conclusion:

> Yet there are times when hopes for the future, as well as contrition over past misdeeds, must be subordinated to the urgent, immediate task. In this instance, the immediate task is the defeat of Nazi tyranny. If this task does not engage us, both our repentance and our hope become luxuries in which

we indulge while other men save us from an intolerable fate, or while our inaction betrays into disaster a cause to which we owe allegiance.[13]

Our sense of spirituality and hope for the future does not relieve us from our duties to work for love and justice on earth but calls us to action. God has placed us here on the planet Earth in the twenty-first century, and we are called to do God's work right here and right now. Another balance that Thor strives to maintain is a balance between his seemingly epic battles as Thor and his seemingly more mundane tasks as Donald Blake. In one tale, Thor again angers Odin by deciding to stay on Earth for a while, saying, "Here in the mortal office of Dr. Don Blake, there is much good that I can do!"[14] Contrasted to visions of the glory of heaven and superspirituality, our tasks on Earth may seem quite mundane, but there is dignity and value in those tasks as well. The well-known preacher and homiletics scholar Fred Craddock has talked about our desire to live out superspiritual lives such as those lived by Albert Schweitzer, Mother Theresa, or missionaries who travel to the ends of the earth for Christ. He recalls that, as a boy, he was more than ready to give his life for Christ in some grand gesture. In his imagination, he pictured people coming to have their picture taken in front of a monument built in his honor. Although now it sounds a bit humorous, he says he was sincere then. As an adult, however, he realized that giving his life to Christ more often means living it out every day, in small as well as in big ways. He reflects that it might be easier to give his life in one grand gesture or, as Craddock puts it, to write one big check. He wrote, "'I give my life,' but nobody warned me that I could not write one big check. I've had to write forty-five years of little checks: 87 cents, 21 cents, a dollar three cents . . ."[15] Craddock's point is that often we need to live out our faith by being faithful in the small, everyday matters, and not just through grand gestures.

There may not be much glory in trying our best to be a good friend or a good parent every day. Faithfully doing our jobs to the best of our ability each day may not win us eternal glory in the halls of Asgard. Teaching a Sunday school class to the best of our ability, working for justice by writing letters, or helping fix up the home of someone in our neighborhood may not seem as glamorous as winning an epic battle on a faraway world. These are all tasks we are called to do, though, and they are acts that do have eternal consequences.

Thankfully, we do not have to choose between heaven and earth. We are not called just to live in the heavenlies and to wage epic battles, but to live our lives on earth doing great and mundane things for God and others. It is great to have faith that there is a heaven waiting for us after we die, but our calling and our prayer is to see God's will be done on earth, as it is in heaven.

"To Live as an Immortal!"

While it is true that we should not get caught up in the heavenlies and forget to live out our missions in life, at the same time we must never forget our connection to the God of heaven.

While we should appreciate our life on earth, people of faith know that there is more to life than what is seen. Human life is of far greater worth than is often recognized. While living our lives on earth, we should not lose sight of the fact that we are children of the God of Heaven and are made in God's image.

While Thor appreciated his earthly life, he also appreciated that he was not just a mortal being. In *The Mighty Thor* #337 (November 1983), writer-artist Walt Simonson began his acclaimed run on the title by having Don Blake walk through Grant Park in Chicago thinking, "On a beautiful day like today, I almost envy every mortal I see."[16] Still, he ponders, he likes his life and his dual nature. The people he sees around him are all tied to the Earth, yet he knows there is more to life than what is seen through earthly eyes. He is glad that he has the power and freedom to roam the glory of the heavens when he chooses. Still, his sense of responsibility to Earth keeps him here to protect it.

By the end of the issue, however, Thor has lost all connection to the heavenly realm. He fights an epic battle against the mighty and noble alien Beta Ray Bill. At a crucial moment he accidentally transforms into Don Blake, which allows Beta Ray Bill to defeat him and grab his hammer. In an instant, Thor loses the battle, his powers, and worst of all, his enchanted hammer Mjolnir. It is the first time that anyone besides Thor or Odin has been able to carry the hammer, which bears the famous inscription, "Whosoever holds this hammer, if he be worthy, shall possess the power of . . . Thor." When Odin calls Thor home, it is now Bill who appears in Asgard, while human Don Blake is left marooned on earth without his godly identity. The issue ends with Blake realizing all he has lost and calling out, "Odin was here! His presence still lingers! And he did not take me! Only a few hours ago, I nearly envied the mortals around me! And now, I may have to join them . . . forever! Father! Hear me! Do not forsake me here! FATHER!"[17] It is one of the most humbling times of Thor's life, and he fears that he has lost his connection to Odin and Asgard. While he enjoys his life on earth, he is devastated when he loses his connection to the heavenly realm.

In 2007, writer J. Michael Straczynski began the new series *Thor* with the premise that the residents of Asgard were trapped in the minds and souls of mortals. They were nobles of the realm of Asgard but did not know it. It is almost as though they were sleepwalking through their lives. In *Thor* #3 (2007), for example, Thor finds a man named Ezra on a bridge in New Orleans, who is watching over and guarding his community. Ezra has seen the death and devastation caused by Hurricane Katrina and has almost given up hope. Thor realizes who he is, and Ezra is awakened to realize he is Heimdall, guardian of the Rainbow Bridge into Asgard.

We are not gods! It is important, however, that we do not forget our own connection to the God of heaven. At times, we can forget how special we are as human beings. The scriptures teach us that humans are not forgettable, irrelevant beings, but rather holy people, fearfully and wonderfully made (Ps. 139:14). The Bible teaches us that human beings are created in the image of God (Gen. 1:26). While theologians debate the exact meaning of that phrase, most agree that it affirms the great value and dignity of all human life and our relationships with God and others.

As a pastor, I ministered to a number of people who had once known, but then had lost, that sense of a connection to God and spiritual things. Because their lives had fallen on hard times, they felt that God had forsaken them. They talked about the wasted years in which they felt they were not worth much to themselves or to other people. As were the Asgardians who were trapped on Earth, they were sleepwalking through life, forgetting their connection to God.

Part of our hope as people of faith is that we know there is more to this world than what we can see. We may not be able to cross a Rainbow Bridge and visit the heavenly realm, but we have faith that there is a God of love looking over us. We believe in a God who has blessed this earthly life and called it good. God has called us to the vocation of living out our faith, not in the heavenlies, but on this earth with all of its wonder and sorrow. Our calling, then, is to recognize that we are special, gifted by God, having the potential to do great things for God and our fellow humans. We can strive to find opportunities to serve in ways that are both mundane and great. A turning point in the early tales of Thor came with the story "To Become an Immortal," from *The Mighty Thor* #136 (January 1967). In those early years, Thor often evoked the wrath of his father Odin because of his love for a mortal woman, Dr. Don Blake's nurse, Jane Foster. Thor begs his father to allow him to marry her, and finally Odin seems to relent. In the story, Thor brings Jane to Asgard so that she can see his home and meet his father. Jane is overwhelmed by what she sees. In order to make her a suitable bride for his son, Odin transforms Jane into an Asgardian and gives her the power of flight. He tests her by sending her into a locked chamber to face a monster named, significantly, the Unknown. Jane, however, cannot handle the wonders of Asgard or her newfound gift and she is paralyzed with fear of the Unknown. She pleads to be allowed to leave Asgard. So she is returned to Earth with no powers and no memory of Thor or Asgard. She soon happily starts a new life as a nurse at another doctor's office. Lee and Kirby must have realized that the character of Jane Foster was not catching on and, at the end of the very same issue, Thor is introduced to a new love interest, the Asgardian warrior Sif. The issue is a melancholy one, with a major character in the series leaving because she prefers a mundane, earthbound life over the wonders of Asgard. She could not handle the opportunity to be more than a mere mortal.

Thor often makes a distinction between mortals, the humans of earth, and immortals, the gods of Asgard. The Christian doctrine of eternal life teaches that in this sense we are all immortal, affirming the value and preciousness of the human soul. Further, it affirms that we all have gifts that can be used to do great things. So while we may be called to do everyday tasks for the sake of our faith, we should not put a limit on the great things that God can do through us if we are willing and if we are not afraid of the unknown. We can take our place among the saints, both living and dead, who have served our God and our world.

We are not gods, nor are we even superpowered Asgardians, but belief in eternal life suggests that human beings are precious and of great worth. We may not have the power to create thunderstorms at will or the power of flight, but with an eternal perspective we know that our lives are precious and connected to God, and that we can do great things on earth.

Pride and Humility

Thor has not been a character with problems regarding his own self-esteem. As a matter of fact, he is one of the few characters in Marvel Comics who exhibits a great deal of pride and self-confidence in who he is. Stan Lee clearly had fun in scripting Thor's self-confident pronouncements. Thor introduces himself to immensely powerful aliens who have imprisoned the planet Earth by saying, "My name is Thor . . . my rank . . . Prince of Asgard . . . my heritage god of thunder! I command thee to remove yon space lock from the planet earth or suffer my boundless wrath! Thus speaks the son of Odin!"[18] He later proclaims, "No matter how great thy strength, I am the mighty Thor!! Mine is the power of Asgard . . . the fury and majesty of the storms of space! By the bristling beard of Odin, none may conquer Thor!"[19] He tells the Absorbing Man, "You presume to think yourself the equal of Thor??! Such base insolence must not go unpunished!"[20]

To be fair, Lee also had Thor repeatedly extol the dignity and value of human lives as well. He has said, for example, "The humblest life is more precious by far than the treasure of a thousand galaxies,"[21] and, "Men, how frail and fragile is their lives. And yet, how tinged with grandeur their dreams, their destiny! Men! In their very weakness there is strength and in their courage unending glory!"[22] (Figure 9). Thor also demonstrates that he has great respect for the dignity of his mortal Avenger teammates, at times showing greater respect for their dignity than they show for themselves.

This sense of personal nobility and self-esteem helps him accomplish great things. He does not shy away from difficult tasks and his sense of honor allows him neither to give up nor to give anything less than his best to a task. Still, at times, Thor's pride gets him and those around him into trouble. At times, he has taken offense to an insult or imagined offense to his dignity and has rushed into battle before his Avengers teammates would have hoped. At other times, he has responded in anger when patience would have been the better tack.[23] As worthy as Thor might be of great honor, one of his biggest weaknesses has been that he had not learned the lesson of humility.

When Thor is smarting over his loss to Beta Ray Bill and the fact that another has been found worthy of wielding his hammer, Odin tells him, "Thor, humility is a lesson even gods can learn. Such was the meaning of Mjolnir's spell wrought long ago."[24]

Figure 9. *The Mighty Thor* #158 (November 1968), page 2; Marvel Comics. Stan Lee script, Jack Kirby art. During a turning point in the life of the Mighty Thor, he returns to Earth from the heavenly realm of Asgard and reflects on the nature of humankind. Kirby uses just four panels rather than the usual nine for the page, which allows him to give the figure of Thor more power and nobility, though Vince Colletta's inking of the page seems to leave out some of the details of Kirby's artwork. Copyright ©1968 Marvel Comics, all rights reserved.

The story of Mjolnir's spell is another classic tale in the history of Thor. As Lee and Kirby developed Thor's personality and told stories of Thor's childhood in Asgard in their "Tales of Asgard" stories, they were compelled to explain how Thor could have existed before Donald Blake found the enchanted cane. Blake begins to wonder why he cannot remember much of his life before finding his enchanted cane. In the story "Who Is the Real Don Blake?" from *The Mighty Thor* #159 (December 1968), Odin explains to Blake that as a young man Thor was proud and headstrong. He recounts a time when he had to tell Thor, "Thou art lacking in humility!"[25] So Odin told Thor, "Though thou art supreme in thy power and thy pride . . . thou must know weakness . . . thou must feel pain!"[26] So, Odin explains, he created the Donald Blake persona and arranged for him to find the enchanted cane in order to teach Thor humility on another world. Odin told Thor, "'Tis known as Earth . . . where fragile mortals dwell! And there shalt thou reside . . . and there shalt thou learn that none can be truly strong unless they be truly humble!"[27] As comic book historian Les Daniels notes, "Marvel's reworking of Thor's story had taken on overtones of a more exalted ancient tale, one in which God sent his only son to earth to serve mankind."[28]

Now Blake understands why he cannot remember his life before Thor and ponders that "even my injured leg has an Odinian purpose . . . to teach me that any handicap can be endured . . . and overcome."[29] Thor learns the lesson of humility but does not confuse it with a sense of weakness or timidity. In the very next issue, Odin sends Thor off to defend the world from no less a threat than Galactus himself!

Too much pride in our standing with God can lead us to begin to think of ourselves as having a special status, blessed by God and superior to others. This can lead us to look down on others, disregarding their needs and feeling justified in hating them. The danger is that we will begin to see ourselves as the chosen, the blessed, and fail to remember that everyone is created in the image of God. To think we are without sin can lead us into Manichaeism, discussed in the introduction to this book, and we can begin to justify all sorts of evil in order to defeat our enemies.

On the other hand, if we allow ourselves to dwell on our sinfulness, we may not have the proper respect for ourselves or for others as children of God. In 1960, feminist theologian Valerie Saiving offered a helpful perspective on sin. Many theologians at that time (mostly male) had identified sin with pride and self-assertiveness. Saiving pointed out that those assumptions were based on the male experience of life. Women, however, were often in a place where they needed to be more self-assertive, not as a way of lording over others, but of being all they could be.[30] As a result, they may not have had the confidence necessary to carry out the tasks they were called to undertake.

While self-confidence is a good thing, it is still helpful for us to remember that humility has been long considered one of the Christian virtues. First Peter 5:5 calls us to clothe ourselves in humility. Proverbs warns us, "Pride goes before destruction, and a haughty spirit before the fall" (Prov. 16:8).

Jesus provides us with a helpful example. Jesus confidently claimed his special status as God's son. He did not shy away from trying to do great things. At the same time, he demonstrated great humility. He repeatedly told his disciples that any leadership role or status that they had should not motivate them to lord it over others but instead to be humble servants to others (Mt. 20: 25–28; Mt. 23:10–12; Mk. 9:33–37; and Lk. 22: 24–27). When his disciples gathered for the Passover meal, Jesus took on the role of a servant and washed the dirt off his disciples' feet. The disciples were taken aback, because to them it seemed that Jesus was too important a man to take on such a humble role. Jesus told them, "You call me Teacher and Lord—and you are right, for that is what I am. So if I, your Lord and Teacher, have washed your feet, you also ought to wash one another's feet. For I have set you an example, that you also should do as I have done to you" (Jn. 13: 13–15).

A rabbi once said that people should carry two stones in their pockets. On one stone should be inscribed "I am but dust and ashes." On the other, "For my sake was the world created." According to the rabbi, we should use each stone as we need it. The Bible teaches us that human beings are created in the image of God (Gen. 1:26), a teaching that affirms the great value and dignity of all human life and our relationships with others. This is good reason for both great pride and great humility. People of faith are called on to humbly acknowledge that they are special and capable beings created by God. At the same time, we are called on to acknowledge that everyone else is special as well, and of great worth as creatures of God.

Questions for Reflection

- If you were the Mighty Thor, would you want to spend more of your time in Asgard or on the Earth?
- In your struggle to find a balance between dwelling too much on heavenly things or too much on earthly things, what do you tend to overemphasize? What might you do to correct this imbalance?
- Are there times when you are tempted to retreat from the world into a Christian counterculture? Is it ever OK to do so? When does it become a problem?
- What are the important but seemingly mundane things you are called to do by God on earth?
- Can you think of some great things that you might be called to do on earth? What might those things be?
- Has there been a time when you were sleepwalking through life, not living as though you were a child of God?
- Can you recall a time in your life when you felt especially close to God and especially loved by God? What was happening at that time in your life and what might you have been doing to help you feel that way?
- Do you tend to have too much pride or too low self-esteem? Is it possible to have both? How can you work to improve this?

Captain America and the Falcon

Serving God and Country

Marvel's Captain America has been both hailed and criticized as the ultimate U.S. soldier and patriot. During World War II, his comic books and his Sentinels of Liberty club for patriotic children served as positive propaganda for the U.S. war effort. Since his revival in the 1960s, Captain America has had a much more ambivalent relationship with his country and its leaders. Sometimes Captain America's strong allegiance to the best ideals that the United States embodies, what he calls the American Dream, leads him to defend the United States with his very life. At other times, his strong belief in the ideals he represents leads him to distance himself from his country's leaders and its policies. As we reflect on Captain America's adventures, we might ask what our relationship should be to our country. As people of faith seek to serve God, how should they live out their faith as citizens of their countries?

The Falcon presents readers with another perspective on America. For nearly forty years, Captain America and the Falcon have presented comic book readers with a model of interracial friendship and partnership. At times, however, despite their respect for each other, their different backgrounds and different experiences of America create tensions between them. How do we learn to live together in a multicultural, multiracial society? This chapter focuses on issues particular to people of faith in the United States, but many of the issues are relevant to people of faith in other countries as well.

Golden Age Origin

In *Captain America Comics* #1 (March 1941), Jack Kirby and Joe Simon told the story of Steve Rogers, a scrawny but patriotic young man who tries to volunteer for military duty. Rogers is turned down because he is not deemed physically fit for service. Instead, he volunteers for the top-secret Super Soldier Project, in which the government is attempting to develop a whole corps of supersoldiers. Rogers is injected with the Super Soldier Serum and transforms into an extremely muscular and fit man, the perfect U.S. soldier. At that very moment, a Nazi spy yells, "Death to the dogs of democracy!" and shoots and kills the only scientist who knows the details of the secret serum, leaving Steve Rogers as the world's sole super soldier.[1] Rogers is given a red, white, and blue costume, a shield, and a new role as Captain America, the Sentinel of Liberty.

As mentioned in the introduction to this book, the cover of the first issue of *Captain America Comics* featured Captain America punching Hitler in the jaw. Inside the issue, Captain America battled Nazi soldiers, including the villain who would become his archnemesis, the Red Skull. The adventures of Private Steve Rogers and his alter ego Captain America were tremendously popular during the war. Bucky Barnes, a boy who is the camp mascot, discovers Steve's secret identity and joins him as his costumed partner Bucky in dangerous adventures, both stateside and behind enemy lines. Soon, both in the comic book and the real world, Captain America became the symbol of the courage and fighting spirit of the American people.

Silver Age Origin

Captain America's popularity waned after the end of World War II, and Marvel soon stopped publishing his adventures. The company tried to bring him back for a few issues in the mid-1950s, but his new stories did not have good sales and they were cancelled again. After the revival of Marvel superheroes in the 1960s, however, the time seemed ripe to bring Captain America back once again.

Avengers #4 (March 1964), written by Stan Lee and penciled by Captain America's original co-creator Jack Kirby, opened with the Sub-Mariner (another revived Golden Age character) finding a tribe of people worshipping the figure of a man encased in ice. In a rage, the Sub-Mariner inexplicably takes the frozen block of ice and tosses it into the sea. The block of ice melts and the man is left adrift under the sea. Just then, the Avengers happen by in an undersea craft and see him. They rescue the man and discover that he is the legendary hero of World War II, Captain America. Inside the submarine, Captain America finishes thawing out and wakes up healthy and ready for battle. Captain America tells the Avengers that, the last he recalls, it was the 1940s and World War II was still going on.[2] He and his partner Bucky had just jumped onto an explosive-filled Nazi drone plane in hopes of stopping it when it suddenly burst into flames, killing Bucky and sending Captain America to the bottom of the sea where he was frozen in ice. He reasons, "All those years of being in a state of suspended animation must have prevented me from aging!"[3]

When they get back to civilization, Steve goes outside to see a world that he does not know. The New York City skyline has changed and the styles of cars and clothing have changed. He realizes that he is a man out of time. A recurring theme in Captain America's stories is that he is a throwback, a man who embodies the values and virtues of a bygone era. He soon discovers that those values and virtues are still needed in the world today.

While he has great acrobatic skills and hand-to-hand combat techniques that have been gained through hours of rigorous training, Rogers has almost never had the level of strength or powers of most Marvel heroes. His greatest asset has been the content of his character. It is his courage, integrity, persistence, and leadership skills that make Captain America Marvel's quintessential winner. Captain America may not be the most powerful person in the fight, but he never gives up and he always finds a way to win.

God and Country

Along with Captain America's adventures with the Avengers, World War II veterans Lee and Kirby also began to tell stories of his solo adventures. These stories, which began in *Tales of Suspense* #59 (November 1964), frequently recounted new "untold" stories of his World War II adventures. Even when these stories were set in the present day, he often fought escaped Nazis such as Baron Zemo and his old nemesis, the Red Skull.

Captain America sometimes serves alongside American soldiers and speaks with patriotic fervor. After defeating the Red Skull yet again, for example, he tells a group of sailors, with humility and pride, "I'm no more a hero than any man who fights for justice, and freedom, and brotherhood! So long as we cherish liberty . . . so long as the bitter weed of tyranny can never take root upon our shores . . . then all of us are heroes and the dream which is America will long endure!"[4]

In most of his incarnations, Captain America does not carry a gun.[5] Instead, he carries a defensive weapon only, his shield, which he occasionally throws to knock down enemy soldiers or to knock the guns out of their hands. He almost never gets shot himself and is able to defeat those with guns using only his fists and his shield. This allows him to take a primarily defensive, nonviolent stance and still defeat the enemy. By extension, his stories portray him as nonviolent and nonaggressive but successful in war.

Captain America is generally seen as an inspiring symbol that honors the courage of American soldiers, but his stories have also been criticized for trivializing the realities of war and the true sacrifice of soldiers. There is some wish fulfillment in watching the fantasy of an American soldier who can dodge bullets and win a war without ever having to fire a shot. Such depiction of war is a fantasy. The deadly violence of war is very real, however, and the sacrifices that soldiers make, both in risking their own lives and being asked to take other lives, are very real and should not be trivialized or overlooked.

Captain America has also been criticized as a symbol of blind patriotism and as a symbol of the way the United States has been willing to fight at all costs to preserve the American way.[6] This may indeed be the way that Captain America functioned in World War II and the way he still functions in the mind of many Americans today. Since Captain America's revival in the 1960s, however, he began to develop a more ambiguous relationship with his country and its leaders.

At the end of the 1960s and the beginning of the 1970s, the United States was in the midst of assassinations, riots, and war protests. The country was changing, and Lee had Captain America, a throwback to an earlier age, begin to struggle with those changes. In *Captain America* #122 (February 1970), Captain America has a troubling encounter with some rebels. As he walks down the street afterward, he thinks, "Who's to say the rebels are wrong? But, I've never learned to play by today's new rules. I've spent a lifetime defending the flag and the law. Perhaps I should have battled less and questioned more."[7] Lee says he thinks that last line is one of the best lines he has ever written.[8]

Perhaps the most shocking story of Captain America being at odds with his country came in the wake of the Watergate scandal. In 1974, writer Steve Englehart and artist Sal Buscema stunned readers with a story line that in some ways paralleled the events of the time and led to Steve Rogers giving up his identity as Captain America. The "Secret Empire" saga ran in *Captain America and the Falcon* #169–176 (January–August 1974). It tells the tale of the Secret Empire, a mysterious organization that frames Captain America for a murder and tries to turn public opinion against him. Captain America tries to clear his name by discovering the identity of the organization's mysterious leader, "Number One." When Captain America finally unmasks Number One, he recoils in shock. He says, "But you . . . you're . . ." The unseen man says, "Exactly! But high political office didn't satisfy me! My power was still too constrained by legalities!"[9] While the issue does not come out and say it explicitly, it was clear to most readers, reeling from the scandal of Watergate, that Number One was the president of the United States himself. Captain America is devastated. He feels that if the president could be corrupt, then everything he has stood for has been a sham. In the next issue, *Captain America and the Falcon* #176 (August 1974), Steve Rogers decides to give up his identity as Captain America because he does not know what America he is supposed to symbolize (Figure 10). For several issues, starting with issue #180 (December 1974), Steve Rogers dons a new costume and takes on the identity of Nomad, a man without a country.

When the Red Skull reemerges, however, it becomes clear that the world still needs Captain America. Steve reclaims the mantle of Captain America and says that this time he will not be naive. He now realizes that America the reality does not always match America the dream, but he will continue to fight for the dream.[10]

Today, Americans are unfortunately only too familiar with scandals involving their elected leaders. At the time, however, the nation's consciousness was taking a hit from the events of the Watergate scandal and the fallout from its cover-up. Perhaps one lesson we can learn is that we should not become too devoted to individual politicians or even to political parties. Instead, we can remain devoted to the best ideals of our countries. Perhaps, at times, we, too, should battle less and question more.

The theme of duty to the American dream versus unquestioning loyalty to government agencies has been a recurring theme for Captain America. During

Figure 10. *Captain America and the Falcon* #176 (August 1974), cover; Marvel Comics.
Steve Englehart script, Sal Buscema art. In the wake of the Watergate scandal, Steve
Rogers is disillusioned by a fictional presidential scandal and renounces his role
as Captain America. Rogers would later reclaim the role, reasoning that he could
represent the American spirit even if he did not always agree with the policies of the
United States government. Copyright ©1974 Marvel Comics, all rights reserved.

the 1980 presidential campaign, writer Roger Stern and artist John Byrne wrote a story in which the New Populist Party tries to recruit Captain America to be their candidate for president. There is a groundswell of support for his candidacy among the public. It troubles Steve that even though they do not know his stance on foreign affairs, energy, or inflation, they are ready to vote for him simply on the basis of the image he projects. After thoughtful consideration, he declines the nomination, explaining, "My duty to the [American] dream would severely limit any abilities I might have to preserve the reality."[11]

In 1987, Mark Guenwald, who wrote Captain America's adventures for over a decade, collaborated with artist Tom Morgan to tell the story "The Choice." Captain America is summoned to a presidential commission at the Pentagon. It informs him that since the government funded the project that gave him his powers, created his uniform, and even gave him his name, therefore he must, from now on, take his orders from them. They tell him that he does not have a choice. In response, Captain America tells them that of course he has a choice. The United States is a free country. He wants to serve his country, but he concludes, "No, those men are not my country. They are only paid bureaucrats of the country's current administration. They represent the country's political system. While I represent those intangibles upon which our country was founded . . . liberty, justice, dignity, the pursuit of happiness."[12] He says, "By going back to my wartime role as an agent of America's official policies, I'd be compromising my effectiveness as a symbol that transcends politics."[13] As a consequence of his decision, Steve Rogers gives his uniform and shield back to the commission. For the next year and a half of his comic book adventures, Steve Rogers fights on as "The Captain," while the government tries to replace him with men who do not have the talent or, more importantly, the character to fill the role. Finally, in issue #350 (February 1989), the commission gives Steve back his identity as Captain America.

In the 1990s, in Captain America #450–453, writer Mark Waid and artist Ron Garney told the story "Man Without a Country." After Captain America is forced to fight briefly alongside the Red Skull, he is arrested and tried for treason. The president revokes Captain America's citizenship and sends him to Europe and into exile. His citizenship is eventually reinstated, but once again Captain America recognizes that his relationship to his country is complex.

One of Steve Rogers' most difficult decisions in his efforts to balance his loyalty to his country and its ideals came during Marvel's 2006–2007 company-wide crossover event, "Civil War." In the story, the United States government implements a Superhero Registration Act that calls for all superpowered individuals to register their secret identities with the government and submit to governmental supervision of their activities. The act would not have that much personal effect on Steve Rogers. The government already knows his secret identity and he has already followed the government's rules. Rogers, however, comes to see the act as a violation of his friends' and colleagues' civil rights. It would have been very easy for him to say "that's their problem," but Rogers is concerned for their rights as well. When the government orders him to hunt down his fellow heroes who are in defiance of the Superhero Registration Act, Steve refuses and chooses to go AWOL, gathers a resistance movement, and becomes an enemy of the government in the process. By way of explanation, he quotes Thomas Payne's famous line, "Those who expect to reap the blessings of freedom must undergo the fatigue of supporting it."[14]

For the sake of his country, Steve Rogers eventually submits to arrest, knowing that the mood of the country and the public trial that awaits him put his life into great danger. In *Captain America* vol. 5, #25 (March 2007), titled "Death of the Dream," Steve Rogers is assassinated while being marched into the courthouse. The story, by writer Ed Brubaker and artist Steve Epting, received great media attention, including the lead front-cover story of the *New York Daily News* and thoughtful analysis in *Time Magazine*, *Newsweek*, *U.S. News and World Report*, *Wall Street Journal*, and many other newspapers, magazines, and television news programs. Captain America was just a fictional comic book character, but he had become a symbol of the American spirit, and his death was cause for reflection. Months later, in *Captain America* vol. 5, #34 (2008), Steve Rogers' former partner Bucky Barnes, who like many other once-dead comic book characters is once again alive, took on the mantle of Captain America. The spirit of Captain America, it seems, is not linked to just one man but to an ideal.

Based on these story lines alone, it may seem as though Marvel's Captain America has been a cynical, almost anti-American comic book. That is not the case. Most of his stories through the decades depict Captain America honoring and serving his country and its leaders. The stories described earlier, however, demonstrate that it is also not accurate to portray him simply as a symbol of blind patriotism.

In 1976, to commemorate the Bicentennial of the United States, Jack Kirby wrote and penciled a special oversized "treasury" edition comic titled *Captain America's Bicentennial Battles* (July 1976). In the story, a mystical character sends Captain America through time to different points in American history. He meets Benjamin Franklin in Philadelphia in 1776, where his costume serves as an inspiration to Betsy Ross for the design of the new nation's flag! He travels to the old west, where the Chiricahua Apache leader Geronimo teaches him about the cost of liberty. He travels to the mid-1800s and helps a slave escape with the help of John Brown's son. In the process, he is shown both good sides and bad sides of America. Still, he is not disillusioned. He says, "I've never been fool enough to believe that this country is made of heroic monuments of fanciful accounts created to inspire people to patriotic fervor."[15] When the mystical character puts Captain America in the middle of a parade scene worthy of the finale of a patriotic Hollywood musical, he calls for it to stop. He says he wants to find "the truth at the heart"[16] of America. In the story, Captain America finds that truth in the real lives and real struggles of Americans of all races, all cultures, and all backgrounds. He says, "That's America! A place of stubborn confidence . . . where both young and old can hope and dream, and wade through disappointment, despair and the crunch of events . . . with the chance of making life meaningful."[17]

While Captain America struggles to balance allegiance to the U.S. government with allegiance to the higher ideals of what he calls the American dream, people of faith struggle to balance allegiance to their faith and ideals with loyalty to their nations.

Even if one views Captain America as the heroic symbol of the American dream rather than as a symbol for its current policies, people of faith should be hesitant to embrace such zealous nationalism. Overly passionate nationalism, the belief that our country's values and policies are vastly superior to all others, can lead to xenophobia. While there is a great deal to admire and to support in the United States' best ideals and its heritage, we serve a God who is the God of the entire world and we are called to be citizens of that world. As people of faith, we know that we pledge our ultimate allegiance to an authority that is even higher than our country.

How, then, have people of faith served both their God and their country? Israel's prophets repeatedly spoke out against the leaders of other nations and of their own nation for the way they were neglecting the poor and for other unjust policies. This was not a very popular thing to do. Those who listened to the prophets enjoyed it when they criticized other nations but were not very happy to hear them criticize their own country. The prophets were often risking their lives to speak up for God.

The Jewish people of Jesus' day faced a dilemma when it came to paying their taxes. Some believed that to pay taxes to an oppressive emperor would be to compromise their faith, since only God was truly their sovereign. Others thought that withholding taxes was being unnecessarily disloyal to the empire and would bring with it the danger of imprisonment, or worse. According to the Gospel of Matthew, the Pharisees tried to entrap Jesus by making him take sides in this partisan issue. They asked, "Is it lawful to pay taxes to the emperor, or not?" (Mt. 22:17). Jesus was aware of their malice, and his answer surprised them: "'Why are you putting me to the test, you hypocrites? Show me the coin used for the tax.' And they brought him a denarius. Then he said to them, 'Whose head is this, and whose title?' They answered, 'The emperor's.' Then he said to them, 'Give therefore to the emperor the things that are the emperor's, and to God the things that are God's.' When they heard this, they were amazed; and they left him and went away" (Mt. 22:19–22). According to New Testament scholar Warren Carter, Jesus' answer calls his followers to obey the law of the empire and pay the tax but, at the same time, to recognize that God has far greater authority over their lives than the empire.[18] As Carter puts it, "Instead of paying taxes as an act of submission to the empire, this community is to pay them as an act which recognizes God's sovereignty over the earth (Mt. 17:24–27; 22:15–22)."[19] This approach to taxes could be seen as part of a larger "nonviolent subversion of Rome."[20]

From the very founding of their nation, people of faith in the United States have had a complex relationship with their country. The founders of the nation drew their values from various faith traditions, but they also insisted that people in this nation would have the liberty to worship as they pleased and that the nation would never establish an official religion.

Some Christians may try to escape the conflict by suggesting that the United States should be a specifically Christian nation, allowing them to make their patriotic loyalty to their country part and parcel of their devotion to God. The founders of the nation, however, made it clear that this should not be the case. For one thing, many of the founders of our nation were not Christians, at least in the way most of us think of Christianity today. Both Thomas Jefferson and Benjamin Franklin were deists who believed in the work of providence in the world and believed that Jesus of Nazareth was a great moral teacher but did not believe that Jesus was the Son of God. John Adams and Thomas Payne were Unitarians.[21] Many of the founders who were Christians had suffered religious oppression in England and therefore wanted to establish a nation with religious liberty for all. The First Amendment to the Constitution reads, "Congress shall make no law respecting an establishment of religion, or prohibiting the free exercise thereof." The two clauses of the amendment, known as the establishment and free exercise clauses, have sparked debate through the years as the country has struggled to balance its efforts to allow people to freely exercise their own faith and yet not to do so in a way that officially establishes any faith or imposes any faith on others. As Jon Meacham writes, "The Founders repay close attention, for their time is like our time, and they found a way to honor religion's place in the life of the nation while giving people the freedom to believe as they wish, and not merely to tolerate someone else's faith, but to respect it."[22]

How then should Christians live out their faith in a country that celebrates the free exercise of religion but does not establish Christianity as the official religion of the country? In his book *God in Public*, religious historian Mark Toulouse traces the variety of ways in which Americans have practiced their faith in relationship to their country.[23] He holds up the example of the Black Church during the civil rights movement, which spoke prophetically to the country as a whole. As with Jesus' followers, those working with the Black Church in the civil rights movement did not subvert their faith to the current laws of the land, nor did they attempt violently to overthrow the government. Instead they lived out their faith through nonviolent subversion of unjust laws and practices. In Toulouse's view, such practices of faith are not disloyal to the nation but part of being citizens in a country that respects freedom of expression of religion while not officially establishing any one religion.

The Reverend Martin Luther King Jr. serves as a helpful example of this type of faith in action. King believed in the United States and the dream of America. But King's first loyalty was to God and God's justice. He was not beholden to any one political party and he did not just follow any one political leader. With values that he unapologetically drew from his faith, he called his country to be faithful to its own best ideals.

During the Vietnam War, King spoke on the subject of "Youth and Social Action." He spoke about how some young radicals were resorting to violence to try to change their society. Meanwhile others, those known at the time as "hippies," were disavowing any responsibility to society by dropping out of it. King, of course, endorsed neither of these approaches. Instead, he encouraged young people to stay engaged with their society through peaceful and nonviolent means. He said, "When an individual is no longer a true participant, when he no longer feels a sense of responsibility to his society, the content of democracy is emptied."[24]

Christian social ethicist Stephen Charles Mott suggests that even acts of civil disobedience can sometimes be patriotic acts. He argues that civil disobedience should be used only after all other nondisobedient recourses have been exhausted, but that such acts can actually help a government avoid greater problems down the road. Protesters can help motivate leaders to address problems before resentment at injustices builds up and is expressed in less constructive ways. As Mott writes, "Thus, civil disobedience can truly be a way of paying our obligations of respect and honor to the political system (Rom. 13.7)."[25]

Through the last several decades, Captain America discovered that his devotion to his country could not be blind. Even when he disagreed with the leaders of his country, he discovered that he needed to keep working to preserve its ideals. For those of us who are citizens of the United States, this means that our faith is a helpful source of values and principles to draw upon as we do our civic duty and strive to make our country the best that it can be.

In a democratic society, then, the church and its members have not only permission but also a duty to draw upon their faith to motivate them to speak up and act for the cause of justice. It is not our duty to undermine the founding principles of our country by trying to get it to endorse any one religion, but it is our duty to draw upon our faith for insight and inspiration and to call our country to live out its ideals of liberty and justice for all. At times this calls us to support our government's policies and its leaders; however, at times, it also calls the church to question government policies in order to help us create a better life together.

America in Black and White

One of the most profound issues facing the United States today and throughout its history has been the issue of race. This book's earlier chapters on the Fantastic Four and the X-Men reflect on issues of multiculturalism. This section will reflect briefly and particularly on the relationship of white Americans and African Americans in the United States.

It is clear from Stan Lee's monthly "Stan's Soapbox" columns, which appeared in every issue of Marvel comics in the late 1960s and early 1970s, that he was deeply concerned about race relations in the United States. During that time, Lee's columns seemed to call for tolerance and understanding with an increasing sense of urgency.[26] Dealing with race in America was part of being a good citizen, and Lee apparently felt that *Captain America* was the appropriate forum in which to deal with the issue directly.

In *Captain America* #117 (September 1969), Lee and artist Gene Colan introduced Sam Wilson, an African American man from Harlem, and his trained falcon Redwing. By issue's end, Sam became the costumed hero the Falcon. Soon afterward he became Captain America's partner and, with issue #134 (January 1971), the comic book was renamed *Captain America and the Falcon*; it would keep that title for the next seven and a half years.

In *Captain America* #126 (June 1970), the Falcon is framed for murder by a villain, and the police are after him. Steve Rogers helps him out of the situation by giving him his Captain America outfit to put on so he can slip away undetected until his name is cleared. At the end of the story, Sam sees Steve leaving and offers the feel-good sentiment, "Go in peace, my friend! Your skin may be a different color . . . but there's no man alive I'm prouder to call . . . brother!"[27] The relationship between Steve and Sam was a picture of interracial harmony. But Lee's treatment of race relations would soon become more complex.

In *Captain America and the Falcon* #143 (November 1971), Lee and artist John Romita Sr. told a story in which Sam's girlfriend gets involved with a radical group that Sam calls a black hate group. The group is led by a masked man who teaches them to despise all white people as well as any black person who works with them. They even take Reverend Garcia, an African American minister who runs a Harlem Boys Club and cooperates with whites, as a hostage. When Sam tries to reason with the members of the group, they beat him up. Soon, the group's masked leader is revealed to be the Red Skull, a Nazi white supremacist. The Falcon and Captain America are able to defeat him and those who have been a part of the group are released from the Red Skull's control. Once things settle down, Steve suggests to Sam that they will have to keep an eye on the African Americans in the community. Steve says, "Who knows what little something it will take to make them explode again." Sam responds, "I don't think I like the way you put that partner! They . . . we . . . got reason to blow up." Sam leaves his partnership with Captain America saying, "I got some value reassessing to do. I'll get in touch when I know where I stand."[28] Captain America, meanwhile, is forced to do some thinking of his own. In the next issue, #144 (December 1971), Steve apologizes to Sam. "About what I said after the near-riot the other night. I'm sorry. I didn't mean it the way it sounded. I know it's tough playing the hero role. And being black doesn't make it any easier." But Sam isn't in a conciliatory mood: "You *know*? You know what it's like to be sneered at by your own people? I got news for you! That's the trouble with you whites. You think you've got all the answers . . . when you don't even ask the right questions. On the day you realize that . . . then maybe you'll have the right to say you know how it is."[29] The two men have a civil conversation, and Steve comes to respect Sam's decision to move out on his own as the Falcon, fighting to defend his neighborhood in Harlem. Captain America has to acknowledge that he does not understand what it means to be an African American in the United States. At the same time, as much as the Falcon respects Captain America, he comes to realize that his friend does not and never will be able to understand fully what it means to be black in America.

It would have been tempting for Lee and Romita to show these two noble heroes getting along perfectly well and to simplistically imply that we can all get along as long as we are not raging bigots. Instead, perhaps because the stories were being written in New York City at a time when it experiencing undeniable strain between whites and African Americans, the stories reflected at least some of the complexity of race relations in the United States. For me personally, and I suspect for many other young white Americans who were reading *Captain America and the Falcon* at the time, the comic book served as one of our first exposures to frank conversation about race in America.

Over the years, Steve Rogers has learned a great deal from trying to see America through Sam Wilson's eyes. Sam, meanwhile, has realized that to become his own man he cannot play the role of a sidekick and has found his own way as a hero who defends the people of Harlem. While the two heroes never again have had the simpler relationship of those earliest issues, they have worked out a better, mutually enriching relationship. There continues to be tension in their friendship, but there is also a more honest relationship and a truer partnership.

Race relations in the United States are complex and are certainly not going to be solved on the pages of comic books. Perhaps one initial step forward may be the act of simply acknowledging that racism exists and that we all have prejudices, many of which we may not even be consciously aware.

Another step is being willing to say, "I don't understand." For those who are not African American, that means recognizing that African Americans have lived under the burden of racism for hundreds of years in America and continue to confront racism today in ways that those who are not African American can never fully understand.

Tony Campolo and Michael Battle open their book, *The Church Enslaved: A Spirituality of Racial Reconciliation*, by saying, "As Christians in North America, we must first acknowledge that racism itself is a continuing and deeply embedded issue in American culture."[30] Campolo and Battle go on to explain that some forms of overt racism have given way to more subtle forms of racism in the last fifty years. While it is certainly good that overt racism is not as common today, it does make it more difficult to recognize the many, more subtle forms of racism that still exist.[31]

In writer Robert Morales and artist Kyle Baker's provocative 2004 series *Truth: Red, White and Black,* Steve Rogers discovers some disturbing background to the Super-Soldier Serum, which gave him his powers. The series tells the story that, in the early days of World War II, the United States took two battalions of African American soldiers and secretly used them as unwitting guinea pigs in the early trial-and-error stage of the serum's development. Most of the soldiers died from the experiments. Finally one man, Isaiah Bradley, survives and gains the powers of a supersoldier. Once the military has a successful version of the serum, however, the plan is to use it on a white man, Steve Rogers; give him a red, white, and blue uniform; and make him the symbol of the American spirit. Rogers is given the formula at another location, and is told that he is the only man ever to receive it. When a storm prevents Rogers from going on his first mission, the military sends Isaiah on a secret suicide mission to a concentration camp to destroy the Nazi version of the supersoldier serum. Before he leaves, however, Bradley grabs a copy of the Captain America uniform and shield, making him the first man to bear the mantle of Captain America. The mission does not go well for Isaiah.

A number of the events in this story may seem extreme to some readers, but in the appendix to the Marvel premiere edition of the series, Morales documents historical parallels to many of the events described in the story.[32] Marvel editor Axel Alonso's primary inspiration for the story was the story of the Tuskegee syphilis experiments, which began in the 1930s and continued for decades. During that time, approximately four hundred African American men in Alabama who had syphilis signed up for free medical care but were then left untreated for decades, even after a cure was available, as part of a U.S. Health Service experiment. An estimated one hundred of them died and many more suffered irreversible health problems.[33]

In Morales and Baker's story, Captain America is not directly responsible for the experiments and has no direct knowledge of the experiments until decades later. Still, although he did not commit the acts, Captain America does not shrug it off and just say that it was not his fault. He knows that he has benefited from this history of injustice. So, while he cannot change the past, he knows that he does bear responsibility to make amends in whatever way he can and strive to make sure it does not happen again.

While most white Americans today had no direct part in some of the racist acts and policies of the past, we can all acknowledge that some have gained advantages from those immoral acts and immoral policies. Knowledge of them calls all Americans to take responsibility for what has happened in the past and what is currently happening in the present in order to create a better future for all people. Racism has been called America's original sin, and it is a sin that continues to poison our culture today. Campolo and Battle write about the "ongoing legacies of racism" that continue to affect the African American community and put it at a disadvantage in our society.[34] The effects of racism, past and present, are complex issues both in the comic books and in the real world. One step in heroic living may be simply to acknowledge that the legacies of racism are not as simple as we may wish them to be and that we need to continue the hard work of justice and reconciliation.

Captain America and the Falcon's lives of patriotism in the comic books have not been ones of simplistic solutions or patriotic platitudes. Working out our duty to God and country can be complex as well. God continues to call all of us "to do justice, and to love kindness, and to walk humbly with your God" (Mic. 6:8).

Questions for Reflection

- Have you ever been disappointed by a political leader whom you once supported? Has your disappointment in that leader ever decreased your efforts to work for the causes that led you to support that leader?
- What is our duty to our country when we disagree with our country's policies? Should we always stay quiet out of a sense of patriotic loyalty?

Should we protest? If so, how should we protest? Is violence ever an option? Do different situations call for different responses? Where do you stand?

- When should we take a stand against the policies of our country? When should we do our best to support our country?
- Have you or others that you know ever struggled with their best efforts to build a friendship with someone of another race or ethnic group? What have you learned from these relationships?
- How does the racism of the past and the present affect the United States today? How can we work to counteract the effects of racism?

The Mighty Avengers

Assembling a Community of Saints and Sinners

Working together with a constantly changing group of people who come with different backgrounds and different life experiences can be challenging. Just ask the Avengers. The superhero group has had a revolving lineup of members that has included legendary heroes, former criminals, an android, and young new recruits. Still, time and time again, they find a way to work together to save the world. As we live out our faith, we often do so in churches, workplaces, and charity organizations that also have ever-changing lineups of people from a variety of backgrounds. As we reflect on the Avengers, we can reflect on how we can find the grace and wisdom necessary to welcome new members into our groups and how we can work together for good causes.

The Origin of the Mighty Avengers

In 1963, Stan Lee and Jack Kirby finally got around to creating the type of super-hero team that was along the lines of what publisher Martin Goodman probably had in mind when he first told Stan Lee to create a superhero team back in 1961. Like DC Comic's Justice League of America, Marvel's Avengers were an all-star team of heroes who had their own solo comic book adventures and who teamed up to battle major threats. Unlike DC Comics' Justice League of the time, however, the Avengers often argued with each other and, at times, even fought each other. Still, more often than not, they found ways to work together.

Avengers was quickly established as a comic book where anything could happen. In *Avengers* #1 (September 1963), Thor's archnemesis Loki realizes that he is having no luck defeating Thor on his own. Spying the Hulk, Loki figures that he has discovered someone strong enough to defeat Thor. Loki hatches a plan in which he frames the Hulk for causing a train accident and waits for Thor to engage him in battle. Contrary to Loki's plan, however, Ant Man, the Wasp, and Iron Man also hear of the accident and converge on the Hulk to battle him as well. These heroes spend much of the issue fighting each other. Thor eventually captures Loki and reveals his deception to the others. By the end of the issue, Thor, Iron Man, Ant Man, the Wasp, and the Hulk decide to join forces to become an unbeatable team they call the Avengers.

In *Avengers* #2 (November 1963), a villain known as the Space Phantom tricks the Avengers into fighting each other again. By transforming himself to look like the Hulk, he is able to make the rest of the team fight the real Hulk once again. This time, the Hulk has had enough. At the end of the book he says, "I never suspected how much each of you hates me, deep down! I could tell by the way you fought me . . . by the remarks you made!"[1] He leaves the group and leaps away.

In *Avengers* #3 (January 1964), the Hulk is back, but this time as the Avengers' enemy, teaming up with the Sub-Mariner to defeat them as a first step to conquering the world. The two sides fight an epic battle, but the fight ends in a standstill.

Avengers #4 (January 1964) reintroduced the World War II hero Captain America to the Marvel Universe. Captain America's presence added some stability to the team. In the issues that followed, the team began to focus more on working together and not fighting each other. Since then, a wide range of heroes have responded to their famous battle cry, "Avengers Assemble!"

Assembling a Team

Working with a Changing Lineup

The Avengers are not a stable family like the Fantastic Four. One feature of the Avengers that has kept their stories fresh and interesting is that they are always welcoming new members into their lineup. While Captain America, Iron Man, and Thor have often served as the core members of the Avengers, a large number of heroes have joined the team at one time or another.

The first major change in the team's lineup came in *Avengers* #16 (May 1965). The team's heavy hitters—Iron Man, Thor, and Giant Man—along with the Wasp decide it is time to focus on their individual duties. They leave Captain America in charge of a new team that consists of three former supervillains: Hawkeye, the Scarlet Witch, and Quicksilver. At first the team seems to be arguing constantly. It is to Captain America's credit that he is able to meld these heroes' powers so that, though they are each individually less powerful than the original members of the team, together they are just as effective.

Another significant early change in the Avengers lineup came in *Avengers* #57 (October 1968), when writer Roy Thomas and artist John Buscema introduced readers to the android known as the Vision. One of the Avengers' greatest enemies, Ultron-5, created the Vision with the ability to make his body either as hard as diamonds or intangible enough that he can walk through walls and programmed him to destroy the Avengers. The Vision almost defeats them. Unfortunately for Ultron-5, the Vision seems to carry a hint of emotion in his synthetic soul as well as a sense of right and wrong. By the end of the issue, the Vision shakes off Ultron-5's control and defeats him instead.

In the very next issue, *Avengers* #58 (November 1968), the Vision requests that the Avengers accept him as a member of their team. He knows that he appears to be a risky candidate for membership. He does not claim to have his life completely together. He was only recently fighting them and he admits that there are gaps in his memory. He also knows that he is different from the other members of the group. From a human perspective he is a bit of an oddball. He has an eerie, ghostly appearance, an unnatural voice, and he shows little emotion. After careful deliberation, however, the other Avengers tell the Vision that he has been accepted. As Giant Man suggests, the Avengers have always had a diverse membership. He says, "The five original Avengers included an Asgardian immortal and a green-skinned behemoth!" Hawkeye, referring to the fact that Captain America was fighting Nazis back in World War II, adds, "Yeah . . . we even let a Methuselah like Cap join!"[2] The Vision stands perfectly still, showing no visible response. He merely says, *"Excuse me . . . please . . . I shall return within a moment."*[3] As he leaves the room, Iron Man comments on how cold and emotionless he seems. Readers, however, see that once he is alone, the Vision is overcome with emotion. The final page of the issue is a full-page illustration of the Vision weeping at the team's grace toward him, as the caption explains, "Even an Android can cry."[4]

The Vision went on to become one of the most powerful and most popular members of the team. Since he joined the Avengers, he has had quite a convoluted history. His program has changed through the years and he has taken on different personalities. At one point he was so "human" that he married the Scarlet Witch. At other times he has seemed so machinelike or ghostlike that his presence unnerved new members of the team. The more established members, however, do not try to fix the problem by asking the Vision to change or by making him feel unwelcome. Instead, they serve as good examples to the newcomers of an inclusive spirit. They model an attitude of acceptance and respect for all members, which new members soon seem to embrace.

Over the last forty years, there have been many more shakeups in the team's line-up.[5] During all of these changes, the Avengers have struggled with personality conflicts, but they have learned to work together. Over the years there have been a large number of heroes who have served as Avengers at one time or another. Given their creed, "Once an Avenger always an Avenger," there is a very large gathering when they are all called together. In *Avengers* vol. 3, #1 (February 1998), for example, it is hard for all the former Avengers to fit into the Avengers Mansion.

Like the Avengers, our churches, workplaces, and community organizations are faced with the challenge of working with ever-changing lineups of people. This is perhaps more often the case today than ever before. A generation ago, many churches had memberships that had been composed primarily of members of the same families for years. Today, people are more transitory and many churches are faced with the challenge of congregations in which some longtime members no longer recognize many of the people who attend their worship services. Ministry teams are continually losing key members and trying to integrate new ones. There may be a temptation to close ourselves off from all this change. We may wish to resist new members, in the desire to be a close-knit group of people. Some church growth experts have even suggested that churches should target just one demographic and develop programs for just one kind of person. Churches that are welcoming to only one kind of person, however, are churches that become stagnant and fail to live out the calling of the church to welcome people of all kinds. In our desire to be close, we should not become closed off from new and different people.

From ancient times, the people of God were asked to show special hospitality to strangers (Ex. 22:21; Deut. 11:19). According to the Gospel of Matthew, Jesus said that the kingdom of heaven is like a mustard seed that grows into a large tree so that many birds can make their nests in its branches (Mt. 13:31–32). He later described the kingdom of heaven as a net that is cast out wide to catch every kind of fish (Mt. 13:47–48). Paul told the Romans to "extend hospitality to strangers" (Rom. 12:13). Christians are people who, from the start, were called to spread out a large welcome mat.

When we are disinclined to welcome someone new into our church or community group because they seem different, it may help us to reflect, as did the Avengers, on how many different personalities our groups already include. Adding new and different people to our groups strengthens us by adding new gifts and new perspectives to our work together. It may also be an act of grace that touches those we accept, more than we may know. Like the Vision, who walked out of the room to cry, we may never know how much our acceptance and camaraderie means to others. When we show grace and accept people into our group, we are doing God's work. To accept people fully, however, we must not only accept them as though we are committing an act of charity but also learn to respect them as colleagues and integrate them into the life and ministries of our churches as well. A great way to integrate people into the lives of our congregations and communities is to put them to work. When we provide people with opportunities to become coworkers with us, we are best able to appreciate all that they add to our group.

Welcoming Saints and Sinners

Reading the adventures of the Avengers through the years, one very specific thing that stands out about the team is that they have had a large number of former villains in their ranks.

As mentioned in previous chapters, Lee repeatedly returned to the theme that people could turn their lives around. As Lee put it, he liked to do stories that showed that "somebody who had made some mistakes in his life, or done some wrong things in his life, that there is still hope for this person, that he can be redeemed, that he can be turned around, so to speak, and become a good guy."[6]

As mentioned earlier, the second lineup of Avengers featured Captain America and three former supervillains: Hawkeye, the Scarlet Witch, and Quicksilver. Like many people who have committed crimes, all three had experienced unfortunate circumstances that led to their crimes. In Hawkeye's first appearance in *Tales of Suspense* #57 (September 1964), he has every intention of becoming a costumed hero. When he stops a jewel thief, however, a policeman assumes that he is the crook and runs after him. The villainous Black Widow helps Hawkeye get away and uses her charms to convince him to help her defeat Iron Man. The Scarlet Witch and Quicksilver first appeared in *X-Men* #4 (March 1964) as part of Magneto's Brotherhood of Evil Mutants. The teenage sister and brother were alone in the world and scorned as mutants when Magneto took them in and protected them. In joining the Avengers, all three former criminals wanted to make amends for their past misdeeds and work for what was right.

Through the years, the Avengers have continued to integrate former enemies into their team. *Avengers* vol. 3, #10, celebrated the thirty-fifth anniversary of the team with a special issue in which New York City throws them a ticker-tape parade. During the parade an announcer says, "Their greatest triumph may be the former foes who have become Avengers themselves, and fought on the side of justice . . . including Wonder Man, the Black Widow, the Swordsman, the Living Lightening, and more!"[7]

In 1997, award-winning writer Kurt Busiek began a critically acclaimed five-year run on *The Avengers.* The Avengers' habit of integrating villains into their team gave him an idea for a story line that he ended up telling in a brand new comic book about a seemingly brand new group of heroes known as the Thunderbolts. *Thunderbolts* #1 (April 1997) took the comic book world by surprise when, on the very last page, it was revealed that the Thunderbolts were actually a group of established supervillains. I asked Busiek about this story line.

> RUSSELL DALTON: This book explores how the Avengers have integrated a number of former criminals and enemies into their fold who now work for what is right and then reflects on how we might do the same in our places of work, community organizations, faith communities, and in society in general. While this wasn't a major theme in your run on the *Avengers*, you really took the theme to a whole new level in your work on *Thunderbolts*. The Thunderbolts were a group of villains who were pretending to be heroes as a cover to their evil plans, but then at least some of them liked the idea of being good guys so much that they decided to try it for real. How did you come up with the idea for this series? What do you think allows some characters in the *Thunderbolts* . . . to make the transition to being heroes, and what prevents others from doing so? What were the unique challenges to changing their ways that you tried to explore with those characters?
>
> KURT BUSIEK: The two most direct influences on *Thunderbolts* were an old TV series called *Alias Smith and Jones*, about two Western outlaws trying to win a pardon by going straight, and the period of Avengers history when Captain America was the leader and Hawkeye, Quicksilver, and the Scarlet Witch were all former villains proving themselves as heroes. I enjoyed both, but thought it would have been more fun to see Hawkeye and company actually deal with the process of reforming rather than

just have it happen overnight. So *Thunderbolts* (and another series I'd done earlier, *The Liberty Project*) was a direct attempt to explore that scenario. Plus, I'd had an idea years back about the Masters of Evil slowly infiltrating the Avengers, disguised as heroes, until things built to the point that the team consisted of Captain America and a bunch of villains, all of whom were ready to take him down. In the wake of Marvel's "Onslaught" event, which left the Marvel Universe without their most famous heroes, I combined the two and built a series around villains posing as heroes, only to have some of them discover that they liked it, and that maybe they wanted to stay that way.

In doing that, I simply went back to the earliest appearances of the characters to see what motivated them. MACH-1, as the Beetle, became a villain because he wanted respect and validation. Being a superhero got him exactly what he craved, so he'd be tempted to stay a hero. Baron Zemo, on the other hand, is a megalomaniac—I didn't think he'd reform for a moment (though Fabian Nicieza did a lot with him in that area after he took over the series). Similarly, Moonstone was crafty and controlling and out for herself—being a superhero was just another guise to her, just a way to feather her nest. She wouldn't reform. But Atlas, I discovered, wasn't at heart a bad guy. He generally did bad things because it was the only way to get out of a jam, or someone told him to, so he took orders. He was a follower, not a leader, and if he was put into situations where he had to think about who to follow and why, that might be interesting. The Fixer was a villain because he liked the challenge; he liked to prove how smart he was. This made it easy for him to act as a hero—as long as he got challenged where he could prove his genius, he'd be happy—but it wasn't exactly a moral transformation. He was still the same guy, still wanting the same thing.

That's what made *Thunderbolts* work as well as it did, I think. Everyone had different motivations, which pushed them in different directions. It made the series unpredictable, because you didn't know what the characters would do next. Would Atlas overcome his weak-willed nature? Could MACH-1 be strong enough to make a moral stand? Would Moonstone manipulate everyone into acting as heroes when it served her interests, or as villains when things changed? The answer to any of these could go either way, unlike a conventional superhero, where we expect them to live up to a particular moral code.[8]

One of the profound teachings of the Christian faith is that God is a God of second chances. While all people are sinful, all people are also redeemable. Even if we have gotten off on the wrong track, or even if we have blown it in the past, we can still choose to do the right thing. We can have a conversion. When we do choose to turn our lives around, God not only accepts us but also uses us as well.

The Letter to the Ephesians says, "For by grace you have been saved through faith, and this is not your own doing; it is the gift of God not the result of works, so that no one may boast" (Eph. 2:8–9). New Testament scholar Jennifer Berenson comments that these verses assert that "deliverance to a new life is due solely to God's mercy and benevolence, and precludes boasting."[9] The very next verse makes it clear, however, that relying on God's mercy does not mean that we are to remain passive in our lives of faith. It reads, "For we are what he has made us, created in Christ Jesus for good works, which God prepared beforehand to be our way of life" (Eph. 2:10). As Berenson puts it, "a new, divinely inspired lifestyle is the appropriate result of salvation."[10] Another way of putting this is that God has designed heroic lives for all of us to live, regardless of the sins of our past.

The Bible is full of examples of people who had sinful or criminal pasts and yet were used by God. Moses killed a man and was on the run for years (Ex. 2:11–12), yet God chose him to lead the people of Israel out of bondage in Egypt. King David abused his power in one of the most atrocious ways imaginable when he had a man killed to cover up an affair he had with the man's wife (2 Sam. 11), but he still went on to lead Israel and was called a person after God's own heart (1 Sam. 13:14). Paul had been an enemy of the gospel and stood by and watched approvingly as Stephen was stoned to death (Acts 8:1–3), yet God used him to spread the good news of God's grace far and wide and the early church graciously accepted him as one of their leaders.

It makes sense that ministry to and with people who have a criminal past was such a focus in the Bible and has continued to be an important ministry of the Church through the ages. The Church, after all, is characterized by love and grace. It is a community whose members realize that they have all sinned and fallen short of God's glory and that we are saved only through the grace of God. It is a community that believes that every life is precious and that no one is disposable. Jesus is not calling people to an exclusive righteousness club, or else none of us would measure up. The four walls of a church are not built to keep sinners outside, but as a home where all are welcomed.

Just as the Avengers seem to have a special interest in former villains, the scriptures have a special interest in ministry with prisoners. Psalm 69:33 states, "For the Lord hears the needy, and does not despise his own that are in bonds." As one reads the New Testament, there is a great deal of focus on ministry with prisoners. In the Gospel of Luke we are told that Jesus began his public ministry by taking the scroll of the prophet Isaiah, and reading,

> The Spirit of the Lord is upon me, because he has anointed me to bring good news to the poor. He has sent me to proclaim release to the captives, and recovery of sight to the blind, to let the oppressed go free, to proclaim the year of the Lord's favor. (Lk. 4:18–19)

In the Gospel of Matthew, Jesus underscores the importance of prison ministry by saying that when the Son of Man returns, whether or not one ministers to those in prison will be one of the criteria he will use to separate the sheep from the goats. He says that people who minister to people in prison are ministering to him and that those who do not minister to those who are in prison are neglecting him (Mt. 25:35, 39, 44). Peter and John were imprisoned (Acts 4:3) and Paul himself was in prison while he wrote some of the epistles. The book of Hebrews asks readers to empathize with prisoners by stating, "Remember those who are in prison, as though you were in prison with them" (Heb. 13:3). Sometimes it is suggested that these passages on prison ministry refer only to people who have been imprisoned unjustly or imprisoned because they have preached the gospel. The writers of the scriptures, however, do not stipulate that our concern for prisoners should be limited to those who have been imprisoned on religious grounds.

Larry Nielsen, a retired law enforcement officer, has written a helpful book for lay volunteers titled *Thinking about Jail and Prison Ministries*. Nielsen notes, "I am not a 'bleeding heart' or a prisoner's advocate. I have seen the blood, the misery, the cost in suffering and resources that these men and women have left in their wake."[11] Nielsen goes on, however, to tell moving, heartbreaking stories of the troubled lives that led many prisoners to commit crimes and many heartwarming stories about how encounters with God through jail and prison ministries have helped heal those lives. Local churches can undertake a variety of ministries to those who are in jails and prisons, including holding worship services, writing to inmates as pen pals, conducting faith-based recovery groups for those battling addictions, conducting Bible studies, and more. A good first step is to contact local jails and prisons and ask them what needs exist and how volunteers can help make a difference.

People of faith can also work to prevent people from falling into lives of crime in the first place. Theologian Andrew Sung Park reflects that good Samaritans today can take a step even beyond that of the Samaritan in Jesus' parable. They can look at the wider sociological forces that underlie robberies. Park writes, "Beyond the biblical story, we realize 'Samaritans' need not to be attentive to healing victims only; they also need to pay attention to robbers. They must see who the robbers are, why they rob strangers, and how such robbery can be prevented in a systematic way. With the present social condition, more evildoers will rise and 'rob' people. More racial eruptions are expected in the future. It is important for 'Samaritans' to change the social system that produces robbers."[12]

I recall being nervous the first time I visited someone in prison as part of my ministry. I soon discovered that the work is sometimes uncomfortable, but my visits to jails and prisons became some of the most rewarding work of my ministry. Furthermore, I have had the privilege of working with churches that welcomed people who had criminal pasts and who had spent some time in prison. Some of the most effective lay leaders in the churches where I have been were people who had spent time in prison. They were people who knew the pitfalls of life and who truly knew God's grace and wanted to share it with others. While they regretted the crimes that they had committed, their experiences gave them useful perspectives that they brought to our ministries.

The Avengers seem to have their own special jobs program for former criminals. They probably know they are going to get burned occasionally, but they decide that they would rather take the risk than turn people away. Our churches would do well to follow their example in this regard. Ministry to those in jail and prison and to those who are being released from jail and prison may seem like innovative work to some, but it is part of a centuries-old tradition of the church.

Working with a Team

Learning to Work Together

The challenge for our churches, workplaces, and community organizations is not only to accept new people into membership but also to make them integral parts of our team. In their comic book adventures, the Avengers have found ways to overcome personality conflicts and a changing lineup to do just this. The group of Captain America, Hawkeye, the Scarlet Witch, and Quicksilver has become known by fans as "Cap's Kooky Quartet." The group faced a number of obstacles. For one thing, three-quarters of the team was composed of brand-new members. Those same three members were also former villains who were just getting used to playing the part of the hero. Perhaps most challenging of all was the fact that all four members of the team had very strong personalities, and those personalities did not naturally blend together. It is to their credit, then, that they quickly learned to work together so well.

In *Avengers* #20 (September 1965), written by Stan Lee and penciled by Don Heck, the villainous Swordsman captures Captain America, ties his hands behind his back, and makes him walk to the edge of a plank on the top of a building. The Swordsman tells the rest of the team to surrender or else he will shove Captain America off the building. Instead of risking the chance that his teammates might give in to the Swordsman's demands, Captain America shows great trust in his new teammates by jumping off the building himself. The rest of the team immediately jumps into action (Figure 11). Quicksilver uses his superspeed to run in circles directly beneath Captain America to create a vortex of wind that slows his fall. Hawkeye shoots an arrow with perfect accuracy that cuts through the rope that binds Captain America's hands. The Scarlet Witch uses her hex power to make one of the building's girders fall out below Captain America, providing him with the opportunity to use his acrobatic skills to twist his body and land on it. The Swordsman watches in amazement and thinks, "They're far more dangerous than I thought! Individually, each one is an enemy to be respected. But, as a team, they're practically unbeatable!"[13] As a team they are greater than the sum of their parts. They are able to work together and blend their individual powers and abilities in amazing ways to save Captain America from a deadly fall. In a similar way, when we work together and coordinate the use of our gifts and talents, our churches and community organizations can be greater than the sum of their parts as well.

Figure 11. *Avengers* #20 (September 1965), page 2; Marvel Comics. Stan Lee script, Don Heck art. The second wave of Avengers does not have as much raw power as the original team, but the new group works well together. Here, as Captain America falls from a building, Quicksilver creates a wind gusher to slow his fall, Hawkeye shoots an arrow to free his hands, and the Scarlet Witch causes a girder to fall into place so that Captain America can land on it. Copyright ©1965 Marvel Comics, all rights reserved.

Writer Kurt Busiek placed an interesting mix of personalities into the group during his time writing *Avengers*. I asked Busiek about his approach to how these Avengers learned to work together.

> RUSSELL DALTON: Sometimes we have to work with people who we do not get along with very well, even when we are all working for a good cause . . . This seems to be a common theme in all Marvel team books, namely that we need to overcome our disagreements and personality conflicts in order to work for a common cause. From your perspective, what are some of the most helpful ways that heroes find a way to do this?
>
> KURT BUSIEK: As for ways heroes find to get along and accomplish things, I don't think heroes do it any differently than normal people. They're all individuals, and so Captain America is going to be reasonable, and Hawkeye is going to be belligerent, and Iron Man is going to be kind of autocratic, and Hellcat is going to try to jolly everyone else along and appeal to their better nature . . . and so on. They all come from different places, and they're all going to deal with things in their own way. That's what makes them interesting—that they do act like individuals, rather than all falling into the same mold.[14]

Our different personalities keep it interesting. We learn that we are stronger not despite our differences, but because of our differences. Christians today sometimes idealize the early Church, envisioning it as a group of people who were always polite and always got along with each other. The early church, however, like many of our churches today, was often filled with conflict. From its earliest days, the church was a diverse institution composed of people from a wide variety of racial, ethnic, sociological, and religious backgrounds. Sometimes this made for very serious, wide-ranging conflicts over religious practices, such as those that confronted the Council at Jerusalem in Acts 15. At other times there were more personal conflicts, such as the one between two women in the church at Phillipi, Euodia and Syntyche, whom Paul urges to get along (Phil. 4:1–9). The challenge that faced those early Christians, and still faces us today, is to find a way to welcome all sorts of people and still find a way to work together.

Finding Our Place, Doing Our Part

Busiek brought an interesting perspective to the Avengers stories he wrote by letting readers experience the legendary group through the eyes of its two newcomers, Justice and Firestar. Both heroes had been members of a group of young heroes known as the New Warriors, but now they were moving up to the big leagues by being part of the Avengers. In *Avengers* vol. 3, #4 (May 1998), they are named reserve members as they alternatively try to prove themselves and to decide whether they want to stay. I asked Busiek about the two characters.

RUSSELL DALTON: Sometimes we are hindered in our efforts to do what is
    right because we do not feel that we measure up to others around us
    at work, in the charity organization we work for, our faith community,
    or even our circle of friends. In your run on the *Avengers* you featured
    two new members, Justice and Firestar, and told stories about how they
    didn't feel like they really belonged. Justice struggled with feelings that he
    didn't measure up to legends like Captain America and Thor. Meanwhile
    Firestar just wasn't sure that she really wanted to be there. By the end of
    your run on the *Avengers*, however, both of them were valued parts of the
    team. What was it, in your mind, that helped them overcome their initial
    hesitancy and become confident and competent members of the team?
KURT BUSIEK: Experience, mostly. We wanted some new heroes on the
    team so we could show the reader how important being an Avenger is
    through other eyes, through eyes that weren't yet used to it. So Justice
    was chosen because he'd dreamed of being an Avenger for years—and
    for him, with all due respect to the New Warriors, this felt like being
    promoted from the minor leagues to the New York Yankees, and sharing
    a locker room with his childhood idols. If you look, you'll see that he's
    nervous about not measuring up, but he never actually screws up—
    right from the beginning, he's a good and effective Avenger, he's just so
    nervous he can't see it. And Firestar never had that same dream, and is
    tortured by being a superhero because using her powers is damaging
    her health. She too does the job well, but she doesn't want to be there.
        And Firestar discovers that being an Avenger really does mean
    more than she thought, as Hank Pym almost casually cured her health
    problems, and she learns that being an Avenger may be a heavy
    responsibility, but it brings you heavy support, which thrills her. And
    Justice gets further and further into a funk, until he's injured (not due
    to his own error) and feels like he's useless, until he's taken away from
    the constant battle and has time to think—and hits on the solution that
    wins the day against Ultron. So that moment, where he fully participates
    and is validated, is the moment he stops feeling like a rookie and starts
    feeling like he belongs. Both of them go through arcs of discomfort,
    and then discover that they do belong after all.[15]

Like Justice, some members of churches or community organizations hang
back because they do not think they are up to the task or because they are simply
not used to taking on responsibility. Our culture celebrates youth, but often it does
not do so in ways that encourage younger people to take on responsibility. Instead,
young adults and even middle-aged baby boomers tend to think of themselves as
the new kids on the block and leave the work and responsibility to the older, more
established members of their congregations or community organizations. While it
is fine to think of ourselves as young and vital, we cannot expect our elders to do

all the work. Whatever age we are, we should not wait until we reach some magic age before we embrace the fact that we are capable members of our congregations or community organizations and decide to do our part. The young minister Timothy was told, "Let no one despise your youth, but set the believers an example in speech and conduct, in love, in faith, in purity" (1 Tim. 4:12). Timothy was young and inexperienced and needed advice and support, but he was told not to shrink away from doing the job set before him because of his youth and inexperience. While we should respect the wisdom and experience of the older members of our congregations and organizations, those who are younger should also be ready to do their part.

There are others who, like Firestar, avoid becoming fully involved in a group because they are unsure whether they want to make a commitment or are unsure whether it is worth the effort. Some value their privacy and independence at the cost of community. Like Firestar, they may discover that there are benefits to being part of a group. Ecclesiastes tells us, "Two are better than one, because they have a good reward for their toil. For if they fall, one will lift up the other; but woe to one who is alone and falls and does not have another to help" (Eccl. 4:9–10). When we join a church, we can accomplish more by working with a team of people. When we join a church, we have the added benefit of being able to give and receive support from others. Jesus Christ did not plan for his followers to serve as individuals, but to worship and serve in community as the church.

The Avengers were wise to make Justice and Firestar reserve members before giving them too much responsibility. In churches and nonprofit organizations, it is helpful to find good entry-level positions in which people can start their work and find their place. Neither Justice nor Firestar were ready, for different reasons, to jump into full-fledged membership, but the Avengers provided them with a role to play. Too often our churches and community groups are so desperate for warm bodies to fill certain roles that we throw new members in over their heads and overwhelm them before they have begun. Instead, a new church member may be invited to be a Sunday school teacher's assistant, for example, before they are asked to teach a class themselves. A new person may be invited to volunteer as a meal server at a soup kitchen for a number of months before being asked to lead or organize some aspect of that ministry. When they are provided with entry-level opportunities, new members are better able to ease into being an active part of a ministry. The goal of such positions is not to enable people to hang back or to help them avoid taking on responsibility, but to help people get acclimated and grow into new roles and responsibilities.

Taking a Leadership Role

The Avengers rotate the leadership of the team, with the Wasp and Captain America among those who have served most often as the team's chairperson. Captain America is perhaps seen as the ultimate leader of the Avengers. Early in his days of leading Cap's Kooky Quartet, Captain America came on pretty strong. He felt he had to prove that he was in charge and stifle Hawkeye and Quicksilver's constant questioning of his authority. Over the years, however, Captain America learned to have the more collaborative, less authoritative approach to leadership that the Wasp had modeled for him. He commands respect but does not constantly demand it.

In the 1984 limited series *Marvel Super Heroes Secret Wars*, a large group of Marvel's superheroes and supervillains are transported to a strange planet known as Battleworld and forced to fight each other. The heroes soon decide that they need a leader. Mr. Fantastic first suggests the Hulk, who at the time had Bruce Banner's intellect. Even though the Hulk is one of the smartest and strongest of the heroes present, he suggests that Captain America would be a better choice. The Wasp and Professor Xavier, the current leaders of their respective teams, concur. Only the Wolverine protests, arguing that they should pick a leader who has greater superpowers. "Wait a minute!" he says. "He's the least of us! He can't do anything! I won't follow him!" Thor replies, "I will! I am a prince of the gods! I do not pledge my allegiance to many of mortal stature. This man I will follow through the gates of Hades!"[16] Though he is not the most powerful, Captain America has earned the respect of his peers. A good leader is not necessarily the strongest or most talented member of a group but rather a person who is respected and well-suited to coordinate or guide the efforts of others.

In 2003–2004, writer Kurt Busiek and artist George Perez presented a long-awaited crossover event, *JLA/Avengers*, in which DC Comics' and Marvel Comics' most famous teams meet, fight each other, and then work together to save their universes. When the teams stop fighting and start working together, they decide to choose a leader for their combined team. The Justice League of America's (JLA's) Superman immediately says that the leader should be Captain America, and Batman immediately agrees. Captain America humbly acknowledges that there are others qualified for the job. Once he realizes that he is the consensus choice, however, he does not shy away from being the leader. He has no sense of superiority, but he also has no false modesty or insecurity that might hamper his abilities as a leader. He immediately assesses the strengths and experiences of the heroes, invites their input, and then confidently lets them know what to do. Seeing this, the JLA's Atom says, "I'll say this—the man knows what he wants. He always this impressive Vision?" The Avengers' Vision simply replies, "Always."[17]

When we are invited to take on a role of leadership at work, school, church, or as part of a nonprofit group, we would do well to follow Captain America's example. When he is asked to take on the role of leader, he serves in that role with confidence. When others take a turn at leading the Avengers, he follows their lead as a good team member. According to the Gospel of Luke, Jesus told his disciples that status and leadership are not things that should be lorded over others (Lk. 22:25). Instead, "the greatest among you must become like the youngest, and the leader like one who serves" (Lk. 22:26). Leadership, then, is not something to be lorded over others, but it is also not something that we should avoid, if we are qualified for the role.

Closing

Iron Man, Thor, and Captain America are formidable heroes on their own but they, along with many other Marvel heroes, have realized that they are able to do more by being a part of a team. They did not create a team like an exclusive, private club that allowed only elite, established heroes into membership. By welcoming a wide variety of people with a wide variety of backgrounds, the Avengers have been able to accomplish great things. In our churches, community groups, and workplaces, we can assemble together and do the same.

Questions for Reflection

- Have you ever been part of a ministry at your church, a community group, or a group at school that changed its lineup significantly, with some people leaving and others joining? What challenges did the group go through as it changed and evolved?
- Have you ever had to work together with someone with whom you did not get along? If you were able to work together for a common cause, what made it possible to do so? If you were not able to work it out, what got in the way?
- Have you (or someone you have known) ever been denied opportunities to work for a good cause because of the sins of your past?
- What opportunities are there in your community to minister to those in jail or prison? What opportunities are there to help those who are released from prison to transition back into society?
- What do you think are the greatest obstacles that prevent people in churches from working together effectively?
- Have you ever felt restricted in what you could accomplish in a church or community group because you felt did not have enough experience or qualifications?
- Have you ever avoided playing your part in an important ministry? If so, what do you think was holding you back from doing your part?
- Have you ever been asked to take on a leadership role at school, at work, with a charity group, or at your church? What do you think are the qualities of a good and effective leader?

9

Daredevil

Vengeance or Mercy?

In the superhero Daredevil's earliest adventures, he was often portrayed as a fun-loving, swashbuckling adventurer. Like most other superheroes, he was also depicted as a pillar of virtue. The contradictions in Matt Murdock's life were apparently too great to ignore, however, and writers and artists soon began to present a more complex perspective on the character. By day, Matt Murdock is a lawyer who fights against crime and corruption from within the legal system. He seeks justice for those who have no other advocate by taking on their cases when no one else will. By night, however, Matt dons a red devil costume and fights outside the law as a vigilante. He beats up and captures criminals who have escaped from the legal justice system. To some extent, all superheroes are vigilantes. None of Marvel's other longtime heroes, however, have struggled more with his or her identity than has Daredevil. Matt Murdock is often portrayed as a tortured soul, and readers are shown his moral failures, when he betrays his own heroic ideals, as well as his moral victories.

People of faith are not always perfect pillars of virtue either. We are called to fight for justice and at the same time to show mercy. How can we do both of these things with integrity? How do we live up to the call of the prophet Micah, who says, "He has told you, O mortal, what is good; and what does the Lord require of you but to do justice, to love kindness, and to walk humbly with your God?" (Mic. 6:8).

The Origin of Daredevil

Stan Lee has said that when he first decided to make his new hero Daredevil a blind man, he meant it as a positive statement about people who are physically challenged. He worried, however, that people might be offended, thinking that some might take his stories of a blind man swinging around the flag poles of Manhattan with his hooked cane as trivializing the very real obstacles faced by those who were blind. He was pleased, then, to receive many letters from blind people and organizations for the blind that thanked him for creating Daredevil.[1]

157

Daredevil's origin story was first told in *Daredevil* #1 (April 1964), written by Lee with art by comic book legend Bill Everett.[2] Each subsequent retelling has added more details to the story. Matt Murdock grows up the son of a widower, a small-time boxer known as Battling Jack Murdock. Young Matt wants to grow up to be just like his dad. His dad, however, wants Matt to study and grow up to use his mind as a doctor or a lawyer. He insists that Matt never fight, box, or join the football team. As he says to Matt in the film *Daredevil* (2003), "You don't hit nuthin' but the books, you get me?"[3] As a result, Matt stays away from physical activities, and the other kids in high school tease him constantly for being a bookworm and never taking chances. They sarcastically call him "daredevil" since he is so passive and never fights back. Still, while his dad's away, Matt works out in a gym to stay in top physical form while still getting straight As in school. One fateful day, Matt sees a blind man walking in front of an out-of-control truck. Matt jumps in front of the truck and heroically knocks the blind man out of the way and to safety. Matt, however, is not so lucky. The truck is carrying radioactive materials that strike Matt in the eyes, blinding him. He soon discovers, however, that the radioactive materials have greatly increased his other senses, giving him a radar sense of everything around him.

Later, gangsters try to force Matt's dad to throw his next fight. They want him to "take a dive" so that they can make money betting on the fight. Jack refuses. He knows that he is risking his life, but Matt is at the fight and Jack wants to make his son proud. So he wins the bout. Unaware that his dad was supposed to throw the fight, Matt tells him, "You proved nothing's impossible if a man has the courage! If a man's not afraid!"[4] That very evening, while Jack is walking home, gangsters shoot and kill him in retaliation for his refusal to throw the fight.

In his grief, Matt remembers the promise he made to his dad to use his brains and not his muscles to succeed in life. He goes on to college, graduates from law school, and starts a law firm with his college roommate, Foggy Nelson. Still, he wants to get vengeance on his dad's killers, so he creates an alternate identity. He reasons that Matt can continue to fight crime with his mind, while Daredevil can use his muscles and his fists. As Daredevil, he finds his father's killers and brings them to justice. Although it seemed like a reasonable solution in that first issue, Matt's dual identity has caused him a great deal of emotional and moral turmoil through the years.

Identity Issues

Although Daredevil started out as a fun-loving person, his stories grew increasingly somber and thoughtful. A key recurring element of the Daredevil mythos has been Matt Murdock's struggle to balance his public identity as a lawyer with his secret identity as a costumed vigilante.

During Lee and artist Gene Colan's classic run on the book, Matt Murdock's law partner Foggy Nelson and their secretary Karen Page grow suspicious that he is really Daredevil. In *Daredevil* #25 (February 1967), Matt decides to create yet another secret identity to cover up the fact that he is Daredevil. Somber, responsible Matt began to masquerade as his own identical twin brother, the brash playboy Mike Murdock, in order to convince Foggy and Karen that it was Mike, and not Matt, who was really Daredevil. Matt struggled with the pressure of juggling three identities and, in *Daredevil* #41 (June 1968), he staged Mike's death (actually Daredevil's death, knowing Foggy and Karen would think it was Mike). Still, the weight of keeping so many secrets eventually got the best of Matt and in *Daredevil* #48 (January 1969), he ends up losing Foggy as a friend and Karen as a "love interest." At one point he decides to give up being Daredevil. He says, "Daredevil! He's already caused me to lose the girl I love . . . and my best friend as well!"[5]

After *Daredevil* #51 (April 1969), Lee stepped down from his long tenure as the writer on the series, and the new writer, Roy Thomas, immediately began to explore Daredevil's moral ambivalence. In his second issue, *Daredevil* #52 (May 1969), Thomas told a story in which Daredevil captures a criminal who has discovered his secret identity. At the end of the story, Daredevil allows the criminal to go free, reasoning that if he brings the criminal in to the police, the criminal will reveal Daredevil's secret identity to the world. As the story ends, Daredevil questions his actions and is plagued with self-doubt. In the very next issue, *Daredevil* #53 (June 1969), Daredevil comes to the troubling conclusion that it is Matt Murdock who is the problem and decides to rid himself of the Matt Murdock identity.

As seen in his origin story, Matt thinks he can split his personality. He reasons that as lawyer Matt Murdock, he can keep his hands clean and work for justice through the law by using his mind. When he puts on the mask, however, he convinces himself that he is no longer Matt but Daredevil and therefore can terrorize villains. He soon discovers that this compartmentalization of his life into separate identities takes a toll on his emotional health.

The stories of Daredevil's identity problems are cautionary tales. They remind us of the damage we do when we try to compartmentalize our lives or to have secret lives "on the side." Daredevil is not clear about who he is. He tries to live his life by using different moral codes, depending on the situation he is in. As a result, he is often in danger of cracking under stressful situations.

We may not leave our day jobs and dress up in costumes at night to go around fighting crime, but it is helpful to ask ourselves whether we have a secret identity of our own. Do we live by one set of rules in one aspect of our lives but live by another set of rules in another area of our lives? Some people have been known to live by one set of values in their church and home lives but then compromise those values in their business dealings. Others try to justify living by one set of values while they are at home but indulging in immoral behavior when they are traveling. Still others carry out double lives, not letting their friends and family know about their secret life online or out on the town. Splitting our identity can torture our soul and ruin our self-esteem. News reports repeatedly tell sad tales of the secret lives of politicians, entertainers, and professional athletes and the damage and disgrace they bring upon themselves and their families. When we try to compartmentalize our life, we can forget who we truly are and in the process harm our friends and families and damage our relationship with God.

Psychologist David Elkind has written about how stress can affect our identity formation and how, on the other hand, a healthy integrated sense of identity can help us deal with stress. Elkind writes about the dangers of what he calls a "patchwork identity," an approach to life in which a person has no clear identity but simply tries to change who they are depending on the situation in which they find themselves or the people they are around. While taking such an approach can occasionally get people through some stressful situations, it does not lead to a healthy approach to life or a good sense of self-esteem. Instead, Elkind speaks of the need to develop an "integrated sense of identity . . . bringing together into a working whole a set of attitudes, values, and habits that can serve both self and society."[6] Elkind writes, "The attainment of such a sense of identity is accompanied by a feeling of self-esteem, of liking and respecting oneself, and of being liked and respected by others."[7] One's faith, and the support of a community of faith, can be invaluable in developing a healthy sense of self. Our faith can help us know who we are and the values by which we live.

Justice or Mercy?

Daredevil would continue to struggle with his identity in the decades to come. Two related recurring motifs have emerged in Daredevil's stories. The first is that Matt repeatedly faces overwhelming tragedies in his personal life and the second is that, under the pressure of these tragedies, he struggles to reconcile his passion for justice and vengeance with his commitment to the heroic ideals of mercy and abiding by the law.

Frank Miller and the Death of Elektra

Writer-artist Frank Miller, who would later become well-known for such graphic novels as *Batman: The Dark Knight Returns*, *300*, and *Sin City*, first made a name for himself with his work on *Daredevil*. Miller's stories were controversial at the time, as he was one of the first writers and artists to bring graphic violence, sexual content, and moral ambiguity to a mainstream superhero comic book. Miller figured that most of *Daredevil*'s readers were adults and so did not hesitate to add mature content to his stories. His first extended story line told the story of Daredevil's love for Elektra, an assassin, and her murder by the supervillain Bullseye. The story served as the primary source for the film *Daredevil* (2003).

In Miller's earlier stories, Daredevil held to the superhero ideal. He would capture villains, but he would not kill them. He resisted the role of the vigilante. Instead, he tried to help society solve its problems through legal means and did his best to protect everyone, including villains.

In *Daredevil* #169 (March 1981), Daredevil and the police discover that the murderous Bullseye, who is a fugitive from the law, is unaware that he is very ill and needs surgery in order to survive. A grizzled detective named Manolis hopes

Bullseye will die before they can find him. Daredevil disagrees, saying, "Any death is a loss, Manolis." Manolis argues, "Nuts. Killing is like breathing to that slime. He doesn't deserve to live." Daredevil responds, "That's not for either of us to decide. We have to save him."[8]

Daredevil then risks his own life to save Bullseye from getting run over by an oncoming subway train when he could easily have left him on the tracks to die. He explains to Manolis that it is not their place to carry out vigilante justice. "If Bullseye is a menace to society," he says, "it is society that must make him pay the price. Not you . . . not me." He adds, "I'm not God . . . I'm not the law . . . and I'm not a murderer."[9]

One year later, however, in *Daredevil* #181 (April 1982), after Bullseye has killed Elektra, the great love of Daredevil's life, Daredevil finds himself hanging on a wire high over the streets of New York and facing a moral dilemma. He is holding onto Bullseye's hand, preventing him from falling to his death. After thinking it through for a moment, Daredevil intentionally lets go of the hand. As Bullseye falls to his death, Daredevil says to him, "You'll kill no one . . . ever again."[10] Daredevil has been pushed to the limit and has seemingly betrayed the very values that he once held dear.

Pushed to the Limit

If the "Death of Elektra" story line seemed to push Daredevil to the limit, it was only the beginning of what writers had in store for the character. It also seems to have started a recurring motif for Daredevil in which writers take Matt's life and turn it upside down, stripping him of anything that brings him happiness. If Peter Parker is Marvel's Charlie Brown, the boy for whom nothing goes right, then Matt Murdock has become Marvel's Mr. Bill, the 1970s *Saturday Night Live* character made of modeling clay who is repeatedly smashed and crushed in more and more elaborate ways. The story lines put Matt through the ringer to see how far he will go to get his life back and get revenge on those who harm the people he loves.

After leaving the book for a time, Miller returned to write *Daredevil* #227 (February 1986) to #233 (August 1986), this time with artwork by David Mazzucchelli. The story line, known as "Born Again," is full of religious imagery and explores Matt's Roman Catholic faith. It is a moving story of betrayal, gracious love, and forgiveness. As the story begins, Matt's former girlfriend, Karen Page, sells him out. She has become a drug addict and sells a dealer the information that Matt Murdock is Daredevil in exchange for another fix. That low-level dealer sells the information to someone else, and eventually the information comes to Daredevil's greatest nemesis, Wilson Fisk, the infamous Kingpin of Crime. Fisk proceeds to do what he does best. He begins working behind the scenes, bribing and threatening business owners and government officials, in order to ruin Matt's life. Six months later Matt wakes up one morning to discover that his bank account has been frozen by an IRS audit, his bank has no records of his payment of monthly bills, he has been framed for misconduct as a lawyer (which eventually strips him of his license to practice law and make a living), and later his home is destroyed by a bomb. For a time, Matt becomes paranoid and thinks that everyone is in on the conspiracy to take him down. He alienates his friends and begins to doubt his own sanity. In an inspiring display of willpower, however, he keeps going, keeps working, and eventually, with the help of friends, overcomes incredible obstacles to get his life back. He also risks his life to save Karen, even though he knows that she is the one who has betrayed him. Matt is not the only heroic figure in the story. Ben Urich, a newspaper reporter with no superpowers, goes to the police and clears Matt of his crimes, despite the fact that the Kingpin's agents have threatened to kill him if he does so. Urich is almost killed but decides it is worth the risk to defend a good, honest man. In this story, with the support of friends, Matt seems to do an admirable job of enduring the crucible of pressure without compromising his moral integrity.

In later story lines, Matt repeatedly faces horrendous circumstances and does not always do as well in maintaining his integrity. In these stories, it is often left up to the reader to determine whether Matt is acting like a hero or like a vigilante who has lost his way.

Writer Brian Michael Bendis explored these themes in his run on the book. This time, Matt's secret identity is revealed not only to the Kingpin but also, through one of the Kingpin's underlings, to the police and then to the whole world. Newspaper headlines declare that Matt Murdock is Daredevil, and Matt, his friends, and his family all face danger from both Daredevil's enemies and the law. Matt feels that his only recourse is to lie and deny the charge. Matt's dual life, his identities as both a lawyer and a costumed vigilante, are forced to come together. The result puts Matt under great stress. His longtime friend and law partner, Foggy Nelson, advises Matt that it is time to give up his Daredevil identity. He points out that it has not served Matt or others very well. In *Daredevil* vol. 2, #34 (August 2002), Foggy says, "When it comes down to it, this life you've chosen brings you nothing but a vicious cycle of pain. I wasn't going to go into this with you, Matt, but seeing as we are where we are . . . Here's the thing . . . You created it. A cycle of pain. And it starts . . . brand new . . . every time you put on that costume."[11] But Matt has pledged to protect the citizens of Hell's Kitchen, the tough neighborhood in New York City where he lives, and the pressure in his life seems to drive him to take extreme measures. In *Daredevil* vol. 2, #49 (September 2003), Daredevil tortures a revived Bullseye (in comic books, as in soap operas, no interesting character stays dead for long) to get revenge. Alex Maleev's artwork makes Daredevil appear to be a demon as he brutally punches Bullseye in the face. In *Daredevil* vol. 2, #50 (October 2003), Daredevil apparently decides that if you can't beat them, you should join them. He declares himself the new Kingpin of Hell's Kitchen. He says, "I am not protecting this city any more. I am running it! And I say: the people of Hell's Kitchen are my people. This is my territory now."[12] He proceeds to go on a violent rampage, beating up criminals in an effort to clean up the neighborhood. Meanwhile, he continues to do good deeds as a lawyer and defends those in need. In *Daredevil* vol. 2, #56 (March 2004), for example, Matt uses the hundreds of millions of dollars that he has earned from a large lawsuit to fund a neighborhood program that provides good low-income housing and builds a library for Hell's Kitchen. Still, when superhero friends such as Luke Cage, Reed Richards, and Spider-Man confront him on his vigilante tactics, Daredevil dismisses them in anger. Eventually, however, he hears his friends' concerns. He admits that they are right and asks them for their help.[13]

In the 2006 story "The Devil in Cell-Block D," writer Ed Brubaker pursued a similar theme. In *Daredevil* vol. 2, #82 (February 2006), Matt is in prison when his best friend, Foggy Nelson, visits him. As Foggy leaves the prison, he is stabbed and left for dead. Inside the prison, surrounded by criminals, Matt begins to escape from his cell at night, sneak around, and beat and torture other inmates who were in on the murder. He hits them in all the right places to inflict maximum pain, in order to get his revenge.[14] The Punisher, Frank Castle, is Marvel's quintessential murderous vigilante. He gets himself arrested and sent to the prison in order to help Matt. When Matt asks him why he is there, the Punisher tells Matt that he wanted to see for himself, "What it looks like when you turn into me."[15] The conversation shakes Matt to the core. Revenge at all costs comes naturally to the Punisher, but it apparently is not how Matt wants to see himself. Matt's new wife, Milla, sees this too. She knows that Matt is seeking revenge for Foggy's death and urges him to stay true to his identity. She says, "So this is who you want to be? Like the rest of the men in here? This is who Foggy died for? Remember who you are, my love . . . remember why I love you."[16] He eventually does and is released from prison.

Later, however, in *Daredevil* vol. 2, #101 (November 2007), when Milla is poisoned by Mr. Fear, Matt once again resorts to vigilante tactics. He breaks the fingers and arms of low-level thugs in order to get information on how to get an antidote for his wife. In *Daredevil* vol. 2, #104, Matt says, "I don't enjoy torture. But tonight I don't care." When he tortures the villain, the Ox, into giving up some information, he says, "I should feel sick. I should, but I don't. I just feel more angry . . . ready for a new target. And I don't even wonder what that says about me."[17] In these cases, when villains have taken so much from Matt, one of the greatest tragedies is that Matt has allowed them to rob him of his character and his soul. Matt has left behind his moral compass and given in to his anger.

Struggling with Our Identity as People of Love and Justice

Matt Murdock's passion for justice is admirable, especially his passion for justice for those who have the least power in society. Social ethicist Stephen Charles Mott writes, "Justice is a chief attribute of God. God is the one who vindicates the oppressed and defends the weak."[18] According to Mott, it follows that people of faith should have the same passion for justice. He writes, "In Scripture, the people of God are commanded to execute justice because God, after whom they in grace and love pattern their lives, executes justice. Since God has a special regard for the weak and helpless, a corresponding quality is to be found in the lives of God's people (Deut. 10.18–19). The justice which they are to manifest is not theirs but God's, the 'lover of justice'" (Ps. 99:4).[19]

A passion for justice, however, can sometimes lead to merciless acts. In the film *Ghost Rider* (2007), written and directed by Mark Steven Johnson and starring Nicolas Cage, the devil gives Ghost Rider the power of the Spirit of Vengeance. A villain says, "Have mercy." Ghost Rider responds, "Sorry. All out of mercy," whips a flaming chain around him and incinerates him alive. Later, he catches a mugger and looks into his eyes, making the mugger feel the pain and fear of each of his victims. The mugger dies in horror. At the end of the film, Ghost Rider says he is going to use the power to fight the devil. "Wherever innocent blood is shed . . . you'll find me there. The Spirit of Vengeance, fighting fire with fire."

Superheroes and action heroes can appeal to an unpleasant side of our personalities, that part of us that may like the idea of hurting criminals to punish them and get justice. As noted before, most costumed superheroes are really vigilantes. They operate outside the law and use their fists, power blasts, or other means to subdue villains. The Punisher and Ghost Rider represent a new breed of Marvel hero created after Lee and Kirby stopped actively creating Marvel's comic books. These heroes are unabashedly violent vigilantes who justify their actions by their desire for justice and vengeance.

It may seem naive to suggest that conflicts with criminals can be solved without resorting to violence. Most superhero comic books, however, have been set in a fantasy world in which the superhero usually captures villains and then hands them over to the police so they will go to court and be convicted of their crimes. In most stories, the superheroes do this without resorting to undue violence and they do it in order to maintain law and order. The writers and artists of *Daredevil*, however, have explored the darker side of a hero who dresses up in a mask and goes out at night to carry out vigilante justice. In the real world, of course, the police and members of the military use force to carry out their duties, and they usually do so to maintain law and order. Daredevil's efforts, however, are not always in the service of the law. Sometimes he inflicts pain upon criminals with the motivation of punishment or revenge. The story of an otherwise good and decent man who is driven to resort to such acts raises interesting questions. How do we fight for justice while staying true to the call to be merciful?

Jesus Christ, Mahatma Gandhi, and Martin Luther King Jr. are three examples of people who passionately sought justice in their times but did so in merciful and nonviolent ways. Gandhi and King both read and adhered to Jesus' teachings on nonviolent resistance. They spoke truth to power, stood up for those who were being marginalized, and protested unjust policies, but they did so in nonviolent ways. They did not seek revenge upon those who had wronged them.

One of Jesus' very first followers, Paul, examined the issue of vengeance in Romans 12. He encouraged his readers to be passionate, even zealous in their faith (Rom. 12:9–11). For Paul, however, zeal for the truth and for one's faith did not lead to acts of vengeance against others. He called upon his readers to bless those who persecute them (Rom. 9:14). He wrote,

Do not repay anyone evil for evil, but take thought for what is noble in the sight of all. If it is possible, so far as it depends on you, live peaceably with all. Beloved, never avenge yourselves, but leave room for the wrath of God; for it is written, "Vengeance is mine, I will repay, says the Lord." No, "if your enemies are hungry, feed them; if they are thirsty, give them something to drink; for by doing this you will heap burning coals on their heads." Do not be overcome by evil, but overcome evil with good. (Rom. 12:17–21)

The good news for people of faith is that it is not up to us to defend God's honor by making sure that those who do evil things receive their due punishment. We are not called to be agents of God's righteous vengeance. We do not have the burden of getting vengeance on everyone who is immoral or does wrong. We can focus on working toward justice for all without the obligation to punish our enemies or those we might perceive to be enemies of God. We don't need to get an eye for an eye to make everything right in the world. God has it all covered. We can focus on working for God's justice through acts of love and grace, not acts of violence and vengeance. We can work toward seeking justice while forgiving those who have wronged us. We can work to ensure that our criminal justice system leads toward justice for victims and correction of criminals rather than just serving as a means of punishing those who commit crimes.

Living by the principles of our faith can be relatively easy when our lives are going well. The challenge comes when we face trials and tribulations. People of faith are not promised an easy life with no problems. The stories of Daredevil in which his personal life is torn apart provide readers with an opportunity to reflect on how they might react in the worst of circumstances. Our God is not a God who swoops down to make everything better for us whenever we face hard times, but God does promise to be with us. Our faith in God can inspire us to work for justice and to do so with mercy, even when we are tempted to resort to acts of vengeance. Faith in God's presence and a commitment to live faithfully through hard times can help us endure the trials we face.

The Temptations of Film

The films *Daredevil* (2003) and the *Daredevil: Director's Cut* (2004) DVD that followed provide an interesting case study for the way in which certain aspects of the commercial film industry can drive filmmakers to tell stories that focus on violent resolutions and vengeance, rather than stories of people working within the law and with other people to change society for the better.

The film *Daredevil* was directed by Mark Steven Johnson and starred Ben Affleck as Daredevil and Jennifer Garner as Elektra. It was based on Daredevil's origin tale and on writer-artist Frank Miller's famous Elektra saga in *Daredevil* #168–182 (January 1981–May 1982). The film includes many religious images and explores themes of sin and guilt, justice and mercy, and revenge and forgiveness.

Much of the film takes place at a Roman Catholic Church and the parish priest, Father Everett,[20] plays a significant role in the film. The film opens with a shot of Daredevil clinging to a cross at the peak of a large church. He slips off the cross and crashes to the floor in pain.

Early in the film, as an attorney, Matt Murdock cross-examines a criminal named Quesada in court. Quesada is clearly guilty of abusing a woman. Quesada, however, has a high-priced lawyer and is found not guilty. Seeing that the law has not worked, Matt Murdock puts on his Daredevil costume and follows Quesada to carry out some vigilante justice. He finds him in a bar with a rough clientele. There, Daredevil soon gets into a fight with the customers, beats them up, breaks some bones, and leaves the bar in flames. When Quesada runs from the bar and into a subway station, Daredevil follows him. He chokes Quesada and knocks him onto the subway tracks as a train is coming through the tunnel. He tells Quesada, "Hey. That light, at the end of the tunnel. Guess what. That's not heaven. That's the C train." Unlike the similar situation in the comic book, Daredevil here does not save the criminal. Instead, he lets the train run over him and kill him.

Matt goes to confession that day, and the priest, Father Everett, who has figured out Matt's secret identity, is frightened for Matt. He tells him that he will hear his confession but he will not give his approval for what Matt is doing. Matt says, "Justice isn't a sin, Father." Father Everett replies, "No, but vengeance is. You see it on the street every day. Violence just begets more violence. Is that how you want to live your life? A lawyer by day, then judge and jury by night?"

Other events also make Matt wonder whether his life is on the right track. A young boy sees Daredevil roughing up a thug and cries out to Daredevil, "Don't hurt me." Matt is taken aback and says, "I'm not the bad guy, kid. I'm not the bad guy." Seeing Matt's devil costume and his violent behavior, however, the boy remains unconvinced.

In the film, as in the comic book, the Kingpin hires Bullseye to kill Matt's girlfriend Elektra. After he kills Elektra, Bullseye meets Daredevil in the church sanctuary for a final showdown. The two fight to the finish. In the comic books, even in the heat of battle, superheroes usually find a way to restrain their enemies without killing them. The code of the superhero is clear: superheroes do not kill. As Daredevil and Bullseye fight, a policeman shoots at them and the bullet goes straight through the palms of both of Bullseye's hands, leaving him incapacitated. He holds out his bloody hands, in a classic stigmata pose, and pleads, "Show mercy." Daredevil responds by throwing Bullseye through the church's stain glass windows to his death.

A few minutes later in the film, with little time for any new epiphany on Matt's part, he confronts Kingpin in his office. In the film, the Kingpin is not only responsible for ordering the hit on Elektra but also the gangster who killed Matt's father years earlier. Daredevil and the Kingpin fight a brutally violent fight, taking turns pummeling each other. When Daredevil finally wins the upper hand, he grabs a steel bar and prepares to deliver the deathblow to the helpless Kingpin. He says, "I've been thinking about this day since I was 12 years old." At the very last moment, however, he holds back the bar. Fisk says, "I don't understand." Daredevil just smiles and says, "I'm not the bad guy." Instead of killing the Kingpin, Daredevil waits for him to be arrested. He knows the Kingpin will eventually get out of prison, but he vows that he will be ready to respond. He says to the Kingpin, "And I'll be waiting. Justice is served."

If the message to be taken from the film is that Matt has learned that violence does not work, and that mercy is better than vengeance, then the message is, at best, a bit muddied. Viewers still have had the chance to cheer on Daredevil in his violent fights. Daredevil gets his deadly revenge upon Bullseye for killing his girlfriend, an act for which he apparently shows no remorse. Moments later, he beats up the Kingpin to the point of death but then has a sudden change of heart. One is left to wonder whether the film is suggesting that it is acceptable to kill Bullseye, the blue-collar criminal who murdered Elektra, but unacceptable to murder the Kingpin because he is the white-collar criminal who ordered the hit. If so, there would be good reason to question such moral distinctions. If the viewer is supposed to see Daredevil have a change of heart, and reject his quest for vigilante justice, then that does not come through clearly.

Still, the film did raise some intriguing questions. It did not present Daredevil as a perfect role model of human decency. For an action film, it did a commendable job of raising the themes of sin and guilt, justice and mercy, and revenge and forgiveness; and of questioning the heroism of a vigilante. As Julien R. Fielding wrote in her review of the film for the *Journal of Religion and Film,*

> Moviegoers still want their superheroes but they no longer get ones placed in a world of black-and-white dualism. *Daredevil* reminds its audience that no one is innocent, but whether that is because of "original sin," it does not say. What it does tell us, though, is that "revenge won't make the pain go away" and that "a man without fear is also one without hope." Murdock sets out to save the city but with Elektra's love also saves himself. Sometimes, he says, faith is all you need.[21]

The theatrical release of *Daredevil* (2003) met with mixed reviews. As described earlier, the film seems disjointed. One moment Daredevil gets his revenge by killing a villain, and the next moment he grants mercy to another. Most critics gave the film negative reviews and even those who were generally positive seemed to suggest that the film fell short of the potential of the character.

The screenwriter and director, Johnson, actually agreed with that evaluation. He said he loved the version of the film that was released in theaters but admitted that it was flawed.[22] So, in 2004, Johnson released a director's cut of the film on DVD that used previously unseen footage and was edited in a way more in keeping with his original vision. This version of the film, *Daredevil: Director's Cut* (2004), was received more positively.

In a featurette on the DVD called "Giving the Devil His Due," Johnson explained how the pressures of the studio and the limitations of commercial film pressured him to change the film significantly from the one he had originally intended to make. Johnson was very frank in his comments. He confessed, "In the process of making a film you can forget what got you into making it in the first place."

In the case of *Daredevil*, Johnson explained that he always admired Matt Murdock's work as a lawyer. He said, "One of the things I always loved about Matt Murdock was the way he always would stand up for the little guy and how he'd take the case that no one else would take." It was one of the reasons he wanted to make the film. So Johnson included in his script an extended story line in which Matt takes on a case involving a murdered prostitute. It was a case that no one else cared about, and it was an example of Matt fighting for those who would otherwise have no one to stand up for them. Through this seemingly insignificant case, Matt made connections that would eventually help him take down the Kingpin of Crime himself. Unfortunately, the studio executives who influenced the final cut of the theatrical version of the film had Johnson cut those scenes. They felt the story line of the court case took too long to unfold and viewers would lose interest. As Johnson said, "Almost all of that got taken out of the film for pace." In his director's cut of the film, Johnson was able to put some of the courtroom scenes back into the film.

Two significant aspects of commercial Hollywood films are that they are time-limited and they are visual in nature. Films generally have only approximately two hours to tell their story, so filmmakers tend to want to keep the story moving quickly, and they gravitate toward captivating visuals to keep viewers interested. As a result, many scripts are simplified. In the case of *Daredevil*, this meant that the slightly complicated and thoughtful court case Johnson had shot was jettisoned in order to focus more on Matt's physical and colorful activities as Daredevil. The studio may have felt, understandably, that viewers would find a man dressed in a red devil outfit punching out criminals to be much more visually interesting than a lawyer standing in a courtroom and making legal arguments.

The highly visual and time-limited character of film also leads many Hollywood films to tell stories about individuals rather than communities. The trailers for many Hollywood films have their deep-voiced narrators breathlessly telling the audience that the film is the story of "One man, alone, in a world that . . ." In the world of motion pictures, stories are often told about an individual who gets angry and fights on his or her own. In the case of *Daredevil*, Johnson explained that many of the scenes that he shot of Matt Murdock's friends and colleagues, such as Foggy Nelson, Ben Urich, and others, were deleted from the theatrical release and put back into the film for the director's cut. In the real world, our problems are most often solved when people come together and work within social structures to change society.

The director's cut also included more scenes in which Father Everett talks to Matt of God's mercy and Matt's need to connect to the community of faith and attend church on Sunday mornings. The following piece of dialogue, for example, was deleted from the theatrical release but reinserted into Johnson's director's cut of the film:

MATT: This is my confession, Father.

FATHER EVERETT: God's mercy is infinite. All ya gotta do is ask.

MATT: Everything I had has been taken from me. Now I'm supposed to ask for mercy? I don't ask for mercy . . . people ask me."

FATHER EVERETT: Oh, is that a fact?

This short piece of dialogue does little to move the plot along, but it adds complexity to Matt's character in the film. It shows viewers that, at this point in the story, Matt refuses to accept God's mercy for himself and is unwilling to show mercy to others. As such, it brings to the fore a significant flaw in Matt's personality and adds considerable depth to the character. Yet the studio apparently felt so compelled to keep the story moving quickly that they deleted this seventeen seconds of dialogue from the theatrical release.

The visual and time-limited nature of film also affects the way the medium explores love and sex. To show true love developing as it does in the real world would take filmmakers hours of showing two individuals meeting, talking, going out on dates, and getting to know each other over time. Many filmmakers apparently feel that the best way to establish quickly that two people have fallen in love with each other, and to do so in a clear, visual way, is to show them in bed together soon after they meet. In the film *Daredevil* (2003), Daredevil and Elektra meet on a rooftop and feel a romantic connection with each other. With his hypersensitive hearing, Daredevil hears a crime victim calling for help on the streets below. He starts to go, but Elektra asks him to stay. The next scene shows the two in bed together in a love scene.

It is interesting, then, to discover that the scene as it appears in the theatrical release is diametrically opposed to Johnson's original vision for the scene. In the version of the scene that was in his script and that is included in the director's cut, Daredevil also hears the call for help. In this version, however, when Elektra asks him to stay, he puts the needs of others before his own happiness. He leaves Elektra in order to help the crime victim. When the studio executives saw an early cut of the film, they had another idea. They knew they had two beautiful actors in Ben Affleck and Jennifer Garner and thought viewers would want to see them in a love scene. So they asked Johnson to change it and went to the expense of having the actors come back to shoot a love scene. In the featurette, Johnson said that, of course, he knows why they wanted that scene in the movie, but that the new scene undermined the character of Daredevil.

Film's visual and time-limited nature also leads to films that tell stories in which conflicts are resolved in violent ways. In the real world, resolving conflict takes time. It usually takes a great deal of talking, of negotiating back and forth, and finding compromise. In a two-hour film, filmmakers often find that they just have enough time to create a conflict, establish a good guy, establish a bad guy, and to try to resolve that conflict in an exciting and emotionally satisfying way. Watching people sit down together in a room, talk through their problems, reach a compromise, and perhaps create some new laws takes too long and is simply not as visually interesting or emotionally satisfying as watching a colorful and attractive hero punch or shoot a villain. In many films, the conflict is supposedly resolved when the villain dies. This is the case not only in many action films but also in many animated children's movies such as Disney's *Beauty and the Beast* (1991) and *The Lion King* (1994). In the case of *Daredevil* (2003), the story was reshaped to deemphasize Matt's efforts in the courtroom and to focus on the way he's able to kill Bullseye and beat the Kingpin within an inch of his life.

Johnson realized that the process of filmmaking resulted in a film that did not tell the story he set out to tell. He said, "The big difference for me is that the theatrical cut felt very much more like a revenge story of 'who got my girlfriend?' And that was never what the movie was supposed to be. It was supposed to be about the hero of Hell's Kitchen. The guy who stands up for the underdog. The guy who's gonna go up against the biggest crime boss the city's ever seen. That's what I think is accomplished in this [The Director's Cut] version."

While there are many films that tell poignant and meaningful stories of the human condition, and others that celebrate the best and most beautiful aspects of life, many films follow patterns of conflict resolution that are problematic to people of faith. They seem to celebrate vengeance and model violent action as the only way to resolve conflicts. These aspects of film are not the result of some Hollywood conspiracy to undermine the values of people of faith. Instead, the nature of commercial film seems to tempt studios into telling stories that focus on individuals over community and that show conflicts being resolved in quick, visual, and often violent ways. As people of faith, we should be aware that the films we watch often tell stories that do not model our beliefs in this regard.

Faith and Fanaticism

Writer Kevin Smith and artist Joe Quesada's story "Guardian Devil," told in *Daredevil* vol. 2, #1–8 (November 1998–June 1999), explores Matt's faith as both a potential source of strength and a potential source of delusion and sin. In the story, Matt Murdock's life is turned completely upside down yet again. Karen Page, the love of Matt's life, leaves him and then returns to tell him she is HIV-positive. Then his best friend and law partner, Foggy, is framed for murder. Next, Matt is forced to quit his job in order to defend his friend. Then, things get even worse!

The story opens with a young teenage girl presenting Matt with a baby girl who she claims is the result of a virgin birth. She tells Matt that angels have revealed to her that the baby is the redeemer of the world, sent to save the world in the final days. The angels also revealed to her, she says, that Matt is Daredevil and told her that he is meant to be its guardian and keep it safe from harm. Matt believes her. The girl leaves the baby with him and then disappears. Soon, however, a mysterious man arrives and tells Matt that the baby is not the redeemer but actually the Antichrist and must be killed. Matt believes this man as well. Throughout all of this, Matt questions his faith and his own sanity. In the midst of all this pressure and because he believes what the mysterious man has told him about the baby, he does atrocious things. At one point he tosses the baby off a rooftop to kill it. Thankfully, his friend the Black Widow rescues her. Later, he breaks the Black Widow's ankle because he thinks she is in league with evil people who want to protect the baby. In yet another reprehensible act, Matt lashes out at Karen and blames and shames her for her HIV-positive status.

Matt Murdock's Roman Catholic faith plays a prominent role in the story (Figure 12). The story begins and ends with Matt in a confessional talking to a priest. At times, his faith is portrayed as a great source of strength. Throughout the story, Matt grasps a cross necklace, as though he is trying to hold on to his faith in the midst of his many trials. Karen refers to Matt's faith as the source of his power to forgive her and others for how they have wronged him. Faith is seen as a source of his hope to carry on and his will to stand up for what is right. Part of the story takes place at a church mission, where nuns and other church members are shown doing noble work, serving the homeless and others in need. Portions of the story are narrated through Matt's prayers to God, in which he expresses to God his anger and his doubts.

The story also explores the dangers inherent in the sort of faith that leads people to abandon reason and to do atrocious things in the name of God. Matt does terrible things, things that he would likely never do if it were not for his faith. In the story, it turns out that the cross necklace that Matt has been grasping was infused with time-release toxins that make Matt highly susceptible to suggestion. The mastermind behind these events knows of Matt's faith and has exploited his devotion to the cross in order to get Matt to betray his values and to torture his soul. A combination of Matt's faith and the drug led to Matt believing both the girl who said the baby was the savior and the man who said the baby was the Antichrist.

The drug-laced cross in the story can be seen as a potent symbol for the potential danger of religious belief. If we are not careful, our faith can open us up to dangerous suggestions that reason or common human decency would have us question or discount.

The Gospel of Matthew tells of a time when Jesus presented his followers with an intriguing image of the potential of the power of faith to do good things. He said that if people have the faith of a mustard seed—which is a very small seed—they can move mountains (Mt. 17:20). Jesus also, however, repeatedly called his followers to use common sense and common decency in dealing with others.

Unreasonable and uncaring faith also has the potential to do great harm. In Jesus' day, some people were so caught up in the details of their faith that they forgot to care about those in need. According to Matthew, one time when Jesus was at a synagogue on the Sabbath, a man with a withered hand approached him and asked to be healed. Some people asked Jesus whether or not it was lawful to cure on the Sabbath, suggesting that he would be breaking God's law to do so. In reply, Jesus appealed to their common sense and their common decency. He said, "Suppose one of you has only one sheep and it falls into a pit on the sabbath; will you not lay hold of it and lift it out? How much more valuable is a human being

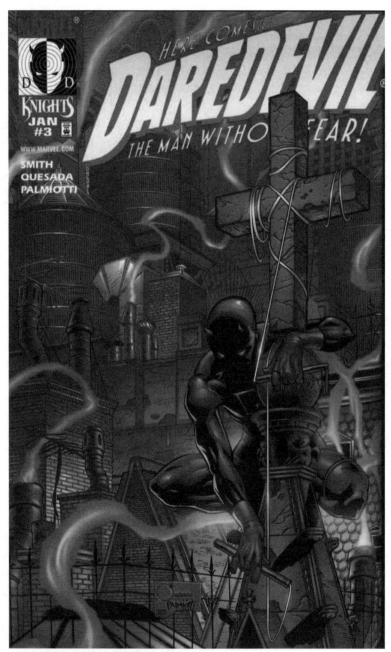

Figure 12. *Daredevil* (vol. 2) #3 (January 1999), cover; Marvel. Kevin Smith writer and
Joe Quesada art. Quesada's cover captures two recurring motifs in Daredevil's stories.
Despite his doubts, Daredevil at times turns to his faith to help him through hard times.
At the same time, he struggles to stay true to heroic ideals rather than becoming a
lawless vigilante. Note how Daredevil looks like a demon even as he clings to the cross.

than a sheep! So it is lawful to do good on the sabbath" (Mt. 12:11–12). For Jesus, the test of whether people were being genuinely faithful seemed to come down to how they were caring for others, even those who might be considered their enemies.

In recent years, in the name of the Christian faith, people have shot a doctor in his church, bombed government buildings, and more. Along with these sensational acts, even more Christians have launched political crusades to hurt people, said things to shame people, and shouted hateful statements toward people. In so doing, they are forgetting that common sense and common decency tell us that faith calls for acts of love and mercy and not for acts of vengeance and hatred.

Courage

The covers of most of Daredevil's comic books proclaim, "Daredevil: The Man Without Fear!" A couple of fan-favorite issues of *Daredevil* have explored Matt's courage.

Early on, in *Daredevil* #7 (April 1965), Stan Lee and artist Wally Wood had Daredevil face the superpowered Prince Namor, the Sub-Mariner. In the story, Namor comes from his undersea kingdom to the surface world and tries to hire Matt Murdock to sue the human race for depriving the people of Atlantis of their birthright, namely total control of the surface world. Matt explains to Namor that any judge would simply throw the case out of court. Namor then tries to get the government's attention by going on a rampage in New York City and getting himself arrested. While waiting for a trial date, he learns that while he has been in jail, the villain Krang, his rival for the throne of Atlantis, has launched a coup and taken over his undersea kingdom. When Namor breaks out of jail to return to his kingdom, the army tries to stop him from escaping. Namor is offended by their actions and plans to destroy them all. Matt understands that a confrontation between Namor and the army could risk the lives of many innocent bystanders, so he changes into his Daredevil costume and convinces the army to let him try to stop Namor first. Daredevil does not have the brute strength of Namor. He is clearly outmatched and he knows it. Still, he does his best to stop Namor, or at least to slow him down, knowing he will probably be hurt in the process. Though he does not win the battle, his courage gains Namor's respect. Namor says, "I have fought the Fantastic Four, the Avengers, and other super-powered humans, but none has been more courageous than he, the most vulnerable of all!"[23] Out of respect for Daredevil, Namor flies over the waiting army and avoids any further conflict with the surface world.

In a classic issue years later, in *Daredevil* #163 (March 1980), writer Roger McKenzie and artist Frank Miller told another story in which Daredevil tries to protect New York City from a superpowered invader. This time the menace is the Incredible Hulk. Once again, Daredevil knows he has no chance to win and knows that he will likely be injured in the process, but he is able to slow the Hulk down just enough to save the city from great destruction.

In these issues, Daredevil is fighting battles that he knows he cannot win. Daredevil does not have a death wish, but he does have the courage necessary to do what he must in order to limit the impact of a destructive force. He usually battles villains that are far less powerful than Namor and the Hulk. More often, he fights the common criminals and gangsters that plague Hell's Kitchen, the rough neighborhood in New York City that he has pledged to protect. In a sense, Daredevil faces the same long odds in his everyday battles as he did against Namor and the Hulk. He does what he can to expose corruption and put criminals in jail through his work as attorney Matt Murdock and to stop supervillains as Daredevil. He must know, however, that he can never completely win the battle. He cannot completely wipe out crime and corruption in Hell's Kitchen. Still, he has the courage and commitment to fight on and do what he can to make things better.

In that way, we may have something in common with Daredevil. Some of us may feel called to work toward eliminating world hunger, homelessness, or poverty. It is easy to become discouraged when we put our hearts and souls into an effort and do not see a clear victory on the horizon. The fact that we may not fully win a struggle, however, should not discourage us from having the courage and commitment to continue in our good work.

One common misunderstanding is that courage leads to violent and aggressive acts. Coaches and political advisors sometimes encourage people to be brave enough to get nasty and mean with their opponents. Too often courage is portrayed as a virtue that leads to violence and aggression. Courage, however, can also lead to acts of love and self-sacrifice. The apostle Paul put the virtues of courage and love together when he wrote, "Keep alert, stand firm in your faith, be courageous, be strong. Let all that you do be done in love" (1 Cor. 16:13–14). Sometimes it takes a great deal of courage to love instead of to hate.

Sometimes courage can drive us to do great things in the face of great danger. People all across the globe have known that they were putting their lives on the line when their faith has called them to stand up for human rights, but they have still taken a stand at the risk of imprisonment or even death. Sometimes courage calls us to make changes in our personal lives. It may take a great deal of courage to quit a job or to leave a relationship that is secure. We may need to have the courage to make these changes, however, if we know they are not healthy for us or our relationship with God. We may need courage to stand up to others at work or school in smaller ways, by refusing to laugh at jokes that demean others, feed into gossip, or go along with unethical plans or policies that would compromise our faith.

As a pastor and a seminary professor, I have been surprised at how often people limit themselves because they are afraid to take a risk or make a change in their lives. They do not apply to a school out of fear that their application will be denied. They do not apply for a job out of fear of being turned down. They do not try to build a friendship for fear of rejection. They miss opportunities because they do not have the courage to try. Fear can limit what we accomplish in our faith vocation as well. Some people lack the courage necessary to make public stands on issues of justice and have confessed to me that they do not feel they are truly living out their Christian faith because of it. Whether we are making bold leaps or taking small steps, we need to have courage to live out our faith. We need to have the courage and willpower necessary to embrace our identity as people of faith and to strive for justice and to do so in ways that model love and not vengeance.

Questions for Reflection

- What would you have done if you had been in Battling Jack Murdock's situation? Would you have thrown the fight and stayed alive to raise your son? Would you have kept your integrity, fought to win the fight, and accepted death as the cost? What other solutions could you have pursued?
- Do you have a disability or limitation that you sometimes use as an excuse for not doing more good in the world? Do you ever look on others and put unjustified limits on what they can accomplish?
- Have you ever tried to compartmentalize your life so completely that it felt as though you had a secret identity? In other words, have you ever tried to live one way with one set of values in one setting but then lived another way by another set of values when you were in another setting?
- Have you observed Christian groups that have set themselves up as the instruments of God's vengeance rather than the instruments of God's justice and mercy?
- How do you integrate your commitment to justice with God's call to show mercy?
- Is there another film you have seen that resorted to violence as an easy, satisfying way to resolve a conflict?
- Have the sights and sounds of a movie ever got you roused into hoping that the bad guy would meet a violent end?
- In what other films have you seen filmmakers use the shorthand of a bedroom love scene to supposedly demonstrate that a couple is truly in love?
- Is there a positive step in your life that you are afraid to take? What are the factors that make it a scary step? What are some things that might give you the courage to move forward?
- When does courage cross over into foolhardiness? When does a healthy sense of self-sacrifice turn into an unhealthy martyr complex?
- Have aspects of your faith ever tempted you to abandon reason in a way that was potentially harmful to you or to others? In your opinion, is faith necessarily a call to abandon reason?
- Matt Murdock had friends and family who helped him find his way back when he had gone astray. Who are some of the people in your life who you trust to help you know whether you are going astray?

The Silver Surfer, Adam Warlock, and Captain Marvel

The View from Outer Space

The heroes of the Marvel Age of Comics were born at the dawn of the space age. It is not surprising, then, that the Fantastic Four traveled into space in their very first issue, *Fantastic Four* #1 (November 1961), and met aliens from outer space, the shape-shifting Skrulls, in their second issue, *Fantastic Four* #2 (January 1962). For most fans, however, Marvel truly went cosmic during the famous Galactus Trilogy in *Fantastic Four* #48–50 (March–May 1966). In that story, in order to defeat Galactus, Johnny is guided by the Watcher to travel to the outer reaches of the universe to Galactus' home planet to find the Ultimate Nullifier, the only weapon that can stop him. When Johnny returns to Earth, it is difficult to tell whether the journey has been more stressful on his body or his mind. He lands back on Earth with the weapon and collapses, saying, "I travelled through worlds . . . so big. . . . so big . . . there . . . there aren't words . . . We're like ants. . . . just ants . . . ants!"[1] The trip is disorienting to Johhny, but it also gives him a helpful new perspective. By seeing a wider universe, he is confronted with the fact that humankind is not the center of the universe and that the world he knows is not the measure of all things. This realization at first overwhelms him, but in the months that follow, Johnny seems to mature. The trip has had a great impact on him, and he is no longer the brash teenager of his earlier days.

One of the benefits of the genres of science fiction and space fantasy is that they can take us beyond the limits of our own lives and into new worlds and new possibilities. They can give us a fresh new perspective from which we can look back at our own world in new ways.

In the late 1960s and early 1970s, Marvel began to explore the outer reaches of space and time with a number of cosmic heroes. The Silver Surfer, a noble being who is marooned on Earth, provides us with an outsider's perspective on the perplexing nature of the human race. Adam Warlock was sent to save Counter-Earth by its creator, the High Evolutionary, and his early adventures provide us with another perspective on the Christ story. The Guardians of the Galaxy, from Earth's future, give us a long-range perspective on our time here on earth and the legacies that we leave behind. Finally, Captain Marvel's universe-spanning adventures provided him, and provide us, with a fascinating perspective on our lives and our inevitable deaths.

Silver Surfer: An Outsider's View of Earthlings

The creation of the Silver Surfer is a fascinating example of the way that Stan Lee and Jack Kirby collaborated on stories at the height of their creative partnership. As mentioned in previous chapters, Lee would often just have brief conversations with artists such as Kirby about the plots of their adventures before the artists went off on their own to plot out and draw the issues. Lee would then receive the pages of art and add captions and dialogue balloons to complete the stories. After Lee and Kirby discussed the plot for the famous Galactus Trilogy, Kirby took a few weeks to finish the drawings for the first issue before submitting them to Lee for scripting. As Lee recalls,

> When he brought it to me so that I could add the dialogue and captions, I was surprised to find a brand-new character floating around in the artwork—a silver-skinned, smooth-domed, sky-riding surfer atop a speedy flying surfboard. When I asked ol' Jackson who he was, Jack replied something to the effect that a supremely powerful gent like Galactus, a godlike giant who roamed the galaxies, would surely require the services of a herald who could serve him as an advance guard.[2]

According to Lee, while he had not even thought of having a character such as the Silver Surfer, Kirby had planned on using him only once or twice, as a supporting character. As he looked over Kirby's illustrations, however, Lee says he saw more potential for the character:

> Studying the illustrations, seeing the way Jack had drawn him, I found a certain nobility in his demeanor, an almost spiritual quality in his aspect and his bearing. In determining what his speech pattern would be, I began to imagine the way that a space-born apostle would speak. There seemed something biblically pure about our Silver Surfer, something totally selfless and magnificently innocent. As you can gather, I was tempted to imbue him with a spirit of almost religious purity. In short, the more I studied him, the more I got into his thoughts and his dialogue, the more I saw him as someone who would graphically represent all the best, the most unselfish, qualities of intelligent life.[3]

Along with the ability to fly through space on his silver surfboard, a nearly invulnerable body, and something called "the power cosmic," Lee and Kirby did give the Silver Surfer a noble character. In *Fantastic Four* #49 (April 1966), he sacrifices his own freedom for the sake of the people of Earth. In *Silver Surfer* #1

(August 1968), it is revealed that he had done the same for the people of his own planet, years earlier.

In *Silver Surfer* #3 (December 1968), readers met Marvel's thinly veiled version of Satan named Mephisto. Mephisto observes the Surfer, and it torments him that one so pure and yet so powerful exists. He brings the Surfer to his netherworld kingdom and tries to tempt him in much the same way that Satan tempted Jesus. The Surfer, naturally, does not give in and stays true to his principles. In Marvel's very first graphic novel, titled *The Silver Surfer* (1978), the Surfer suffers the loss of a great love and yet again sacrifices his own freedom and happiness for the salvation of humankind.[4] In the years that followed, a number of special graphic novels returned to the same theme, with the Silver Surfer sacrificing himself in various ways for the sake of the people of Earth, who often feared and persecuted him in return. Among some fans and artists, these story lines have even earned the Silver Surfer the nickname of "Christ on a Surfboard."[5]

As an alien being who is noble of spirit, but also new to the ways of Earth and naive regarding them, the Silver Surfer became Lee's mouthpiece for his personal reflections on all that was right and wrong about humankind. Like a parent who feels compelled to say he loves all of his children the same, Lee was hesitant to say which character he likes the best, but ended up admitting that it is the Silver Surfer:

> Perhaps it's because I really believe so deeply in the philosophy and utterances of our shiny-domed crusader. Perhaps it's because he comes the closest to articulating my own beliefs and convictions. Perhaps, most of all, it's because, with every word I write, I want to feel that some of this charismatic character's innate goodness will have an effect on some reader somewhere—and perhaps the power of his own deep-rooted morality and concern for his fellow beings will, in some subtle way, help make our own troubled world just a little better for his stories having been told.[6]

In the first Silver Surfer comic book series, writer Stan Lee and artist John Buscema would often show the Silver Surfer flying over the cities of Earth and making observations about humankind. In *Silver Surfer* #2 (October 1968), he says, "Of all the countless worlds I've known . . . of the myriads of planets upon which I've trod . . . never have I known a race so filled with fear . . . with distrust . . . with the seeds of smoldering violence . . . as this which calls itself humanity!"[7] He observes that while the animals of Earth battle for food to survive, "It is man alone who battles in the name of nameless causes. It is man alone who is goaded by emotion, who is driven by savage pride!"[8] Still, he has sympathy for the people and wants to help those "plagued by poverty and want, the cancer of crime, and the brutal scourge of tyranny!"[9]

In a later issue he reflects, "At last I know how Earthmen differ from rational beings . . . They think peace denotes weakness . . . and savagery strength! And none but their very young or very old knows the true meaning of love!"[10] He says to a group of people who are judgmental of others, "You see only good and bad . . . right and wrong . . . do you never see mercy? Are you blind to forgiveness?"[11] As the series continued, the Surfer's frustration with what he saw seemed to grow as did, it seems, Lee's own frustration with the violence and intolerance he was seeing in the world around him. In *Silver Surfer* #15 (April 1970), John Buscema's artwork highlights the Surfer's alien nature as Lee's script has him reflecting on how he is still a stranger in a strange land (Figure 13). The Surfer says, "Despite the long tortured months I have spent observing the human race, I understand them no better now than when I first set foot on their hostile world! They long for peace, yet gird for war! They search for love, yet harbor hate! If man is sane . . . then the universe itself is steeped in madness!"[12]

The Silver Surfer's reflections on humankind were not all negative, however. He often would risk his life for them and made good friends with some humans, including the members of the Fantastic Four. In the Silver Surfer's first solo story, which appeared in *Fantastic Four Annual* #5 (November 1967), Lee and Kirby tell a story in which the Silver Surfer observes his new home planet. He says, "The waves of human emotion which I sense are too overwhelming! Fear . . . envy . . . greed . . . and hatred engulf me in ever-increasing torrents. And yet . . . there is a kindness too . . . and love, fighting to break through the clouds."[13] The Surfer's frustration is palpable in these panels. He is aware of humankind's great potential for good, but at the same time he observes its capacity for evil.

Theologians are aware of this tension in human nature as well. They observe that human beings are fallen and imperfect but that they are capable of great good as well. Theologian Tyron Inbody writes, "One of the most egregious misrepresentations of the faith of the church is the claim that it teaches a pessimistic view of human nature."[14] According to Inbody, the Christian view of humankind is neither overly optimistic nor pessimistic but offers a realistic assessment of the human capacity for evil. He writes, "The Christian concept of sin is bracketed by the two optimistic doctrines that human beings are created in the image of God and are redeemable and redeemed."[15] As he puts it, "Human beings are sinners and saints, destructive and creative, a bundle of tensions."[16] When we acknowledge both sides of our human nature, our great potential to do good and our potential to commit sinful acts, we are in a better position to monitor our own lives and to choose to live lives that reflect God's love and grace.

To be perfectly honest, the Silver Surfer's musings in those early issues could at times seem a bit pretentious. In the series *Stan Lee Meets*, Lee wrote stories in which he is a character who meets some of his most famous creations. In *Stan Lee Meets Silver Surfer* (2006), penciled by artist Mike Wieringo, Lee uses some self-effacing humor to make a point. Galactus complains to Stan about how the Surfer goes on and on about the sorry state of the universe. Galactus says, "Now do you understand? Now do you see how unbearable he is?" He adds, "The worst thing about him is he influences others! Tell me . . . could you stop him from boring you to death with his eternal preaching?" Stan replies, "Preaching? Preaching may be mankind's greatest weapon against the burgeoning cruelty and violence in the human condition. Since the Force has proven useless, perhaps only love, truth,

Figure 13. *Silver Surfer* #15 (April 1970), page 2; Marvel Comics. Stan Lee script, John Buscema art. Buscema presents readers with a more alien-looking Silver Surfer than in past issues, which serves to highlight the Surfer's estrangement from the human race. Lee's script has the Surfer's soliloquy return to one of his most common themes, the hostility and hatred that plague humankind. Copyright ©1970 Marvel Comics, all rights reserved.

and forgiveness shall ultimately prevail."[17] Of course, even the best preaching, whether it comes in a comic book or from behind a pulpit, is effective only if those who hear the message choose to put it into practice.

Adam Warlock: Images of Christ and Church

Like many other Marvel characters, Adam Warlock was introduced by Lee and Kirby in the pages of *Fantastic Four.* Number 67 (October 1967) tells the story of three evil scientists who form a lab they call the Beehive. There, they create a being whom they design to be the perfect man of the future. When the being hatches from his cocoon, he is revealed to have golden skin and great powers, though those powers are not specified. This being would eventually become known as Adam Warlock, but in this story he is known simply as Him. His creators' motives for creating Him, however, are not pure. Once he hatches from his giant cocoon, they plan to have Him conquer the world for them. Unfortunately for his creators, however, Him is both morally and physically superior to them. He is immediately aware of his creators' evil plans, destroys their headquarters, and says, "This planet of humans is not for me. . . . Not yet. . . . Not till another millennium has passed! Thus, I shall take my leave . . ."[18] A couple of years later, in *Thor* #166 (July 1969), Him goes toe-to-toe with the Mighty Thor, and he is shown to have great strength but also a naive innocence about the world around him. Through the years, this character was used to explore religious themes more explicitly than any other Marvel character.

A Christ Figure for Counter-Earth

In 1972, writer Roy Thomas and penciler Gil Kane reintroduced the character Him as the messianic Adam Warlock. While the Silver Surfer certainly had some Christlike attributes, the adventures of Adam Warlock became a full-blown allegory of the life of Christ. Thomas writes that he was influenced by David Lloyd Webber and Tim Rice's rock opera *Jesus Christ Superstar* after he watched Ben Vereen perform on Broadway in the role of Judas. Thomas did not intend to be subtle in his approach. He wanted it to be clear to readers that the gospels were his inspiration for the story. He explains, "I didn't want to be thought sacrilegious; I simply thought that, since there's always been a messianic side to superheroes, which had recently been embodied by the Silver Surfer in particular, perhaps it was time to carry that notion to the next level."[19]

In *Marvel Premiere* #1 (April 1972), readers meet the High Evolutionary. In an earlier adventure,[20] the High Evolutionary had evolved animals into people, much like in the H. G. Wells novel *The Island of Dr. Moreau.* His experiment with a wolf, however, went awry, and the wolf became too advanced and too powerful. The wolf became the Man-Beast and led other creatures in a revolt against the High Evolutionary. It is now years later, and the High Evolutionary wants to create a perfect world that is free from sin. As he is in the midst of doing this, he finds a large cocoon floating in space and senses that the being inside it has a noble spirit. He brings the cocoon into his spaceship for observation. The High Evolutionary then creates Counter-Earth, a world that he would hide from the evils of Earth by placing it on the exact opposite side of the sun. Thomas says that he made sure that the High Evolutionary created his world out of a hunk of rock, "but *not* out of nothingness, since I didn't want to offend Judeo-Christian sensibilities if I could avoid it."[21] Because of the exhausting work of trying to create a perfect world, the High Evolutionary needs to rest. He falls asleep, and the Man-Beast comes onto the ship and introduces evil into Counter-Earth.[22] Readers then see a montage of images sketching the accelerated history of Counter-Earth, featuring murders and wars, as it unfolds. The Man-Beast gloats, "Thus it begins! And now thru twice-lived ages, one crime follows hard upon another even unto the ultimate transgression!"[23] Accompanying these words is the image of Jesus being crucified on a cross. The High Evolutionary then wakes up, and Him, who would soon be known as Adam Warlock, emerges from the cocoon. Together they are able to fight off the Man-Beast, who escapes from the ship. The damage, however, is already done. Counter-Earth is not the sinless utopia the High Evolutionary had hoped for, and he plans to destroy it. Adam Warlock pleads with the High Evolutionary to spare Counter-Earth and to let him go to the planet in order to save it. The people, he says, are worth saving. At the end of the issue, the High Evolutionary gives Adam a mysterious soul gem to wear on his forehead and sends him to Counter-Earth.

In *Marvel Premiere* #2 (July 1972), Adam crashes to the ground and awakes with amnesia. He is discovered by four teenagers, who Thomas says he intended to represent the disciples.[24] The world on which he finds himself is much like Earth, though with small differences, such as the fact that there appear to be no other superheroes. The stories in *Marvel Premiere* were intriguing enough that the character was awarded his own series, and in *Warlock* #1 (August 1972) and the issues that followed, Adam battles the Man-Beast's followers. Along the way, the series raises interesting questions. The High Evolutionary observes the sinfulness of the people on Counter-Earth, and he once again wants to destroy it in order to satisfy his sense of justice. Adam again talks him out of it.[25] When one of Adam's young disciples, Jason, wants Adam to stop battling the Man-Beast's men long enough to help the poor, Adam says, "I cannot while the greater threat of the Man-Beast remains!"[26] Jason disagrees, gets mad, and almost leaves Adam but eventually decides to continue following him. Later, the rulers of the world persecute Adam out of desire to hold on to their own power.[27] As promising as the premise may have been, the series failed to succeed in quality or in sales and was cancelled after *Warlock* #8 (October 1973).

The end of Adam Warlock's quest to bring salvation to Counter-Earth would have to wait to be told in *The Incredible Hulk* #176–178 (June–August 1974), with Roy Thomas now serving in the role of editor, Gerry Conway plotting the tale, Tony Isabella scripting, and Herb Trimpe supplying the artwork. The iconic cover of *The Incredible Hulk* #178 (August 1974), drawn by Trimpe, shows Adam Warlock being crucified on a giant ankh, an ancient Egyptian symbol for eternal life that vaguely resembles a cross (Figure 14). Adam is crucified in front of a live television

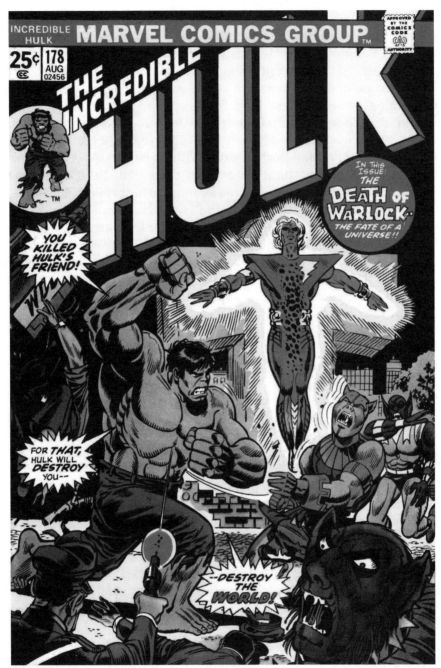

Figure 14. *The Incredible Hulk* #178 (August 1974), page 1; Marvel Comics. Herb Trimpe art, Gerry Conway plot, and Tony Isabella script. Adam Warlock Superstar. The story of Marvel's Christ figure Adam Warlock comes to its predictable climax as he is crucified on a giant ankh on the planet Counter-Earth. Copyright ©1974 Marvel Comics, all rights reserved.

audience and calls out, "High Evolutionary . . . Why have you abandoned me?!"[28] The Hulk had been helping Adam in the preceding issues, so the Man-Beast captures him and, when he has transformed back into Bruce Banner, forces him to watch the crucifixion from the front row. Banner becomes incensed that they are killing an innocent man and transforms back into the Hulk. He breaks free and gets to Adam, but it is too late. Adam has already died and his body has reverted into a cocoon. Not sure what to do, the Hulk grabs the cocoon and leaps away. He meets up with Adam's followers at a cavern, where the Hulk lays down the cocoon. A powerful full-page illustration by Trimpe shows the Hulk dropping to his knees in prayer and mourning as a shaft of sunlight falls on the cocoon. Later in the issue, the Hulk battles the Man-Beast and his minions and gains the upper hand. He holds the Man-Beast over his head and gets ready to throw him down, saying, "Shut up, Man-Beast! Hulk will smash others after he kills you!"[29] Suddenly a voice cries out, "Stop, Hulk! I will have no killing in my name!" The Hulk says, "Huh, who orders Hulk?"[30] It is Warlock, raised from the dead, having emerged from the cocoon. He replies, "I order no one, Hulk. For my friendship and help, both freely given, must be freely accepted!"[31]

Adam's followers want him to stay, but he says, "I have changed. I see things I did not see before. I see other worlds where the Man-Beast has not been recognized and exposed. I must go to those worlds and do as I have done here. I will think of you often, my friends, and for all eternity. And, as you likewise think of me, I will be among you."[32] As Adam leaves he says, "For all living things are kindred to one another no matter their outward form. In helping one, we help all. Remember that always, my friends. If you do I shall never leave you."[33] After Adam leaves, for the first time in a long time, the Hulk is strangely at peace with himself.

Both literary critics and film critics often use the term "Savior figure" or "Christ figure" to describe a character who sacrifices himself or herself to save others or a character who demonstrates one or more of the characteristics of Jesus Christ. The parallels to the life of Jesus Christ are rarely as obvious as they are in the story of Adam Warlock, though sometimes authors or movie directors give a wink to the audience to let them know that a comparison is being made. In the classic science fiction film *The Day the Earth Stood Still* (1951), for example, the character from another planet who offers the world peace but is killed and resurrected from the dead takes on the name "Mr. Carpenter." In a climactic scene in the film *The Truman Show* (1998), the "True Man" is filmed in a way that makes him appear to be walking on water. In the film *The Green Mile* (1999), the man who sacrificially gives of himself to heal others is named John Coffey, sharing the initials J. C. with Jesus Christ. To say that a character is a Christ figure is not to say that they are exactly like Christ or as good as Christ. As a matter of fact, Christ figures often are the most effective when, at first blush, the character seems very different from Jesus Christ, such as Lucas Jackson in the film *Cool Hand Luke* (1967) or R. P. McMurphy in *One Flew Over the Cuckoo's Nest* (1975). These characters give us a different perspective on the life of Christ and motivate us to reevaluate what Jesus was like and what his life was all about.

While the story of Adam Warlock was an interesting attempt to bring a Christ-like figure into the superhero genre, the experiment was not very successful in terms of sales or critical acclaim. Perhaps this was because the story was more an allegory of the life of Christ than a tale about a typical Christ figure. The story covers some of the major plot points of the story of Christ in the gospels but does not evoke many new insights. There were a few interesting aspects to the story, such as the tensions that sometimes existed between Adam and his teenage disciples, but the story did not include many intriguing images that led to in-depth reflection on the nature of Christ or the nature of life in general.

Thomas has revealed that, if he had continued as the writer of the series, he would have ended the story differently. He writes, "I'd intended to have the character cruise through three years' worth of adventures, then be killed. My idea was that he'd come back to life when his four teenage friends, led by the 'Judas' character, Jason, mystically combined to recreate his gold-hued body."[34] This plot would have raised some very interesting themes for reflection. Thomas apparently had planned to have Jason flirt with betraying Adam and yet have Adam accept him and make him the leader of the disciples. If Adam could forgive Jason, how forgiving do we think our Christ is? Are we willing to accept people who have betrayed Christ in the past? Also, Thomas's plans for his story would have introduced the intriguing image of Adam's followers combining to form his body. This would have given a concrete illustration of the words, "Now you are the body of Christ and individual members of it" (1 Cor. 12:27). While Christians today might not literally combine bodies to form the body of one person, we can use the image to reflect on how we join with other Christians in unity to serve as the physical presence of Christ on earth.

Writer and artist Jim Starlin, whose later stories of Adam Warlock will be explored in more detail later, also told a story of Adam Warlock's death. In *Warlock* #11 (February 1976), after Adam realizes that he must die in order to save the universe, Adam enters a Time Probe that transports him forward in time to help bring about the death of his future self. In a bizarre scene, he meets his future self, who is lying on the ground in despair. As he looks at his future self, he wonders aloud how he could have become so distraught in just a few years. His future self replies that he has traveled mere months, not years, into the future. The present-day Adam says, "Months . . . I didn't realize it had happened such a short time ago!" The future Adam replies, "Short time?! You fool! It's been an eternity. During that time, everything I've ever cared for, or accomplished has fallen into ruin! Everyone I've ever loved now lies dead! My life has been a failure. I welcome its end!"[35] To make the scene even more bizarre, a few months later in *Avengers Annual* #7 (1977), readers see the death scene played out again, this time from the point of view of the Adam who is lying on the ground, as he realizes that he has lost everything. The scene is unsettling. Adam's depressed state does not jibe with our usual image of a triumphant superhero. More than that, it does not jibe with our image of Christ. We tend to want to think about Jesus as being someone who happily went to his death for our sakes and always kept a pleasant disposition. We sometimes tell children (unhelpfully) to always try to be pleasant. But a rereading of the gospels reveals that Jesus did not always look on the sunny side of life as he went to his own crucifixion. In Luke 22:42, he pleads to God, "Father, if you are willing, remove this cup from me; yet, not my will but yours be done." He suffered one of the most painful and humiliating deaths in the history of humankind. He was abandoned by most of his followers and friends and asks God why God had abandoned him. Starlin's death scene for his Christ figure helps us consider how comfortable we are with understanding our savior as a man of sorrows (Is. 53) and as someone who was not always upbeat or triumphant. It helps us consider the scourge of the crucifixion.

Other Marvel superheroes have served as savior figures or Christ figures as well. Jean Grey can be seen as a Christ figure. Although her life does not parallel that of Jesus in as many ways as Adam Warlock's did, her story does offer up some images that parallel aspects of the life of Christ. In the comic books and in the film *X2: X-Men United* (2003), Jean sacrifices her life to save her friends and then rises again as the Phoenix. In the early church and into the Middle Ages, Christians used the image of the mythical phoenix as a symbol of Christ. The phoenix is beautiful, sings a beautiful song, and after its death it rises to life from the ashes.

In the film *Spider-Man 2* (2004), Peter Parker struggles with his dual nature as a hero and an average person. In the end, he embraces his nature as a hero. As he is trying to stop a subway train, he is shown in cruciform, holding his arms out wide while in pain as though he is hanging on a cross. This is a common motif for directors who want to cue the audience to Christlike aspects of the character. Peter is willing to sacrifice himself to save the people. As he does so, he seemingly dies. The people gather around him, carry him, and lay him down as if for burial in a tomb, before he rises again.

By being aware of Christ figures, readers and viewers can engage some works of literature and some films on another level. These images of Christ can give us an opportunity to gain a new perspective on the story of Christ. Sometimes people of faith can be so close to the story and so set on our understanding of it that creative images of Christ can help us step back and reflect on the story of Christ in new ways.

The Universal Church of Truth?

After several years without a comic book series of his own, Adam Warlock was revived by writer-artist Jim Starlin. In *Strange Tales* #178 (February 1975), Adam meets a young woman who is being chased by agents of the Universal Church of Truth. She has crossed a dozen galaxies to find Adam and ask him for help. But just as she reaches him, some agents of the Church arrive and Adam fails to stop them from killing her. Adam never learns her name, but after the agents of the Church leave, he uses his soul gem to reanimate her temporarily, allowing her to tell her tale. She tells him of the tyrannical Universal Church of Truth, founded by a being known as the Magus who set himself up as a god over five thousand years earlier.

She says that if everyone lived by the Magus's teachings, the universe would be a place of peace. Unfortunately, those teachings only apply within the church. So, for example, the Universal Church of Truth teaches, "Love your neighbor, as long as he's a fellow Universalite!"[36] She adds that "to question Church doctrine or policy is heresy and may be punished by death!"[37] Over the previous five thousand years, the Universal Church of Truth has amassed great material and political power, enslaved thousands of worlds, and killed those who refused to accept its teachings. When she is finished with her tale, Adam is confronted by the Magus himself, a tyrannical ruler who looks oddly familiar. The horrible truth dawns on Adam. He says, "Magus . . . Magus is Latin for wise man . . . magician . . . Warlock!!!" The Magus replies, "That's right Adam, you and I are one and the same being!"[38] In the issues that follow, Adam Warlock learns that Magus is his future self who went back into time five thousand years and emerged from his cocoon with great power and only a tenuous grasp on his own sanity.[39] In that distant past, the Magus set himself up as a god and founded the Universal Church of Truth to worship and serve him.

In the issues that follow, Adam strives to overthrow the Universal Church of Truth's tyrannical rule. He eventually realizes that the only way to stop it is to make sure that it was never created in the first place, and the only way to make sure that the church was never founded is to make sure that he never turns into the Magus. Furthermore, Adam realizes that the only way to do that is to sacrifice his own life for the sake of the universe. He does so in *Warlock* #11 (February 1976) and in *Avengers Annual* #7 (1977), as described earlier, by ending his own life and absorbing himself into his own soul gem. There, within the world that exists within the gem, Adam finally finds peace and happiness with his friends and enemies who have died before him.

Starlin's story of Adam Warlock and the Universal Church of Truth falls into a subcategory of fictional tales that criticize aspects of Christianity by presenting fantastical versions of the church. Starlin has admitted to using the series to work through some issues he had with his own Catholic upbringing. He writes, "You know, it's no coincidence that the word 'catholic' means 'universal church.'"[40] When Christians watch films or read fictional stories that criticize faith, it is natural to become defensive or even angry that anyone would criticize what we hold dear. There is value, however, in listening to legitimate criticisms of some aspects of the church and of the life of faith. Starlin's church is so corrupt, however, that many readers would dismiss it as being something entirely different from their own church. It would perhaps be more interesting and more thought-provoking to readers if the leaders of the Universal Church of Truth were not quite as ruthless in their quest for power and if, for example, they truly wanted to be good but were misguided and used some corrupt means to try to achieve a noble end.

In the 2008 series *Guardians of the Galaxy*, a reborn Adam Warlock continues to be, in some ways, a Christlike figure. Writers seem to have difficulty topping a death and resurrection scene, and so Adam Warlock has now died and risen again a number of times. As a member of the new Guardians of the Galaxy, Adam has served as the moral and spiritual conscience of the team and has once again taken up his battle against a new version of the Universal Church of Truth. The church's creed is "Convert or Die." The prayers of the faithful are stored in belief batteries, which supply the church with immense power to fly the church's space ships and give incredible power to its superpowered cardinals. While the metaphor may be a bit strained, the image does reflect on the great power that religious institutions can wield in a culture.

While all people of faith should be sensitive to the harm that negative caricatures of the Roman Catholic Church and other religious groups can do, there is also value for all people of faith in recognizing the dangers inherent in religion. In the days following the terrorist attacks on September 11, 2001, some people of faith immediately responded that the brutal attacks had nothing to do with religion. They had a point. Many Muslim clerics who follow the Qur'an's teachings of peace explained that such acts were not in keeping with the teachings of Islam, and many religious scholars from other faiths agreed. Still, several scholars and clergy interviewed for the excellent *Frontline* documentary "Faith and Doubt at Ground Zero" argued that it was also important to acknowledge that religion has a shadow side to it, and the potential harm that shadow side can do. Monsignor Lorenzo Albacete, professor of theology at St. Joseph's Seminary in New York, recalled his thoughts when he saw the Twin Towers in flames:

> From the first moment I looked into that horror on September 11, into that fireball, into that explosion of horror, I knew it. I knew it before anything was said about those who did it or why. I recognized an old companion. I recognized religion. . . . The same passion that motivates religious people to do great things is the same one that that day brought all that destruction. When they said that the people who did it did it in the name of God, I wasn't in the slightest bit surprised. It only confirmed what I knew. I recognized it.[42]

Rabbi Brad Hirschfield, an Orthodox rabbi and vice president of the National Jewish Center for Learning and Leadership in New York City, shared similar reflections. He said, "Look, it's very simple for me. There's no dodging this. This was done in the name of religion, and I care deeply about religion. It's amazing how good [it] is at mobilizing people to do awful, murderous things."[41] He went on to talk about the evil things that have been done in the name of all major religions, including his own. He explained,

> Anyone who loves religious experience, including me, better begin to own [that] there is a serious shadow side to this thing, because it motivates. It mobilizes and it creates big ways of thinking and understanding the world. It creates remarkable cover, because it can divide the world up—who's good and who's bad, who's right and who's wrong; and as long as I'm on the right side, I can do no evil. Right?[43]

Khaled Abou el-Fadl, a Muslim who is a professor at the University of California at Los Angeles and one of the leading thinkers on Islamic law in the United States, pointed out that many atrocities have also been committed by groups that hold to atheistic and nationalistic ideologies. In his opinion, the response to wrongdoing committed in the name of one's own religion is to make sure that we are doing what we can to counteract it and to live out what we believe to be the best tenets of our faith. For him, the response was very personal:

> My son is going to ask me, "How could this have happened in the name of the religion you follow?" How can I justify, not just to neighbors and friends, but how can I justify to my son that this happened in the name of the faith that [I am] committed to? . . . In order to be able to respect myself before my son, I must be able to say, "Here is what I've done." . . . Otherwise, I really don't think you can hold your head high and have a sense of dignity about yourself if you can't clearly confront the fact that this remarkable amount of ugliness was committed in the name of the faith that you believe in.[44]

Many of those interviewed for the documentary talked about the importance of embracing mystery and avoiding absolutism. They talked about religious passions that can lead people to deny the humanity and worth of others who do not believe as they do.[45]

While most of us are not tempted to kill others in the name of our faith, we need to be careful that we are not justifying pride, selfishness, or cruelty to others behind the cover of our faith. When we start to believe that we are the only ones who know the truth, we may start to attack others who do not believe as we believe. Faith, however, is not about the arrogant desire to be the ones with all the answers but rather the acknowledgement that there are some things, indeed there is Some One, who is beyond our understanding. As 1 Corinthians 13:9 puts it, "For we know only in part," and 1 Corinthians 13:12 continues, "For now we see in a mirror, dimly, but then we will see face to face. Now I know only in part; then I will know fully, even as I have been fully known." The final verse of the chapter, 1 Corinthians 13:13, concludes, "And now faith, hope, and love abide, these three; and the greatest of these is love." To the casual reader, verse 13 may not seem to follow from verse 12, but acknowledging that we know only in part can help us be more humble and more loving to others who disagree with us. When we are tempted to go on crusades against others, we can ask ourselves whether we are truly being faithful to our highest ideal, that of love.

The Guardians of the Galaxy: Changing the Future, Leaving a Legacy

In *Marvel Superheroes* #18 (January 1969), writer Arnold Drake and artist Gene Colan introduced readers to an unlikely group of heroes who would come to be known as the Guardians of the Galaxy. Written in 1969, during the time of the first lunar space landings, their story imagined that twenty long years into the future, in 1988, humankind would be ready to put an astronaut into suspended animation and have him fly in a rocket ship for a thousand years until he reached a world in the Alpha Centauri solar system. When that astronaut, Vance Astro, arrived in the Alpha Centauri system, he woke up to discover, to his chagrin, that two hundred years after he was put into his deep sleep, humankind had discovered the secret of flying faster than the speed of light and were already there and had met the native people. They were unable to interrupt his sleep, so when he arrived and woke up he was greeted as a hero. Vance, however, was not pleased. Everyone he had ever known in his former life was now dead, and he felt that his life and his sacrifice had been wasted.

Back in Earth's own solar system, humans had been genetically engineered to survive on various planets. Those born and living on Jupiter, for example, were built strong and stocky to survive Jupiter's gravity, while those living on Pluto had been engineered to have a hard crystal skin to survive the planet's cold, harsh environment. There is some evidence of prejudice and tensions between these races, but when the reptilian alien race known as the Badoon takes over the Solar System, Vance Astro joins his friend Yondu, a blue-skinned native of Alpha Centauri; Martinex, the last free person from Pluto; and Charlie-27, a strong Jovian militiaman, as the last free men in the solar system. The four survivors band together and pledge to fight for Earth's freedom. As the story ends, Vance Astro leads them in a chorus from the civil rights movement of Earth's past, and together they sing "Earth Shall Overcome . . . some day."[46]

After this story, the Guardians of the Galaxy did not appear again until the mid-1970s, when they had guest appearances in several comic books. In *Giant-Size Defenders* #5 (July 1975), they travel back in time from the thirty-first century to 1975 and try to take action to change the future and stop the Badoon invasion before it begins. In *Defenders* #26 (August 1975), Vance even has a chance encounter with himself as a boy. The Defenders soon discover that Vance's presence as two different people at the same moment in time is wreaking havoc on the world's weather. The Guardians of the Galaxy must leave 1975 before they have the opportunity to change their future. The Defenders travel with them into the future, however, and in *Defenders* #29 (November 1975), they help the Guardians liberate the people of Earth. In *Marvel Presents* #3–12 (February 1976–August 1977), writers Steve Gerber and Roger Stern had the Guardians meet the enigmatic Starhawk and travel into outer space to combat threats to their galaxy.

Years later, in *Marvel Two-in-One* #69 (July 1980), Vance Astro once again travels back into time and speaks to his younger self. This time, however, he is able to change the future. Vance talks to his younger self about what the people of Earth need to do differently and talks the younger Vance out of his plans to become an astronaut. As readers of Marvel Comics know, this throws off the timeline of the entire universe. Vance, however, is pleased that, at least in some timeline, his future self will not have to endure what he has endured. While Vance's Guardians of the Galaxy still exist in an alternate future, they no longer exist in young Vance's future. As a result of the conversation, the younger Vance does not grow up to be an astronaut but becomes a superhero instead. He takes the name Marvel Boy and joins a group of young heroes known as the New Warriors. Later he takes on the name Justice and joins the Avengers.

While the Guardians of the Galaxy's earlier stories focused on time travel and alternate futures, writer and artist Jim Valentino's revival of the group in the 1990s focused on the legacies that heroes leave behind. In some cases this legacy is a good one. The Guardians discover that Captain America's long-lost shield has become a legendary symbol of liberty and freedom throughout the galaxy. The series' first story line is a quest to discover that shield and it culminates in *Guardians of the Galaxy* #6 (November 1990), with Vance Astro finding and claiming the shield for their struggle for liberty. Because of the way he lived his life, Captain America's legacy is one of which he would be proud. In other cases the legacies left behind are unintentionally negative. Tony Stark did much good in his life as Iron Man, but his work also left behind many potentially harmful consequences. In *Guardians of the Galaxy* #2 (July 1990), the Guardians must battle a warrior race that calls themselves the Stark. They are a warrior race that discovered some of Tony Stark's armor and weaponry and came to worship him. They polluted their own planet with factories built to produce more and more weapons based on Stark's designs and then used them to terrorize the universe.[47] This is not the legacy that Tony Stark would have been proud to leave behind, but it is one that his work made possible.

The current incarnation of the group, introduced in *Guardians of the Galaxy* vol. 2, #1 (May 2008), features another team of cosmic heroes that includes Star-Lord, Adam Warlock, Drax the Destroyer, Gamora, Captain Marvel's daughter Phyla-Vell (who is the new Quasar), Rocket Rackoon, Groot, and Mantis. The series is set in Marvel's present day. After the universe is threatened, first by a hoard of insectoid military forces from the Negative Zone known as the Annihilation Wave and then by a technologically advanced race known as the Phalanx, the heroes decide that they must band together to ward off threats to the universe in a pre-emptive manner.[48] They are willing to risk their lives to preserve the future of the universe. The series is in many ways a war book set in outer space, with mature content and some ridiculously revealing outfits, and is rated Teen Plus. The series does, however, raise the concept of securing a future by anticipating problems and working to avert them, rather than just taking a "wait and see" approach.

People of faith are time travelers in some regards. We journey into the ancient past in search of wisdom for how to live our lives today. At our best, we also have hope and vision for what the world can become in the future. People of faith can offer prophetic warnings of what the world might become if we do not change direction from some of the paths we are on. We do not need to have visitors from the future to tell us that if we do not get to work on issues such as poverty, the AIDS epidemic, and global warming, that the Earth of the future will be pretty grim in some ways. On a more local level, we do not need a time machine to tell us that there will be more people dying of cancer tomorrow if we do not focus more on finding a cure today. We already know that there will be more people sleeping on the streets of the nearest city tomorrow night if we do not take action to prevent homelessness and help fund shelters today. We already know the tragedies that possible futures hold, and knowing them can help motivate us to create alternate futures of our own. Whatever way we choose to change the world, if we work to make the future a better place, then that is a legacy of which we can be proud.

Captain Marvel: Facing Death

Marvel's publisher Martin Goodman had always been bothered that Fawcett Comics, a rival company, introduced a hero named Captain Marvel months after he entered the comics field with *Marvel Comics* #1 (October 1939). In *Whiz Comics* #2 (February 1940), a young reporter named Billy Batson turned into the superpowered Captain Marvel whenever he uttered the word "Shazam." This Captain Marvel was one of the most popular heroes of the 1940s. DC Comics later sued Fawcett Comics over the character, claiming that he was too similar to their hero Superman. As a result, by 1967, no comic book with a character named Captain Marvel had been published for some time, and Goodman wanted Marvel Comics to stake a claim to the name. So he instructed Stan Lee to come up with Marvel's own Captain Marvel.

Lee and artist Gene Colan quickly introduced a new Captain Marvel in *Marvel Superheroes* #12 (December 1967). In his earliest adventures, this Captain Marvel was a Kree soldier from outer space sent on a mission to observe Earth. In *Captain Marvel* #16 (September 1969), the character went through a significant change. Instead of being a soldier trained in the strategies of war, he became more interested in concepts such as peace and love. He traded in his green and white military uniform for a new red, blue, and gold costume. His existence also became intertwined with a young teen rock star named Rick Jones. Captain Marvel and Rick had to take turns, with one of them living on Earth while the other was forced to live in a harrowing, limbo-like plane known as the Negative Zone. The two would trade places by hitting together the "Nega-Bands" that they wore on their wrists.

Jim Starlin took over as artist with *Captain Marvel* #25 (March 1973) and soon began both writing and drawing what have become recognized as the most creative and well-remembered issues of the series. In Starlin's stories, Captain Marvel is granted "cosmic awareness" and is appointed Protector of the Universe. As the planet-sized collective being known as Eon tells him, "You have lived and accepted the ways of the warrior! The Universe now needs not a warrior, but a protector! He who seeks to protect must first love . . . and there is no love in war!"[49] The issue ends with Captain Marvel literally battling his own inner demons and becoming cosmically aware. In *Captain Marvel* #30 (January 1974), Captain Marvel is no longer a self-righteous and headstrong warrior but a calm and cosmically aware agent of peace. Being a superhero comic book, however, this simply means that he is better able to focus and beat his enemies in hand-to-hand combat. In this way the character was similar to the Shaolin monk Kwai Chang Caine from the television series *Kung Fu* (1972–1975), which aired during the same time period. Fans admired him as a man of peace but loved to watch him beat up his enemies in fight scenes.

Captain Marvel was never one of Marvel's most popular titles, and for all the hero's cosmic battles, he is perhaps best remembered for the way he died. In 1982, Marvel had Starlin return to write and draw the character one last time for the first in a deluxe series of Marvel graphic novels. The story was titled "The Death of Captain Marvel" (1982). What struck many readers most about the story was the cause of Captain Marvel's death. He does not die a hero's death in some epic battle. Instead, he discovers that he is not feeling well and goes home to get a medical scan. His friend Mentor gives him the bad news. He says, "It's a terrible disease. We, on Titan, call it the inner decay. You Kree have named it the Blackend. Earthmen call it cancer."[50] When Mentor asks if the Kree might have a cure, Captain Marvel responds, "No, war has always been the Kree Empire's chief preoccupation. They've never had the spare time or resources needed to find a cure for the Blackend. They're a lot like Earth in that respect."[51] Captain Marvel remains calm in public, but in private he expresses his anger. "Alien invaders, super-villains, monsters, mutants. They all tried. But none of them could kill me. I fought them all and I won! I survived! Who would have thought that, in the end, it'd be my own body that would turn on me and do me in."[52]

Starlin has said, "Writing 'The Death of Captain Marvel' was working out my own father's death. They paid me to do gestalt therapy on myself."[53] The story explores several aspects of death and grief. The young man Rick Jones, who is now free from the Negative Zone and able to live separately from Captain Marvel, nonetheless goes through the stages of grief that dying patients often go through, according to Elisabeth Kübler-Ross. These include denial (this can't really be happening to me), anger (why is this happening to me), bargaining (I promise I'll be a better person if . . .), depression (I just can't do this anymore), and finally acceptance (I accept what is happening to me).[54] Rick is particularly angry with the Marvel heroes who have medical and scientific background, such as Reed Richards, Thor, Tony Stark, the Black Panther, and others. He calls them together and chides them for putting so much effort into their battles and developing new weapons and so little time and energy into finding a cure for cancer. He asks them to find a cure right away. The heroes protest, saying that much is being done and that cancer is a complex disease. After Rick storms out of the room, however, they all acknowledge that Rick is right. While each of them had already been secretly working to find a cure since they heard the news about Captain Marvel, they all know that they could have been doing more sooner. In a very realistic scene, Rick also expresses his anger at the patient, Captain Marvel, for not fighting the disease more or doing something, somehow, to get better. The scene reflects a common phenomenon in which loved ones sometimes get angry at the person who is dying. It is not a logical response, but it is a common one.

The story also has several scenes that poignantly illustrate how different people face death in different ways. When Captain Marvel's friends Spider-Man and the Thing go in to see him, thin and sickly on his death bed, they have very different reactions. The Thing jokes about old times. Spider-Man, however, is overcome with emotion and has to excuse himself from the room. The Thing tries to stop him, but Captain Marvel says, "Ben, let him go. Death touches us all in different ways."[55] The impending death is perhaps hardest on Rick Jones, who enters the room and finally stops being in denial, stops being angry, stops trying to negotiate a cure, and just cries and hugs Captain Marvel. Captain Marvel himself reflects on the way that Adam Warlock died to save the universe, but says, "When death came for him, he welcomed it as a friend. I'll not do so. I've enjoyed this life. It's had its bad moments but it's had far more good moments. I'm going to miss it."[56] Though Captain Marvel was not distraught, he did affirm that life was precious. In so doing, he acknowledged that death was indeed an enemy (cf. 1 Cor. 15:26) and did not try to pretend that he was happy that he was dying.

For most people, the death of a loved one is one of the most difficult things that life brings. Belief in eternal life does not mean that people of faith do not mourn the death of people they love, simply that they do "not grieve as others do who have no hope" (1 Thess. 4:13). Believing in eternal life does not mean that we are not sorry about death, but simply that we have hope that God is there, even beyond the limits of this life. The New Testament assures its readers that "neither death, nor life, nor angels, nor rulers, nor things present, nor things to come, nor powers, nor height, nor depth, nor anything else in all creation, will be able to separate us from the love of God in Christ Jesus our Lord" (Rom. 8:38–39).

In the end, Captain Marvel's death was not due to some grand gesture of heroic sacrifice in battle, such as taking a ray blast to save another or fighting off a whole armada of space ships. Instead, he died in a hospital bed surrounded by friends. His death was heroic because of the way he lived. The way he lived touched others and left a positive legacy behind.

As a pastor I have had the honor of visiting people when they were in the hospital or at a hospice at the end of their lives, often when they were literally on their death beds. The patients I met had a strong desire to talk and to reflect on what made their lives meaningful. Since others seemed uncomfortable with such conversations, I had the great privilege of listening to their stories. One lesson that these people taught me was that they did not regard the big, flashy events for which people receive honors and public recognition as the most important accomplishments in their lives. More often it was the quiet things they did to help others. They talked about the times they did the hard work of being a good spouse by swallowing their pride and asking for forgiveness. They talked about the evenings and weekends they spent leading a scouting troop instead of going to the mall. They talked about the times they worked for justice in the world, worked to feed the hungry, and got involved in a cause that mattered. They talked about when they volunteered to be a Sunday school teacher and took it seriously, taking time early in the week to prepare a lesson. These were the acts in their lives that were heroic (to use my word, not theirs).

These men and women also provided me with a word of caution. They talked to me about how easy it is to get caught in the rut of just living our lives by going through the motions, doing our jobs during the week, watching television in the evenings, and relaxing on the weekends, without stopping to reflect on whether or not we are living our lives in a meaningful way. As Psalms 90:1–10 warns us, our life here is brief. From their perspective, at the very end of their lives, these men and women recognized what was truly important.

Conclusion

One of the most influential photographs ever taken is a photograph of planet Earth rising over the moon. The photograph is known as "Earthrise" and it was taken by astronaut William Anders during the Apollo 8 mission, the first manned voyage to orbit the moon. The photograph has helped us understand that all Earth's inhabitants share the same small, fragile globe that is floating through space. Sometimes we need to travel into space, even if we are just traveling there through fictional tales, in order to gain a fresh view of our lives on Earth. Through the alien eyes of the Silver Surfer we can reflect on how flawed we humans can be yet recognize our great potential as well. Through the other-worldly savior Adam Warlock we are challenged to take another look at the gospel story and the church. Through the time-traveling adventures of the Guardians of the Galaxy, we can reflect on the ways in which our actions today have consequences for generations to come. Through the life and death of Captain Marvel, we can reflect on the ways we choose to live out our lives and the ways we choose to face death. Sometimes the best way to see something clearly is to take a look at it from outer space.

Questions for Reflection

- When is the last time that you read or heard a news story and you took a step back, took an outsider's view, and were shocked at how crazy the world is? When were you last shocked at the cruelty or inhumanity of humankind?
- When was the last time you read or heard a news story that impressed you with humankind's potential to do good and gracious things?
- When was the last time you recognized a Christ figure or savior image in fiction or film? How was the character similar to Christ? How was the character different from Jesus Christ?
- What concerns you the most about Earth's future? What can you do today to make Earth a better place in the future?
- What decisions are you making at this time that will affect your future? What decisions are you making that will affect the future of others? What actions are you taking to affect Earth's future in a positive way?
- If you were to die today, what would be your legacy? Looking back over your life, what difference would you have made in the world and how? What sorts of things do you wish you had done more of? What are some steps you could take in the next couple of weeks to do more of those sorts of things?
- Has someone close to you died? What were the most important things that they left behind?
- What are the different ways you have seen people deal with death and with grieving? Do you know anyone who is grieving right now? How might you help that person?
- Are there any other thoughts or reflections that you have had on these stories or other outer-space adventures?

Afterword

A Call to Heroic Living

This book places the stories of Marvel superheroes, stories that have become a significant part of our popular culture, into dialogue with our faith. It has explored the ways in which Marvel superheroes live out their heroic lives and how their stories might be used to help us reflect on how we are living out our own lives of faith.

As discussed throughout this book, many people of faith are properly concerned about certain aspects of the stories of superheroes. Stories of superheroes tend to divide the world between good guys and bad guys, while our faith teaches us that all of us are sinners and that everyone can be redeemed. Stories of superheroes can also reinforce the view that we solve our problems primarily by defeating or destroying our enemies and they place an emphasis on redemption through violence. Our faith, on the other hand, calls us to work for reconciliation with others and teaches us that redemption is found not through acts of violence, but through acts of love and forgiveness. Stories of superheroes can also leave readers and viewers with the impression that when we face problems the only solution is to wait passively for a hero to come in from outside our community and save the day. Our faith, however, teaches us that we must take the initiative and work together to make our community and our world a better place.

While people of faith should be aware of these concerns, I believe that the heroes of Marvel Comics can also inspire us to good deeds. As they were created and developed by Stan Lee, Jack Kirby, and others, the stories of Marvel superheroes went against the grain of many other superhero stories. They dealt with more realistic issues and obstacles than most other stories. Their heroes struggled to do what is right and struggled with many of the same concerns noted here about the task of being a superhero. Because of this, I believe there are some aspects of these stories that can serve to inspire us to positive actions.

In the film *Spider-Man* (2002), the Green Goblin attacks Spider-Man while he is trying to save Mary Jane and a group of children. A group of New Yorkers watching from a bridge start throwing things at the Goblin, distracting him long enough that Spider-Man is able to rescue both Mary Jane and the children. Instead of just remaining spectators, watching the superhero try to save the day, they were inspired to take action themselves. The same is true for us. We do not have to go through life as mere spectators of the actions of heroes or the events unfolding around us. We can take action ourselves.

While we will never face a Green Goblin riding on a glider to terrorize our community or a Doctor Doom threatening to take over the world, the world still needs heroes. The needs of the real world cry out for our attention and active involvement. The world is confronted with the problems of hunger, homelessness, disease, loneliness, unjust laws, poverty, and natural disasters, and we can respond. As a religious educator, I am concerned that people of faith spend a great deal of time thinking about their faith but not enough time actually living it out in concrete ways. We teach and learn many lessons that talk about the sorts of things we should be doing, but we do not spend enough time actually training ourselves to do those things or developing concrete ways to carry out those ministries together.

Besides being a reflection on the stories of Marvel superheroes, this book is also a call to action. We can all find ways to join together and use our powers and gifts to accomplish great things. Many churches have ministries that can put our gifts and talents to very good use in many different ways. There are also many great community organizations that can use our gifts, our talents, and our passion in ways that help and heal others. Habitat for Humanity, Big Brothers Big Sisters, Amnesty International, Second Harvest, Compassion International, the Boys and Girls Club of America, and many other community organizations can use volunteers and donations to help carry out their good work in the United States and around the world. The U.S. government Web site http://www.serve.gov and the related Web site http://www.AllforGood.org allow people to choose an issue that they care about, such as hunger, health care, or mentoring, and state their location in order to see information on nonprofit groups in their own community that can use volunteers to address the issues they care about.

When I was about eight years old, my best friend's older brother tried to convince me that Marvel heroes were based on real people. He said that the Hulk was based on a real-life soldier who painted himself green and, though he was not as strong as the Hulk in the comic books, he could break a tank with his bare hands. He said that Spider-Man was based on a policeman in New York City who used acrobatic moves to catch criminals and who had such a strong grip that he could climb up the sides of buildings. He didn't fool me for a second. At that age, I read my Marvel comics so thoroughly that I even read the small print that was on the bottom of the front page of every issue. There it said, in very small letters, "No similarity between any of the names, characters, persons and/or institutions in this magazine with those of any living or dead person or institution is intended, and any such similarity which may exist is purely coincidental." Even at that young age, I knew that Marvel superheroes did not exist in the real world.

While the superheroes of Marvel Comics are not real, I will let you in on a secret. Heroes really do exist in the real world. I know. I have met them.

I have met women and men, children and teenagers who were fantastic. These people found ways to use the gifts and abilities God had given them, not for personal gain but to help others. I have seen them love their neighbors and even step outside their comfort zones to show love to strangers and compassion toward their enemies. I have seen amazing people who, even when times were tough, kept going and carried out their responsibility to help others. I have known incredible people who allowed their anger at injustice and suffering to motivate them to action, and others who took steps to control their anger so that it was not expressed in harmful ways. I have been part of churches and seminary communities that made uncanny efforts to be diverse and inclusive communities that accepted people for who they were. I have known people who had an iron-clad commitment to be good stewards of what God had given them, using their money, their talents, their possessions, and the body God had given them to do good work and support good works. I have known mighty people who humbly acknowledged that they were not God yet did not place limits on the great things God could do through them. I have worked with people who loved their country, and at the same time worked hard through social and political action to help their country live up to its best ideals. I have seen teams of people coordinate their gifts and talents to accomplish more than any one of them could on their own. I have been inspired by people who seemed as though they were without fear and had the courage to show love and mercy to those who had wronged them rather than seeking revenge. I have been inspired by the wisdom of people who, at the end of their lives, had the long-range perspective they needed to see what was truly important about our lives. These people inspired me to think about what I was doing with my life and what legacy I was leaving behind.

We are real people and we face real obstacles in our lives. We do not wear masks and we do not have super powers. We are not perfect, but with God's help we can all be heroes. We can all use the gifts, talents, and resources that God has given us and do our best to live heroic lives in the real world.

Notes

Prelude

1. "2008 National Medal of Arts: Stan Lee," National Endowment for the Arts, accessed March 8, 2009, http://www.nea.gov/news/news08/medals/Lee.html.

2. See Stan Lee, *Stan's Soapbox: The Collection* (New York: Marvel, 2008).

3. In the early days of their marriage, Stan and Joan Lee apparently were the victims of religious discrimination for having a "mixed marriage." See Stan Lee and George Mair, *Excelsior! The Amazing Life of Stan Lee* (New York: Simon & Schuster, 2002), 75.

4. Stan Lee, "God Woke: A Poem," in *Stan Lee: Conversations*, ed. Jeff McLaughlin (Jackson: Univ. Press of Mississippi, 2007), 219–26.

5. Ibid., 225–26.

6. It is worth noting that Lee's primary partner in creating Marvel's new wave of heroes, artist and co-plotter Jack Kirby, explored a similar theme in the illustrations included in *The Kirby Portfolio*. In one illustration titled "God's Vision of the World," a large, muscular male image of God looks sorrowfully toward an earth comprised of images of famine, war, pornography, and starving children, all of which were concerns of Kirby's. The next plate is titled "God Turns His Back on the World" and shows God turning his back on people who angrily cry out to God, demanding God's help from the spiritually barren world they have created. The message, as in Lee's poem, seems to be that humankind should take responsibility for the way it is destroying the earth rather than just appealing to God to free them from it. See Jack Kirby, *The Kirby Portfolio* (Milwaukie, Oreg.: Dark Horse Comics, 1996).

7. Upon rereading many Silver Surfer comic books and graphic novels since this interview, I recognize that many of them depict the Silver Surfer selflessly sacrificing himself in various ways in order to save humankind. So viewing the Silver Surfer as a figure of Christ in this way is not inappropriate.

Introduction

1. Adamantium is a fictional, virtually indestructible metal alloy.

2. In the documentary "Sentinel of the Spaceways: Comic Book Origins of the Silver Surfer," Twentieth Century Fox Home Entertainment, LCC, 2007, available on the second disc of *Fantastic 4: Rise of the Silver Surfer* (2007) 2-Disc DVD.

3. Walter Wink, *The Powers That Be: Theology for the New Millenium* (New York: Galilee Doubleday, 1998), 42.

4. See, for example, Rodrigue Tremblay, "The Manichaeism of Osama bin Laden and George W. Bush," *Freethought Today* 20, no. 2 (2003): 6–7.

5. Cf. Russell W. Dalton, *Faith Journey through Fantasy Lands: A Christian Dialogue with Harry Potter, Star Wars, and The Lord of the Rings* (Minneapolis: Augsburg, 2003), 80–81, 108.

6. John Shelton Lawrence and Robert Jewett, *The Myth of the American Superhero* (Grand Rapids, Mich.: Eerdmans, 2002).

7. The book does not reveal great familiarity with superheroes. It refers to "Spiderman" rather than "Spider-Man," a cardinal sin among comic book fans, and talks about "episodes" rather than "issues" of the comics.

8. Lawrence and Jewett, *Myth of the American Superhero*, 6.

9. Ibid., 7.

10. Ibid., 14.

11. Mark Evanier, *Kirby: King of Comics* (New York: Abrams, 2008), 56.

12. It is a sad part of the heritage of comic books that they, like most popular visual media of the time, portrayed many ethnic groups, even American ones, as offensive racial stereotypes. African Americans in particular were drawn and written of in very demeaning and troubling ways.

13. Fredric Wertham, *Seduction of the Innocent* (New York: Reinhart, 1954), 192, 234–35.

14. Les Daniels, *Marvel: Five Fabulous Decades of the World's Greatest Comics* (New York: Abrams, 1991), 84.

15. Ibid., 84.

16. For more on Kirby's genius see the excellent documentary "Jack Kirby, Storyteller," on the *Fantastic Four* extended edition DVD, directed by Tim Story (Los Angeles: Twentieth Century Fox, 2005) and the book by his former assistant, comic book writer and historian Mark Evanier, *Kirby: King of Comics*.

17. In *Fantastic Four* #511 (May 2004), as a tribute to Kirby, Mark Waid and Mike Wieringo had the Fantastic Four meet God. In the story, in order to relate to them, God appears in the form of one of their creators, Jack Kirby. During the visit he receives a call from his "collaborator" Stan Lee.

18. As discussed in later chapters, there were limits to the diversity of the early Marvel heroes. In the early 1960s, all of the Marvel superheroes were white and most of them were male.

19. Daniels, *Marvel*, 85.

20. Ibid., 85.

21. Ibid., 85.

22. Ibid., 84–85.

23. Although accounts vary, Jack Kirby may also have played some part in the creation of Spider-Man.

24. Stan Lee, introduction to *Marvel Masterworks: The Amazing Spider-Man Nos. 1-10 and Amazing Fantasy No. 15* (New York: Marvel Comics, 1987), n.p.

25. See Ronin Ro, *Tales to Astonish: Jack Kirby, Stan Lee, and the American Comic Book Revolution* (New York: Bloomsbury, 2004), 163.

26. "Jack Kirby, Storyteller," *Fantastic Four* DVD, extended edition (2005).

27. Stan Lee, "Stan's Soapbox," *Marvel Comics* (April 1972).

28. Ronin Ro, *Tales to Astonish*, 244.

29. Marvel Comics' current rating system for comic books includes "All Ages," "A" for books appropriate for ages nine and older, "Teen+" for ages thirteen and older, "Parental Advisory" for books deemed appropriate for most readers age fifteen and older, and "MAX: Explicit Content," sold only to customers eighteen years and older.

30. *X-Men* #9 (January 1965): 20.

31. *New X-Men* #46 (January 2008): 23.

32. The nature of film is discussed in some depth in this book's chapter on Daredevil.

33. Chris Claremont, phone interview with the author, 17 November 2008.

34. Herb Trimpe, phone interview with the author, 20 November 2008.

35. Ibid.

36. Kurt Busiek, e-mail interview with the author, 22 December 2008.

Chapter 1

1. *Fantastic Four* #1 (November 1961): 9.

2. Ibid., 13. Note that it was not out of desire for high drama that Stan Lee ended every sentence with an exclamation point. The limited printing capabilities and pulp paper used in the production of comics in those days meant that simple periods would often disappear when printed and therefore were not used. Also, readers today might be surprised to note that Lee and Kirby took only five pages to tell this origin story and establish the characters' distinct personalities. The same sort of plot often takes three or four full issues to tell in comics today.

3. *Fantastic Four* #507 (2004).

4. See *Fantastic Four* #18 (September 1963) and #32 (November 1964).

5. *The Last Fantastic Four Story: World's End* (June, 2007).

6. *Fantastic Four* #72 (March 1968): 13.

7. See John Shelton Lawrence and Robert Jewett, *The Myth of the American Superhero* (Grand Rapids, Mich.: Eerdmans, 2002), 6.

8. In a memorable cameo appearance, even Stan Lee and Jack Kirby showed up to the ceremony, but the agents of S.H.I.E.L.D. guarding the door would not let them in because they did not have an invitation. This scene is recreated in the film *Fantastic Four: The Rise of the Silver Surfer* (2007), with Stan Lee unable to get into the ceremony, though sadly Jack Kirby had passed away in 1994 and so was not present to take part.

9. Jon B. Cooke, "From This Day Forward: How Marriage Changes Everything (Even for the FF)," in *The Fantastic Four Omnibus*, vol. 2 (New York: Marvel, 2007).

10. Ibid.

11. This is a recurring motif in the Fantastic Four's adventures. See, for example, *Fantastic Four* #40 (July 1965) and #79 (October 1968).

12. *Fantastic 4: Rise of the Silver Surfer*, directed by Tim Story (Los Angeles: Twentieth Century Fox, 2007), DVD.

13. Ibid.

14. See writer Paul Jenkins and artist Jae Lee's *Inhumans*, vol. 2, #1–12 (1998–99), which explores aspects of the Inhumans' culture that are very foreign to our own.

15. Jack Kirby was plotting much of the story at this point and, according to Mark Evanier, Kirby's inspirations for the story included the public's fear of aliens from outer space and the more earth-bound threat of corporations that take over companies and suck them dry. This latter threat was on Kirby's mind as rumors swirled that publisher Martin Goodman was looking to sell Marvel to a large corporation. Mark Evanier, "Wonders Aplenty," in *The Fantastic Four Omnibus*, vol. 2 (New York: Marvel, 2007).

16. Ibid.

17. *Fantastic Four* #49 (April 1966): 4.

18. Ibid., 11.

19. *Fantastic Four* #50 (May 1966): 2.

20. Stan Lee, introduction to *Marvel Masterworks: Sgt. Fury and His Howling Commandos,* vol. 1 (New York: Marvel, 2006).

21. *Sgt. Fury and His Howling Commandos* #6 (March 1964): 23.

22. Stan Lee, introduction to *Marvel Masterworks.*

23. The naming of the Black Panther had no connection to the Black Panther Party founded by Huey P. Newton and Bobby Seal, which rose to national attention at about the same time. As a matter of fact, in *Fantastic Four* #119 (February 1972), in an apparent effort to distance the character from the group, Marvel briefly changed his name to the Black Leopard, with the character explaining that in the United States the name Black Panther had too many political connotations. His name was soon changed back to the Black Panther.

24. *Fantastic Four* #52 (July 1966): 2.

25. It seems that heroes in the Marvel Universe almost always fight when they first meet.

26. See, for example, *Fantastic Four* #53 (August 1966): 5–6.

27. The Black Panther and Storm were married in *Black Panther,* vol. 4, #18 (2005).

28. *Fantastic Four* #544–50 (2007).

29. This is according to comic book writer and historian Mark Evanier's April 14, 2009, comments on his site POV Online at http://www.povonline.com/alternate/Alternate06.htm.

30. Reginald Hudlin, "The Start of a Revolution," in *The Fantastic Four Omnibus,* vol. 2 (New York: Marvel, 2007).

31. Ibid.

32. Ibid.

33. See Warren Carter, *Matthew and the Margins: A Sociopolitical and Religious Reading* (Maryknoll, N.Y.: Orbis Books, 2000), 154.

34. Victor Paul Furnish, *The Love Command in the New Testament* (Nashville: Abingdon, 1972), 60, 202.

35. Stan Lee, *Stan's Soapbox: The Collection* (New York: Marvel, 2008), 8.

36. *Fantastic Four* #1 (November 1961): 22.

37. Ibid.

38. *Fantastic Four* #89 (August 1969): 14.

39. Ibid., 17.

40. Ibid., 18.

41. Ibid., 18.

42. *Fantastic Four* #87 (June 1969): 17.

43. Chris Claremont, phone interview with the author, 17 November 2008.

44. The Sub-Mariner appears in *Fantastic Four* #4 (May 1962), #6 (September 1962), #9 (December 1962), #14 (May 1963), *Fantastic Four Annual* #1 (1963), #27 (June 1964), and #33 (December 1964).

45. *Fantastic Four* #14 (May 1963): 22.

46. *Fantastic Four Annual* #1 (1963): 33.

47. *Fantastic Four* #51 (June 1966): 18.

48. Stan Lee, phone interview with the author, 3 March 2009.

49. Carter, *Matthew and the Margins,* 151.

50. Ibid., 151.

51. Ibid., 155.

52. Ibid., 155.

53. Stephen Charles Mott, *Biblical Ethics and Social Change* (New York: Oxford Univ. Press, 1982), 50.

54. Ibid.

55. Carter, *Matthew and the Margins,* 156.

Chapter 2

1. Stan Lee, *Origins of Marvel Comics* (New York: Simon & Schuster, 1974), 135.

2. Ibid., 135.

3. *Amazing Fantasy* #15 (August 1962): 1.

4. Ibid., 3.

5. In the comic books, it is science class honor student Peter Parker who invents web shooters to enhance his power. In the films, this power is organic, a result of the radioactive spider bite.

6. *Amazing Fantasy* #15 (August 1962): 8.

7. Ibid., 11.

8. Roy Thomas and Stan Lee, *Stan Lee's Amazing Marvel Universe* (New York: Sterling, 2006), 51.

9. *Amazing Fantasy* #15 (August 1962): 11.

10. Peter Sanderson, *Marvel Universe* (New York: Abrams, 1996), 79–80.

11. *Amazing Spider-Man* #1 (March 1963): 1.

12. This became a common theme for Marvel's superheroes. Many of them, including the X-Men, Silver Surfer, Hulk, and others, were mistrusted and feared by the public and even wanted by the police.

13. *Amazing Spider-Man* #1 (March 1963): 2.

14. Ibid., 11.

15. Ibid.

16. *Amazing Spider-Man* #7 (December 1963).

17. *Amazing Spider-Man* #12 (May 1964).

18. *Amazing Spider-Man* #13 (June 1964).

19. *Amazing Spider-Man* #39 (August 1966).

20. *Amazing Spider-Man* #43 (December 1966).

21. *Amazing Spider-Man* #44 (January 1967).

22. *Amazing Spider-Man* #48 (May 1967).

23. The script says that it is the George Washington Bridge, but it is clearly the Brooklyn Bridge pictured in the story.

24. *Amazing Spider-Man* (June 1973): 19.

25. For background on the decision to kill off Gwen Stacy, see John Romita, "Marvels Commentary," in *Marvels: 10th Anniversary Edition,* ed. Kurt Busiek and Alex Ross (New York: Marvel, 2004), 321; Les Daniels, *Marvel: Five Fabulous Decades of the World's Greatest Comics* (New York: Abrams, 1991), 208; and Thomas and Lee, *Stan Lee's Amazing Universe,* 171 and audio commentary 61.

26. Kurt Busiek, e-mail interview with the author, 22 December 2008.

27. *Amazing Spider-Man* #122 (July 1973): 11.

28. Ibid., 11.

29. Ibid., 17.

30. Ibid., 19.

31. *Amazing Spider-Man* #33 (February 1966): 4.

32. Ibid., 19.

33. Ibid., 20.

34. Ditko's commitment to Objectivism and the ways in which it influenced his work in comic books is detailed in Blake Bell, *Stranger and Stranger: The World of Steve Ditko* (Seattle: Fantagraphics Books, 2008).

35. Ayn Rand, *The Fountainhead,* 50th anniversary ed. (London: Penguin Books, 1996).

36. Ayn Rand, *Atlas Shrugged,* centennial ed. (New York: Signet Books, 1992).

37. It is interesting to note that the film *Spider-Man* (2002) puts an extreme version of this elitism into the mouth of the villainous Green Goblin. He says to Spider-Man, "Here's the real truth. There are eight million people in this city. And those teeming masses exist for the sole purpose of lifting the few exceptional people onto their shoulders." Spider-Man clearly disagrees.

38. See, for example, *Amazing Spider-Man* #31 (December 1965): 8–11, 13; #33 (February 1966): 17–18; #36 (May 1966): 6; #37 (June 1966): 5; and #38 (August 1966): 11.

39. *Amazing Spider-Man* #37 (June 1966): 5.

40. Bell, *Stranger and Stranger,* 96.

41. *Amazing Spider-Man* #18 (November 1964): 19.

42. Ibid., 22.

43. See Bell, *Stranger and Stranger,* 117–18.

44. Kurt Busiek, e-mail interview with the author, 22 December 2008.

45. *Amazing Spider-Man* #50 (July 1967): 7.

46. Thomas and Lee, *Stan Lee's Amazing Universe,* 142.

47. *Amazing Spider-Man* #50 (July 1967): 14.

48. Ibid., 18.

49. For another, slightly different, perspective on Peter's guilt, see B. J. Oropeza's essay, "Behold! The Hero Has Become Like One of Us: The Perfectly Imperfect Spider-Man," in *The Gospel According to Superheroes,* ed. B. J. Oropeza (New York: Peter Lang, 2005), 135–39.

50. *Amazing Spider-Man* #539 (2007).

51. Ibid.

52. Ibid.

Chapter 3

1. Stan Lee, *Origins of Marvel Comics* (New York: Simon & Schuster, 1974), 75.

2. *Incredible Hulk* #130 (August 1970): 10.

3. Ibid., 17.

4. Herb Trimpe, phone interview with the author, 20 November 2008.

5. Ibid.

6. Kathleen A. Farmer, *Who Knows What Is Good? A Commentary on Proverbs and Ecclesiastes* (Grand Rapids, Mich.: Eerdmans, 1991), 90.

7. Andrew D. Lester, *Anger: Discovering Your Spiritual Ally* (Louisville: Westminster John Knox Press, 2007), 6.

8. Ibid., 43. Italics in the original.

9. Ibid., 13.

10. Ibid., 61–78.

11. Ibid., 84–85.

12. Ibid.

13. Doris Moreland Jones, *God's Gift of Anger* (St. Louis: Chalice Press, 2005).

14. Carroll Saussy, *The Gift of Anger: A Call to Faithful Action* (Louisville, KY: Westminster John Knox Press, 1995).

15. Lester, *Anger*, 14–24.

16. Ibid., 116–19.

17. Ibid., 51.

18. Ibid., 59. Italics in the original.

Chapter 4

1. Stan Lee, *Son of Origins of Marvel Comics* (New York: Simon and Schuster, 1975), 13–14.

2. Stan Lee, introduction to *Marvel Masterworks: X-Men*, vol. 1 (New York: Marvel, 1987). This reprints *X-Men* #1–10.

3. *X-Men* #1 (September 1963): 11.

4. Ibid.

5. *X-Men* #16 (November 1965): 20.

6. Kurt Busiek, e-mail interview with the author, 22 December 2008.

7. *X-Men* #57 (June 1969): 14.

8. Joe Casey, introduction to *X-Men: Children of the Atom* (New York: Marvel, 2001).

9. Chris Claremont, introduction to *X-Men: God Loves, Man Kills* (New York: Marvel, 2003).

10. Chris Claremont, phone interview with the author, 17 November 2008.

11. Stan Lee, *Stan's Soapbox: The Collection* (New York: Marvel, 2008), 16, 18.

12. Ibid., 18.

13. I am indebted to my colleague Stephen V. Sprinkle, associate professor of practical theology at Brite Divinity School, for suggesting this train of thought to me.

14. Claremont, introduction to *X-Men: God Loves, Man Kills*.

15. *X-Treme X-Men* #30 (2003).

16. Chris Claremont, phone interview with the author, 17 November 2008.

17. René Girard, *I See Satan Fall Like Lightning* (Maryknoll, N.Y.: Orbis Books, 2001).

18. David Kinnaman and Gabe Lyons, *Unchristian: What a New Generation Really Thinks about Christianity . . . and Why It Matters* (Grand Rapids, Mich.: Baker Books, 2007), 21–40.

19. Les Daniels, *Marvel: Five Fabulous Decades of the World's Greatest Comics* (New York: Abrams, 1991), 168.

20. Chris Claremont, phone interview with the author, 17 November 2008.

21. Jennifer K. Berenson, "Colossians," in *The New Oxford Annotated Bible*, 3d ed., ed. Michael D. Coogan (New York: Oxford Univ. Press, 2001), 338.

22. Ibid.

23. Michaela Bruzzese, "Who (Doesn't) Belong?" *Sojourners* 38, no. 5 (May 2009): 48.

24. Martin Luther King Jr., "1963 Public Interview at Western Michigan University," Western Michigan University Libraries, Archives and Regional History Collections, accessed December 24, 2009, http://www.wmich.edu/library/archives/mlk/q-a.html.

25. Chris Claremont, phone interview with the author, 17 November 2008.

26. *X-Men: The Animated Series*, season 3, episode 44, aired May 13, 1995.

27. *Nightcrawler* vol. 2, #1 (2002).

28. *Nightcrawler* vol. 2, #3 (2002).

29. *X-Treme X-Men* #30 (2003).

30. Chris Claremont in the documentary "History of the X-Men: The Secret Origin of the X-Men," *X2: X-Men United,* two-disc DVD, directed by Bryan Singer (Los Angeles: 20th Century Fox, 2003).

31. Chris Claremont, introduction to *Wolverine*, premiere hardcover ed. (New York: Marvel, 1987).

32. *Wolverine* vol. 1, #1 (September 1982): 1.

33. Joe Neumaier, "*X-Men Origins: Wolverine* is a 'superhero fiasco,'" *New York Daily News*, 29 April 2009.

34. *Uncanny X-Men* #148 (August 1981): 8.

35. *New Avengers* #6 (2005).

36. Ibid.

37. Bryan Singer, "History of the X-Men: The Secret Origin of the X-Men," disc 2, *X2: X-Men United*, directed by Bryan Singer (Los Angeles: 20th Century Fox, 2003), 2-disc DVD.

38. David Elkind, *All Grown Up and No Place to Go: Teenagers in Crisis*, rev. ed. (Cambridge, Mass.: De Capo Press, 1998).

Chapter 5

1. In 1968, Iron Man left the pages of *Tales of Suspense* and received his own series. In *Iron Man* #1, writer Archie Goodwin and artist Gene Colon retold the origin tale and highlighted the fact that Yinsen's selfless sacrifice motivated Tony to use the armor not only to escape but also to fight crime as well.

2. Kurt Busiek, e-mail interview with the author, 22 December 2008.

3. Cf. James Hudnut-Beumler, *Generous Saints: Congregations Rethinking Ethics and Money* (Herndon, Va.: Alban Institute, 1999), 1ff.

4. Eugene Grimm, *Generous People* (Nashville: Abingdon Press, 1992), 19.

5. Mark Allan Powell, *Giving to God: The Bible's Good News About Living a Generous Life* (Grand Rapids, Mich.: Eerdmans, 2006), 80–81.

6. Ibid., 159.

7. See, for example, Michael Joseph Brown, "Hearing the Master's Voice," in *Engaging Biblical Authority: Perspectives on the Bible as Scripture*, ed. William P. Brown (Louisville: Westminster John Knox Press, 2007), 12–13. (Essay appears on pages 10–17.)

8. *Tales of Suspense* #53 (May 1964): 3.

9. Ibid., 4.

10. Ibid., 5.z

11. For example, see *Iron Man*, vol. 3, #8–9 (1998) and vol. 4, #6 (2006).

12. David Michelinie, "Introduction: Heart of Iron, Feet of Clay," in *Iron Man: Demon in a Bottle* (New York: Marvel, 2008).

13. Kurt Busiek, e-mail interview by author, 22 December 2008.

14. *Iron Man* vol. 3, #25 (February 2000): final page.

15. National Highway Traffic Safety Administration, *2007 Traffic Safety Annual Assessment*, DOT 810 791, Washington, D.C.: U.S. Dept. of Transportation, July 2008. Available at http://www-nrd.nhtsa.dot.gov/pubs/811016.pdf.

16. Larry Nielsen, *Thinking About Jail and Prison Ministries: A Guide for the Lay Volunteer* (Ft. Pierce, Fla.: FBC, 2005), 35.

17. See http://www.aa.org, http://www.na.org, and http://www.al-anon.org.

18. Michelinie, "Introduction."

19. Ibid.

20. Ibid.

Chapter 6

1. Stan Lee, *Origins of Marvel Comics* (New York: Simon & Schuster, 1974), 178.

2. Lee did not like his characters simply to have the power of flight without any further explanation. So it is revealed that the Human Torch can fly because his flames make him lighter than air. The Hulk does not fly but leaps with his mighty leg muscles. Later, the Angel would have wings. Still, Thor's method of throwing his hammer and catching a ride along with it is perhaps his most peculiar explanation for a hero's ability to fly.

3. *The Mighty Thor* #142 (July 1967): 13.

4. Lee, *Origins*, 181–82.

5. *The Mighty Thor* #140 (May 1967): 8.

6. *The Mighty Thor* #143 (August 1967): 2.

7. Ibid., 3.

8. Ibid., 6.

9. Ibid., 6.

10. *The Mighty Thor* #171 (December 1969): 2.

11. Ibid., 3.

12. Karl Marx, *Contribution to the Critique of Hegel's Philosophy of Right: Introduction* (1843), in *The Marx-Engels Reader*, ed. Robert C. Tucker (New York: W. W. Norton, 1978), 54.

13. Reinhold Niebuhr, "The Christian Faith and the World Crisis," *Christianity and Crisis* 1 (February 10, 1941): 4–6.

14. *The Mighty Thor* #145 (October 1965): 5.

15. Fred B. Craddock, *Craddock Stories* (St. Louis: Chalice Press, 2001), 155.

16. *The Mighty Thor* #337 (November 1983): 4.

17. Ibid., 23–24.

18. *The Mighty Thor* #132 (September 1966): 2.

19. Ibid., 6.

20. *The Mighty Thor* #122 (November 1965): 3.

21. *The Mighty Thor* #142 (July 1967): 15.

22. *The Mighty Thor* #158 (November 1968): 2.

23. See, for example, *Avengers* vol. 3, #25 (2006).

24. *The Mighty Thor* #340 (February 1984).

25. *The Mighty Thor* #159 (December 1968): 18.

26. Ibid.

27. Ibid.

28. Les Daniels, *Marvel: Five Fabulous Decades of the World's Greatest Comics* (New York: Abrams, 1991), 92.

29. *The Mighty Thor* #159 (December 1968): 20.

30. Valerie Saiving, "The Human Situation: A Feminine View," *Journal of Religion* 40, no. 2 (April 1960): 100–112.

Chapter 7

1. *Captain America Comics* #1 (March 1941): 6.

2. By doing this, Lee and Kirby effectively ignored Captain America's short-lived revival in the 1950s. In those stories, he often ferreted out and captured Communist spies in the United States.

3. *Avengers* #4 (March 1964): 8.

4. *Tales of Suspense* #91 (July 1967): 10.

5. In a controversial move, the new Captain America who takes Steve Rogers's place in 2008 does carry a gun.

6. See Robert Jewett, *The Captain America Complex: The Dilemma of Zealous Nationalism* (Philadelphia: Westminster Press, 1973) and Robert Jewett and John Shelton Lawrence, *Captain America and the Crusade Against Evil: The Dilemma of Zealous Nationalism* (Grand Rapids, Mich.: Eerdmans, 2003). The books do relatively little analysis of *Captain America* comic books but examine how the image of Captain America could function in America's psyche.

7. *Captain America* #122 (February 1970): 3.

8. Roy Thomas and Stan Lee, *Stan Lee's Amazing Marvel Universe* (New York: Sterling, 2006), 159.

9. *Captain America and the Falcon* #175 (July 1974): 32.

10. *Captain America and the Falcon* #183 (March 1975).

11. *Captain America* #250 (October 1980).

12. *Captain America* #332 (August 1987): 13.

13. Ibid.

14. *Captain America* vol. 5, #22 (2006).

15. Captain America's Bicentennial Battles (July 1976), 62.

16. Ibid., 72.

17. Ibid., 78.

18. Warren Carter, *Matthew and the Margins: A Sociopolitical and Religious Reading* (Maryknoll, N.Y.: Orbis Books, 2000), 440.

19. Ibid., 46.

20. Ibid., 440.

21. Jon Meacham, *American Gospel: God, the Founding Fathers, and the Making of a Nation* (New York: Random House, 2006), 6.

22. Ibid., 8.

23. Mark G. Toulouse, *God in Public: Four Ways American Christianity and Public Life Relate* (Philadelphia: Westminster/John Knox Press, 2006), 193–94.

24. Martin Luther King Jr., "Youth and Social Action," in *The Trumpet of Conscience* (New York: Harper & Row, 1968), 44.

25. Stephen Charles Mott, *Biblical Ethics and Social Change* (New York: Oxford University Press, 1982), 165.

26. Stan Lee, *Stan's Soapbox: The Collection* (New York: Marvel, 2008).

27. *Captain America* #126 (June 1970): 20.

28. *Captain America and the Falcon* #143 (November 1971): 33.

29. *Captain America and the Falcon* #144 (December 1971): 13–14.

30. Tony Campolo and Michael Battle, *The Church Enslaved: A Spirituality of Racial Reconciliation* (Minneapolis: Fortress Press, 2005), 3.

31. Ibid., 4–10.

32. Robert Morales, "Appendix," in *Captain America: Truth* (New York: Marvel, 2009). The book is a collection of *Truth: Red, White and Black* #1–7.

33. For more information see James H. Jones, *Bad Blood: The Tuskegee Syphilis Experiment*, rev. ed. (New York: Free Press, 1993).

34. Campolo and Battle, *The Church Enslaved*, 26–36.

Chapter 8

1. *Avengers* #2 (November 1963): 22.

2. *Avengers* #58 (November 1968): 19.

3. Ibid.

4. Ibid., 20.

5. Some of the other significant lineup changes occurred in *Avengers* #75 (April 1970); #151 (September 1976); #181 (March 1979); #211 (September 1981); #300 (February 1989); vol. 3, #4 (May 1998); and vol. 3, #27 (April 2000); and *New Avengers* #1–5 (December 2004–March 2005).

6. Stan Lee, phone interview with the author, 3 March 2009.

7. *Avengers* vol. 3, #10 (1998): 12.

8. Kurt Busiek, e-mail interview with the author, 22 December 2008.

9. Jennifer K. Berenson, "Ephesians," in *The New Oxford Annotated Bible*, 3d ed., ed. Michael D. Coogan (New York: Oxford University Press, 2001), 322.

10. Ibid.

11. Larry Nielsen, *Thinking About Jail and Prison Ministries: A Guide for the Lay Volunteer* (Ft. Pierce, Fla.: FBC, 2005), 6.

12. Andrew Sung Park, *Racial Conflict and Healing: An Asian-American Theological Perspective* (Maryknoll, N.Y.: Orbis Books, 1996), 136–37.

13. *Avengers* #20 (September 1965): 3.

14. Kurt Busiek, e-mail interview with the author, 22 December 2008.

15. Ibid.

16. *Marvel Superheroes Secret Wars* #1 (May 1984): 17.

17. *JLA/Avengers* #4 (2004).

Chapter 9

1. Listen to Stan Lee's audio commentary #30, in Roy Thomas and Stan Lee, *Stan Lee's Amazing Marvel Universe* (New York: Marvel, 2006).

2. Lee says he actually created the character to have something for Bill Everett to do. Everett created Marvel's first superhero, the Sub-Mariner, back in 1939, but left *Daredevil* after drawing just one issue.

3. *Daredevil*, directed by Mark Steven Johnson (Los Angeles: 20th Century Fox, 2003), DVD.

4. *Daredevil* #1 (April 1964): 12.

5. *Daredevil* #49 (February 1969): 2.

6. David Elkind, *All Grown Up and No Place to Go: Teenagers in Crisis*, rev. ed. (Reading, Mass.: De Capo Press, 1998), 196.

7. Ibid.

8. *Daredevil* #169 (March 1981).

9. Ibid.

10. *Daredevil* #181 (April 1982).

11. *Daredevil* vol. 2, #34 (August 2002).

12. *Daredevil* vol. 2, #50 (October 2003).

13. *Daredevil* vol. 2, #59 (June 2004) and #60 (July 2004).

14. *Daredevil* vol. 2, #84 (April 2006).

15. *Daredevil* vol. 2, #85 (July 2006).

16. *Daredevil* vol. 2, #86 (August 2006).

17. *Daredevil* vol. 2, #104 (March 2008).

18. Stephen Charles Mott, *Biblical Ethics and Social Change* (New York: Oxford Univ. Press, 1982), 60.

19. Ibid.

20. The name of the priest pays homage to Bill Everett, the legendary artist who drew the first issue of *Daredevil*. Many of the minor characters in the film, including the criminal Quesada, are named after Marvel writers and artists who worked on the *Daredevil* comic book through the years.

21. Julien R. Fielding, "Film Review: *Daredevil*," *Journal of Religion and Film* 7, no. 1 (April 2003), http://www.unomaha.edu/jrf/.

22. Mark Steven Johnson, "Giving the Devil His Due," *Daredevil: Director's Cut*, directed by Mark Steven Johnson (Los Angeles: 20th Century Fox, 2004), DVD.

23. *Daredevil* #7 (April 1965): 19.

Chapter 10

1. *Fantastic Four* #50 (May 1966): 7.
2. Stan Lee, introduction to *Son of Origins of Marvel Comics* (New York: Simon & Schuster, 1975), 206.
3. Ibid.
4. See Stan Lee and Jack Kirby, *The Silver Surfer* (New York: Simon & Shuster, 1978).
5. See the documentary "Sentinel of the Spaceways: Comic Book Origins of the Silver Surfer," disc 2, *Fantastic 4: Rise of the Silver Surfer* (Los Angeles: Twentieth Century Fox, 2007), 2-disc DVD. For more on the Silver Surfer as a figure of Christ, see B. J. Oropeza's thoughtful essay, "The God-Man Revisited: Christology Through the Blank Eyes of the Silver Surfer," in *The Gospel According to Superheroes*, ed. B. J. Oropeza (New York: Peter Lang, 2005), 155–70.
6. Stan Lee, introduction to *Marvel Masterworks: Silver Surfer* (New York: Marvel, 1990). This volume is a collection of *Silver Surfer* #1–6.
7. *Silver Surfer* #2 (October 1968): 5.
8. Ibid., 6.
9. Ibid., 11.
10. *Silver Surfer* #10 (November 1969): 17–18.
11. *Silver Surfer* #11 (December 1969): 13.
12. *Silver Surfer* #15 (April 1970): 2.
13. "The Peerless Power of the Silver Surfer," *Fantastic Four Annual* #5 (November 1967): 3.
14. Tyron Inbody, *The Faith of the Christian Church* (Grand Rapids, Mich.: Eerdmans, 2005), 185.
15. Ibid.
16. Ibid., 186.
17. Stan Lee, writer, and Mike Wieringo, artist, *Stan Lee Meets Silver Surfer* #1 (2006).
18. *Fantastic Four* #67 (October 1967): 20.
19. Roy Thomas, introduction to *Marvel Masterworks: Warlock*, vol. 1 (New York: Marvel, 2007).
20. *Thor* #134–35 (November–December 1966).
21. Thomas, introduction to *Marvel Masterworks*.
22. Thomas, in his introduction to *Marvel Masterworks*, says the Man-Beast was Counter-Earth's Satan.
23. *Marvel Premiere* #1 (April 1972): 20.
24. Thomas, introduction to *Marvel Masterworks*.
25. *Warlock* #1 (August 1972): 7–8.
26. Ibid., 9.
27. *Warlock* #5–6 (April–June 1972).
28. *Incredible Hulk* #178 (August 1974): 1.
29. Ibid., 16.
30. Ibid., 17.
31. Ibid.
32. Ibid., 18.
33. Ibid., 19.
34. Thomas, introduction to *Marvel Masterworks*.
35. *Warlock* #11 (February 1976): 27.
36. *Strange Tales* #178 (February 1975): 22.
37. Ibid., 22.
38. Ibid., 31.
39. *Strange Tales* #180 (June 1975).
40. Jon B. Cooke, "CBA Roundtable: The Cosmic Code Authority Speaks!" *Comic Book Artist* 18 (March 2002): 26. (The article is on pp 14–29.)
41. Monsignor Lorenzo Albacete, interview by Helen Whitney, in "Faith and Doubt at Ground Zero," *Frontline*, PBS, winter 2002. Available at http://www.pbs.org/wgbh/pages/frontline/shows/faith/interviews/albacete.html.
42. Rabbi Brad Hirschfield, interview by Helen Whitney, in "Faith and Doubt at Ground Zero," *Frontline*, PBS, winter 2002. Available at http://www.pbs.org/wgbh/pages/frontline/shows/faith/interviews/hirschfield.html.
43. Ibid.
44. Khaled Abou el-Fadl, interview by Helen Whitney, in "Faith and Doubt at Ground Zero," *Frontline*, PBS, winter 2002. Available at http://www.pbs.org/wgbh/pages/frontline/shows/faith/interviews/elfadl.html.
45. See also Charles Kimball, *When Religion Becomes Evil* (San Francisco: HarperSanFrancisco, 2002).
46. *Marvel Superheroes* #18 (January 1969): 22.
47. *Guardians of the Galaxy* #2 (July 1990).
48. For the Annihilation Wave, see the 2006 Marvel crossover series *Annihilation*. For the Phalanx, see the 2007–8 Marvel crossover series *Annihilation: Conquest*.

49. *Captain Marvel* #28 (September 1973).
50. *The Death of Captain Marvel* (1982).
51. Ibid.
52. Ibid.
53. Cooke, "CBA Roundtable," 26.
54. Elisabeth Kübler-Ross, *On Death and Dying* (New York: Macmillan, 1969).
55. *The Death of Captain Marvel* (1982).
56. Ibid.

Bibliography

Albacete, Lorenzo. "Interview with Monsignor Lorenzo Albacete." By Helen Whitney, winter 2002. In "Faith and Doubt at Ground Zero," *Frontline*, PBS. Available at http://www.pbs.org/wgbh/pages/frontline/shows/faith/interviews/albacete.html.

Bell, Blake. *Stranger and Stranger: The World of Steve Ditko*. Seattle: Fantagraphics Books, 2008.

Berenson, Jennifer K. "Colossians." In *The New Oxford Annotated Bible*. 3d ed., edited by Michael D. Coogan. New York: Oxford University Press, 2001.

———."Ephesians." In *The New Oxford Annotated Bible*. 3d ed., edited by Michael D. Coogan. New York: Oxford University Press, 2001.

Brown, Michael Joseph. "Hearing the Master's Voice." In *Engaging Biblical Authority: Perspectives on the Bible as Scripture*, edited by William P. Brown, 10–17. Louisville: Westminster John Knox Press, 2007.

Bruzzese, Michaela. "Who (Doesn't) Belong?" *Sojourners* 38, no. 5 (May 2009), 48.

Campolo, Tony, and Michael Battle. *The Church Enslaved: A Spirituality of Racial Reconciliation*. Minneapolis: Fortress Press, 2005.

Carter, Warren. *Matthew and the Margins: A Sociopolitical and Religious Reading*. Maryknoll, N.Y.: Orbis Books, 2000.

Casey, Joe. "Introduction." In *X-Men: Children of the Atom*. New York: Marvel, 2001.

Claremont, Chris. "Introduction." In *Wolverine*, premier hardcover ed. New York: Marvel, 1987.

———. *X-Men: God Loves, Man Kills*. Graphic novel. New York: Marvel Entertainment, 2003.

Cooke, Jon B. "CBA Roundtable: The Cosmic Code Authority Speaks!" *Comic Book Artist* 18 (March 2002): 14–29.

———. "From This Day Forward: How Marriage Changes Everything (Even for the FF)." In *The Fantastic Four Omnibus*, vol. 2. New York: Marvel, 2007.

Craddock, Fred B. *Craddock Stories*. St. Louis: Chalice Press, 2001.

Dalton, Russell W. *Faith Journey through Fantasy Lands: A Christian Dialogue with* Harry Potter, Star Wars *and* The Lord of the Rings. Minneapolis: Augsburg, 2003.

Daniels, Les. *Marvel: Five Fabulous Decades of the World's Greatest Comics*. New York: Abrams, 1991.

Elkind, David. *All Grown Up and No Place to Go: Teenagers in Crisis*. Rev. ed. Cambridge, Mass.: De Capo Press, 1998.

Evanier, Mark. *Kirby: King of Comics*. New York: Abrams, 2008.

———. "Wonders Aplenty." In *The Fantastic Four Omnibus*, vol. 2. New York: Marvel, 2007.

Fadl, Khaled Abou el-. "Interview with Khaled Abou el-Fadl." By Helen Whitney, winter 2002. In "Faith and Doubt at Ground Zero," *Frontline*, PBS. Available at http://www.pbs.org/wgbh/pages/frontline/shows/faith/interviews/elfadl.html.

Farmer, Kathleen A. *Who Knows What Is Good? A Commentary on Proverbs and Ecclesiastes*. Grand Rapids, Mich.: Eerdmans, 1991.

Fielding, Julien R. "Film Review: *Daredevil*." *Journal of Religion and Film* 7, no. 1 (April 2003). Available at http://www.unomaha.edu/jrf/.

Furnish, Victor Paul. *The Love Command in the New Testament*. Nashville: Abingdon, 1972.

Girard, René. *I See Satan Fall Like Lightning*. Maryknoll, N.Y.: Orbis Books, 2001.

Grimm, Eugene. *Generous People*. Nashville: Abingdon Press, 1992.

Hirschfield, Brad. "Interview with Rabbi Brad Hirschfield." By Helen Whitney, winter 2002. In "Faith and Doubt at Ground Zero," *Frontline*, PBS. Available at http://www.pbs.org/wgbh/pages/frontline/shows/faith/interviews/hirschfield.html.

Hudlin, Reginald. "The Start of a Revolution." In *The Fantastic Four Omnibus*, vol. 2. New York: Marvel, 2007.

Hudnut-Beumler, James. *Generous Saints: Congregations Rethinking Ethics and Money*. Herndon, Va.: Alban Institute, 1999.

Inbody, Tyron. *The Faith of the Christian Church*. Grand Rapids, Mich.: Eerdmans, 2005.

Jewett, Robert. *The Captain America Complex: The Dilemma of Zealous Nationalism*. Philadelphia: Westminster Press, 1973.

Jewett, Robert, and John Shelton Lawrence. *Captain America and the Crusade Against Evil: The Dilemma of Zealous Nationalism*. Grand Rapids, Mich.: Eerdmans, 2003.

Jones, Doris Moreland. *God's Gift of Anger*. St. Louis: Chalice Press, 2005.

Jones, James H. *Bad Blood: The Tuskegee Syphilis Experiment*. Rev. ed. New York: Free Press, 1993.

Kimball, Charles. *When Religion Becomes Evil*. San Francisco: Harper San Francisco, 2002.

King, Martin Luther Jr. 1963 Public Interview at Western Michigan University. Western Michigan University Libraries, Archives and Regional History Collections. http://www.wmich.edu/library/archives/mlk/q-a.html. Accessed December 24, 2009.

———. "Youth and Social Action." In *The Trumpet of Conscience*. New York: Harper & Row, 1968.

Kinnaman, David, and Gabe Lyons. *Unchristian: What a New Generation Really Thinks about Christianity . . . and Why It Matters*. Grand Rapids, Mich.: Baker Books, 2007.

Kirby, Jack. *The Jack Kirby Portfolio*. Ltd. ed. Milwaukie, Oreg.: Dark Horse Comics, 1996.

Kübler-Ross, Elisabeth. *On Death and Dying*. New York: Macmillan, 1969.

Lawrence, John Shelton, and Robert Jewett. *The Myth of the American Superhero*. Grand Rapids, Mich.: Eerdmans, 2002.

Lee, Stan. "God Woke: A Poem." In *Stan Lee: Conversations*, edited by Jeff McLaughlin, 219–26. Jackson: University Press of Mississippi, 2007.

———. "Introduction." In *Marvel Masterworks: Sgt. Fury and His Howling Commandos*, by Stan Lee, Jack Kirby, and Dick Ayers. Vol. 1. New York: Marvel, 2006.

———. "Introduction." In *Marvel Masterworks: The Amazing Spider-Man*, by Stan Lee and Steven Ditko. Vol. 1. New York: Marvel, 1987.

———. "Introduction." In *Marvel Masterworks: The Silver Surfer*, by Stan Lee and John Buscema. Vol. 1. New York: Marvel, 1990.

———. "Introduction." In *Marvel Masterworks: X-Men*, by Chris Claremont and Dave Cokrum with Stan Lee. Vol. 1. New York: Marvel, 2002.

———. "Introduction." In *Son of Origins of Marvel Comics*, by Stan Lee, Jack Kirby, John Buscema, Don Heck, Bill Everett, and Gene Colan. Revised edition. New York: Marvel Entertainment Group, 1997.

———. *Origins of Marvel Comics*. New York: Simon & Schuster, 1974.

———. *Stan's Soapbox: The Collection*. New York: Marvel, 2008.

Lee, Stan, and George Mair. *Excelsior! The Amazing Life of Stan Lee*. New York: Simon and Schuster, 2002.

Lee, Stan, and Jack Kirby. *The Silver Surfer*. New York: Simon & Schuster, 1978.

Lester, Andrew D. *Anger: Discovering Your Spiritual Ally*. Louisville: Westminster John Knox Press, 2007.

Marx, Karl. "Contribution to the Critique of Hegel's Philosophy of Right: Introduction." In *The Marx-Engels Reader*, edited by Robert C. Tucker. New York: W. W. Horton, 1978.

Meacham, Jon. *American Gospel: God, the Founding Fathers, and the Making of a Nation*. New York: Random House, 2006.

Michelinie, David. "Introduction: Heart of Iron, Feet of Clay." In *Iron Man: Demon in a Bottle*, by David Michelinie, Bob Layton, John Romita Jr., and Carmine Infantino. New York: Marvel, 2008.

Morales, Robert, and Kyle Baxter. *Captain America: Truth*. Collected issues of *Truth: Red, White and Black*, nos. 1–7. New York: Marvel, 2009.

Mott, Stephen Charles. *Biblical Ethics and Social Change*. New York: Oxford University Press, 1982.

National Endowment for the Arts. "2008 National Medal of Arts." http://www.nea.gov/news/news08/medals/Lee.html. Accessed March 8, 2009.

National Highway Traffic Safety Administration. *2007 Traffic Safety Annual Assessment*. DOT 810 791. Washington, D.C.: U.S. Dept. of Transportation, July 2008.

Neumaier, Joe. "*X-Men Origins: Wolverine* is a 'Superhero Fiasco.'" *New York Daily News*, 29 April 2009.

Niebuhr, Reinhold. "The Christian Faith and the World Crisis." *Christianity and Crisis* 1 (February 10, 1941): 4–6.

Nielsen, Larry. *Thinking About Jail and Prison Ministries: A Guide for the Lay Volunteer*. Fort Pierce, Fla.: FBC, 2005.

O. Henry. "The Gift of the Magi." In *The Gift of Magi and Other Stories* (Scholastic Classics). New York: Scholastic Paperbacks, 2002.

Oropeza, B. J., ed. *The Gospel According to Superheroes*. New York: Peter Lang, 2005.

Park, Andrew Sung. *Racial Conflict and Healing: An Asian-American Theological Perspective*. Maryknoll, N.Y.: Orbis Books, 1996.

Powell, Mark Allan. *Giving to God: The Bible's Good News About Living a Generous Life*. Grand Rapids, Mich.: Eerdmans, 2006.

Rand, Ayn. *Atlas Shrugged*. Centennial ed. New York: Signet Books, 1992.

———. *The Fountainhead*. 50th anniversary ed. London: Penguin Books, 1996.

Ro, Ronin. *Tales to Astonish: Jack Kirby, Stan Lee, and the American Comic Book Revolution*. New York: Bloomsbury, 2004.

Romita, John, Sr. "Marvels Commentary." In *Marvels,* 10th anniversary ed., edited by Kurt Busiek and Alex Ross. New York: Marvel, 2004.

Sanderson, Peter. *Marvel Universe*. New York: Abrams, 1996.

Saussy, Carroll. *The Gift of Anger: A Call to Faithful Action*. Louisville: Westminster John Knox Press, 1995.

Saiving, Valerie. "The Human Situation: A Feminine View." *Journal of Religion* 40, no. 2 (Apr 1960): 100–112.

Thomas, Roy. Introduction to *Warlock*. Marvel Masterworks, by Roy Thomas, Mike Fiedrich, Ron Goulart, Gil Kane, and Bob Brown, vol. 1. New York: Marvel, 2007.

Thomas, Roy, with audio commentary by Stan Lee. *Stan Lee's Amazing Marvel Universe*. New York: Sterling, 2006.

Toulouse, Mark G. *God in Public: Four Ways American Christianity and Public Life Relate*. Philadelphia: Westminster John Knox Press, 2006.

Tremblay, Rodrigue. "The Manichaeism of Osama bin Laden and George W. Bush." *Freethought Today* 20 (March 2003): 6–7.

Wertham, Fredric. *Seduction of the Innocent*. New York: Reinhart, 1954.

Wink, Walter. *The Powers That Be: Theology for the New Millennium*. New York: Galilee Doubleday, 1998.